CONSCIENTIZATION AND CREATIVITY

Paulo Freire and Christian Education

Daniel S. Schipani

UNIVERSITY
PRESS OF
AMERICA

LANHAM • NEW YORK • LONDON

Copyright © 1984 by

University Press of America,™ Inc.

4720 Boston Way
Lanham. MD 20706

3 Henrietta Street
London WC2E 8LU England

Library of Congress Cataloging in Publication Data

Schipani, Daniel S., 1943–
  Conscientization and creativity.

  Revision of thesis—Princeton Theological Seminary,
1981.
  Bibliography: p.
  1. Freire, Paulo, 1921–   . 2. Education—Philosophy.
3. Liberation theology—History of doctrines. 4. Christian education —Philosophy. I. Title.
LB880.F732S34   1984   370'.1   84-3607
ISBN 0-8191-3881-9 (alk. paper)
ISBN 0-8191-3882-7 (pbk. : alk. paper)

All University Press of America books are produced on acid-free
paper which exceeds the minimum standards set by the National
Historical Publications and Records Commission.

ACKNOWLEDGEMENTS

This book is a revision of a dissertation that I presented to the faculty of Princeton Theological Seminary in 1981. I want to express my grateful appreciation, therefore, to my teachers at Princeton who initially guided this work: Professors James E. Loder, Richard Shaull, and D. Campbell Wyckoff. Each of them provided support, criticism, and orientation concerning creativity and interdisciplinary studies, theological reflection, and Christian education theory and practice. In particular, the personal and professional encouragement given me by Dr. Loder has been greater than anyone could expect.

For the last few years I have been a member of the faculty of Seminario Evangélico de Puerto Rico. The seminary has afforded me time to complete the manuscript by granting a sabbatical leave for which I am very grateful. Special thanks are due to President Luis Fidel Mercado who supported the project and my plans for further research and writing.

To my wife Margaret Anne for her support, patience, and inspiration, in countless ways--including careful manuscript typing--I reserve my deepest gratitude and I dedicate this book.

Daniel S. Schipani, Ph. D.
Río Piedras, Puerto Rico
Thanksgiving 1983

TABLE OF CONTENTS

SECOND PART -- THE THEOLOGICAL FOUNDATION:
EDUCATION AND THE KINGDOM

CHAPTER 3: FREIRE AND LIBERATION THEOLOGY

CHAPTER 4: KINGDOM GOSPEL AND CREATIVITY

THIRD PART -- RAMIFICATIONS
FOR THEORY AND PRACTICE

INTRODUCTION

Paulo Freire is an influencial thinker in the areas of social and educational thought. Although he works and writes out of a Third World perspective, his approach has also had an impressive impact among the more industrialized nations and beyond the field of education in the strict sense of the word.

Freire devised and tested an educational model as well as an overall philosophy of education primarily during several years of active involvement in Latin America. His work was further developed in later assignments at the Department of Education of the World Council of Churches. Freire's educational thrust centers on the human potential for creativity and freedom in the midst of politico-economic and cultural oppression. It aims at discovering and implementing liberating alternatives in social interaction and transformation via the conscientization[1] process. "Conscientization" can be defined as the process in which persons achieve a deepening awareness, both of the socio-cultural reality that shapes their lives and their capacity to transform that reality. It involves praxis understood as the dialectic relationship of action and reflection.[2] That is, Freire proposes a praxis approach to education in the sense of both critically reflective action and critical reflection that is informed by practice. Actually, Freire is today the most significant exponent of such an approach that seeks to keep "theory" and "practice" together as mutually enriching dimensions of the same educational process.

We start this discussion with two major sets of questions. First, we want to explore why the so called "Freire method" has been so successful and how we can comprehend this approach as well as the integrity of Freire's contribution. This is important because the analysis of Freire's work immediately reveals the influence of diverse foundations from the fields of philosophy, linguistics, education, psychoanalysis, sociology and theology. However, those foundations are not explicitly articulated in his writings, which do not include precise and systematic formulations. A special challenge here is to expose and correct some limitations and contradictions in this thrust of "cultural action for freedom." This is due mainly to the uncritical assimilation of Marxism in liberation thought. Interestingly enough, Freire himself has been aware of the need to prevent potential misuse and distortions of the conscientization method and process.[3] The second set of questions refers to how Freire's contribution can inform Christian education, especially in light of the need for integrating theory and practice with sound educational and theological bases.

As we face those major questions, we propose that the dynamics of conscientization need to be understood in terms of creativity and the creative process. Further, we claim that this is the way to illuminate and correct Freire's thought. Then, the educational and theological perspectives can be integrated thus providing and adequate foundation for Christian education. Therefore, our purpose is to re-examine Freire's work with three objectives in mind: (a) to make the integrity of his approach more comprehensive; (b) to spell out further the character and dimensions of creativity; and (c) to make a contribution to Christian education theory.

The two chapters in the first part deal with Freire's methodology, with focus on his view of education as knowing. That is why we refer to this discussion as the epistemological foundation. In chapters 3 and 4-- the second part--we consider the theological base and frame of reference of Freire's approach. In this case, we concentrate on the biblical motif of the Kingdom of God. Analysis and critique are followed by constructive re-statements in both instances. Finally, in the third part we move to spell out implications for Christian education theory and practice on the basis of the previous discussion.

This book is an interdisciplinary study involving topics related to the fields of education, philosophy, psychology and theology. It is written primarily for persons interested in education, and Christian education especially. I have tried to discuss those topics in accessible language and I have used the end notes to refer to sources and to expand certain issues for those who wish to deal with them in a more detailed or technical way. The general reader may skip most of the notes as well as the Excursus section in chapters 2 and 3.

Several essays, books and other materials dealing with different areas of our subject have been written in the last few years. In some cases, Freire's work or certain dimensions of it are analyzed and assessed in depth.[4] In other instances, the focus has been the applicability or transference of this thought and method to the North American scene.[5] A third category includes

comparative studies between Freire and other major fig-
ures.6 The preset study attempts to provide a comprehensive evaluation and reformulation of Freire's methodology and theology, and to suggest an educational model
from the perspective of liberation and creativity.

FIRST PART -- THE EPISTEMOLOGICAL FOUNDATION:
EDUCATION AS KNOWING

We wished to design a project in which we would attempt
to move from naiveté to a critical attitude at the same
time we taught reading. We wanted a literacy program
which would be an introduction to the democratization
of culture, a program with human beings as its subjects
rather than as patient recipients, a program which
itself would be an act of creation, capable of releasing
other creative acts.

                    Paulo Freire
                    Education as the Practice of Freedom

In this part of our study we will concentrate on the epistemological basis of Freire's work and thought. Epistemology is the philosophical discipline which studies the source and nature of knowing and the reliability of claims to knowledge. This is a necessary starting point because, for Freire, education is essentially a certain theory of knowledge put into practice. This is the meaning of the conscientization method and process, which lies at the core of his conception and approach. Freire presents a special understanding of learning and education which involves an explicit epistemological perspective.

> I see "education as the practice of freedom" above all as a truly gnosiological situation . . . In the educational process for liberation, educator-educatee and educatee-educator are both cognitive subjects before knowable objects which mediate them.[1]

Freire's acknowledged contribution to philosophy of education is partially due to the fact that the relationship between philosophy and education is specially clear with regard to the theory of knowing and the theory of learing. Indeed, epistemology has been a fruitful source for a variety of fecund educational ideas.[2]

The first part of the book is divided into two chapters. In chapter I, we will discuss Freire's work and thought by means of an analysis and critique of his approach. In the second chapter there will be constructive reformulation in terms of creativity.

CHAPTER I

CONSCIENTIZATION AND HUMAN DEVELOPMENT

We will begin our discussion with a short presentation of Freire's educational method with the focus on his approach to adult literacy, which is paradigmatic of the thrust of "education for liberation" and "cultural action for freedom." We will then concentrate on the key concept of conscientization as we uncover the developmental structure of Freire's method. In the next step, there will be a reference to a major shift in the epistemological base,which parallels a change toward revolutionary radicalism in his later writings. This reflection will in turn lead us to describe Freire's approach in terms of a reconstructionist perspective. Finally, a critical assessment will underscore some limitations and contradictions that call for the corrective statement to be developed in the next chapter.

A. Freire's Educational Method

The approach and the ideas that Paulo Freire proposes in light of his vision of education and society, need to be perceived within the context of his direct involvement in the struggle for enabling the submerged masses of population to emerge and to "speak their word."[1] Freire affirms strongly that education has the responsibility and the potential for helping to make possible that special cultural and political service. Therefore, as we consider the main features of Freire's pedagogy, we are actually referring not only to a theoretical stance, but also to his educational work in Latin America and elsewhere.

We will indicate in the first place the components of the Freire method. Secondly, we will refer to the phases of the literacy/conscientization program as such in order to illustrate and concretize further our analysis.

1. Components of The Freire Method

a. Limit-Situations: The Challenge for Literacy and Critical Consciousness

From the beginning of his efforts to implement an effective literacy program, Freire tried to ensure that the development of critical consciousness would be built

into the educational project. As stated in the initial
quotation: "We wished to design a project in which we
would attempt to move from naiveté to a critical attitude at the same time we taught reading."2

The lack of literacy skills coupled with other lim-
iting existential conditions is perceived by Freire in
terms of "limit-situation." This concept has a sociological import which point to the recognition of an
oppressive situation:

> . . . limit-situations imply the existence
> of persons who are directly or indirectly
> served by these situations, and of those
> who are negated and curbed by them. Once
> the latter come to perceive these situations
> as the frontier between being and being more
> human, rather than the frontier between being
> and nothingness, they begin to direct their
> increasingly critical actions towards achiev-
> ing the untested feasibility implicit in that
> perception.3

Limit situations, then, do not represent unsurmount-
able obstacles. They are rather problematic and conflict
circumstances which call for a resolution. They are challenges
to further growth, to "being more human " i.e., to
develop one's potential in several dimensions (language,
self, and social participation) as we will see below.
In order for the limit-situations to be recognized as
such and appraised as existencial challenges,Freire
proposed to deal with the historico-cultural "themes"
in a given setting.

b.   Themes - Thematic Universe and Generative Themes

The themes of the epoch are constituted by concrete
representations of common and seminal ideas, values,
hopes and challenges of the people, as well as the obstacles that impede their full humanization.4 "Thematic
universe" is the name for the complex of themes which
vary from one particular context to the other, and that
always needs to be investigated anew. For example, the
thematic universe of a slum would be different from that
of a peasant village. The recognition of the peculiarity
of the thematic universe in a given socio-cultural setting is both a requirement as well as a feature of the
dialogical character of this eductional program and
process.

4

Freire conceives of the themes as located in concentric circles. They are "generative themes" because they move from the general to the particular, and each one of them unfolds, as it were, into new themes. For him the theme of domination and liberation is the broadest generative theme of our time.[5] It may illumine problem situations ranging from the economic development to sex roles, family economics, and the relationship between teachers and students.

The themes can be seen as parts of the larger limit-situations which people may either face more or less critically, naively, or fatalistically. In other words, the themes are contained in the limit-situations. However, the only way to perceive and apprehend the situation is through focusing on the themes. In this sense, as Freire indicates, "The themes both contain and are contained in the limit situations."[6]

c. Thematic Investigation

In light of the previous discussion, the first task in a truly liberating educational program and process is to engage in the investigation of the themes of the reality in which the educational plan is to be implemented. By taking seriously the educatees' actual experience, the danger of "cultural invasion" is minimized.

The investigation of themes is crucial also because problem situations need to be adequately identified. In Freire's terms, the themes contain the "tasks" to be carried out or fulfilled. If themes are not recognized, then the tasks are not known and, consequently, a given situation may remain unchanged. This is another way of affirming from the beginning the integration of action and reflection in an educational process.

Thematic investigation consists not only of a study of the local context or reality, but of the people's perception of their reality. The people's language and thought dialectically refer to their social reality. This is already a part of the educational program and process which, as such, includes direct involvement of the participants from the very beginning. The educators--all usually members of an interdisciplinary team (a linguist, a sociologist, a psychologist, and others)--study the various dimensions of the social life from different perspectives, togehter with volunteers or "co-researchers" from the community. Freire refers to this

5

process of analysis as an "excision" of main lacks and contradictions in the social, cultural, political and economic aspects of the situation.

d. Codification - Decodification

The observations gathered from the analysis by "experts" and "volunteers" especially in terms of conflict situations or contradictions, needs to be "codified." Photographs, drawings, plays, oral presentations, and other means, may be chosen to represent situations that are familiar to the participants. This is done in order to facilitate their direct involvement both as reflecting subjects and as objects of their own reflection. Freire indicates that:

> . . . (the)thematic nucleus be neither overly explicit nor enigmatic. The former may degenerate into mere propaganda with no real decoding to be done beyond stating the obviously predetermined content. The latter runs the risk of appearing to be a puzzle or a guessing game . . .[7]

"Decodifications" should make it possible to move in the direction of other themes while always pointing back to major conflicts and contradictions. The participants may thus be able to deal not just with partial representations of certain sectors of their reality, but with their total existential situation. By reflecting on the codification of their own situations, participants reveal their level of awareness in regard to that reality. The coordinators of these "thematic investigation circles" ask questions about coded situations and they also pose the learners' answers as new problems. coordinators and specialists attending the meetings then record and report their observations. On the basis of those reports, each specialist of the team works on a list of themes implicit or explicit in the previous discussions. The idea is for the specialists to perceive the core or nucleus of the themes and to suggest specific learning "units" i.e., the breakdown of the themes for the conscientization program. Freire suggests that the thematics which have come from the people return to them--not as content to be deposited, but as problems to be solved. [8]

The coordinators need to select the most appropriate ways of representing the new codifications of the existential situations, and of organizing the didactic material. Several factors will determine this selection, such as the characteristics of the participants, the kinds of codified themes, the material resources available, and the educators' creativity. The participants in the learning setting where the literacy/conscientization program takes place--called "culture circles"--will then engage in a constant process of observation, analysis, synthesis, description, and critical reflection of the situations represented in the codifications. They can reflect critically on that reality and also on their own perception and understanding of it.

Generative themes point to new themes. In this way, in the conscientization process the people themselves participate in the three basic moments of the Freire mehod--investigation, thematization, and problematization of existential situations. The educational goal is to facilitate an increasingly critical insertion of the persons in the reality in which they live. They are to know that reality profoundly and they are to be able to transform it creatively.

2. Phases of the Literacy Method

By focusing now on the literacy method, we will be able to illumine Freire's theory of education and social transformation. Several propositions will thus become more meaningful in terms of the central thrust of "cultural action for freedom." Since the method is described in detail in Freire's basic works, we will present here a brief characterization.

a. The Vocabular Universe. The investigation of generative themes discussed above, in the case of the literacy programs, includes also the investigation of potential "generative words." This is done together with an appraisal of ways in which people perceive and assess their reality in terms of prevailing levels of consciousness. Therefore, the first phase in the preparation of the literacy method as such, is the discovery of the "vocabular universe" of the community to be served. They must be typical and common expressions of the people, full of existential meaning for them. Coordinators and experts are to be engaged in a search in which the integrity of the people's language is always respected.

b. The selection of <u>generative words</u> from the popular vocabulary is done according to how charged those words are with meaning and emotional content, in the existential context in which they were studied. This choice is determined by three criteria: (1) "Phonemic richness"--the capacity of the word to include as many of the basic sounds of the language as possible.[9] Freire soon realized that only about twenty carefully selected generative words would suffice, provided that the following two additional criteria are also taken into account; (2) "gradualism" as far as phonetic difficulty of the language is concerned. The presentation of the words must be arranged in an order of increasing difficulty so that the persons learning to read and write may experience success immediately and their motivation may be reinforced; (3) "pragmatic tone" of the words--i.e., the potential that words have to confront and "speak to" the current socio-cultural reality of the learners. The best generative words are those that rate highest in syntactic and semantic criteria and conscientization potential. A collaborator of Paulo Freire thus summarized what he calls the semiotic criterion:

> . . . the best generative word is that which combines the greatest possible "percentage" of the syntactic criteria (phonemic richness, degree of complex phonetic difficulty, "manipulability" of the groups of signs, the syllables, etc.), the semantic criteria (greater or lesser "intensity" of the link between the word and the thing it designates), the greater or lesser correspondence between the word and the pragmatic thing designated, the greater or lesser quality of <u>conscientizaçao</u> which the word potentially carries, or the grouping of socio-cultural reactions which the word generates in the person or grup using it.[10]

c. The third phase consists of the creation of codifications--i.e., representations (drawings,photographs, or other materials) of typical existential situations of the participants. These situations are identifiable in terms of the generative themes discussed before. Hence, there is an intimate relationship between representations, generative themes, and generative words. One generative word may embody the entire situation--e.g. "slum"--or it may refer only to one of the elements in the situation,--e.g. "housing." The teaching material being prepared at this point, then, consists of

8

the codifications. We must emphasize that the pictorial representations should include situations that are entirely familiar to the persons whose "thematic universe" is being explored together with them. The series of representations that are correlated with generative words, should be well arranged, both sequentially and with regard to content.

d. Coordinators, specialists, and volunteers prepare agendas for discussion. These are designed primarily to assist the coordination of the circles of culture in their role as moderators and facilitators of the learning process--i.e., learning to read and write which, in Freire's view, is inseparable from consciousness raising.

e. The final "preparation phase" includes the elaboration of cards or slides with the breakdown of the phonemic families (the syllables) which correspond to the generative words. They will be needed later for observation, selection and combination fo "parts" into words and senteces.

f. The actual literacy/conscientization program starts with thematic investigation, as previously indicated. In a second movement, a series of codified situations is presented and associated with specific generative words. Participants have an opportunity to discuss the situations, to share personal stories related to them, and to reflect critically upon them. For example, in the analysis of the codification of a "favela" (slum), the problem of food, shelter, clothing, health, and education frequently emerge. A slide or card with the word FAVELA is then presented alone, and then another one with the word broken into its three "pieces" (syllables): FA - VE - LA. The presentation of phonetic families then follows:

FA FE FI FO FU

VA VE VI VO VU

LA LE LI LO LU

The learners can immediately recognize the five vowels (which are always pronounced in the same way). They are now ready to start making up their own words, freely selecting and combining syllables. They can produce "real" or "thinking" words (e.g., VELA = "candle",

9

VIVO = "I live", or, "alive") and they can also play with "funny" or invented words. The practice of the mechanisms of word formation continues through the presentation of codifications and generative words. Furthermore, they can start the practice of writing from the very first session. Participants thus discover a numer of language rules while developing a variety of skills together with the realization of their enormous potential for learning.

The adult literacy program is conceived as one dimension--and also a result--of the process of critical reflection in a community learning context. People can reflect on their situation, on their place and role in the world, on their power to transform reality, on the encounter with their own consciousness as they cooperate together in the liberating production of acts of creation.

As we discussed major features of the Freire method, it became clear that the educational process focusses on the expansion of awareness, especially as critical awareness. Learning is understood as the process by which a person moves from one level of consciousness to another. And the content of this consciousness is the view that people have of their own existence in the social reality, and the power that they possess to determine their destiny. The learning process starts with the present level of consciousness as it is manifest in the living conditions, language, self-concept, and world view. In the literacy-conscientization program, people are expected to become more aware of the contingency of social reality and, therefore, of the possibilities for creative and liberating transformation. To the topic of conscientization and development we must now turn our attention.

B.   Conscientization and Development

The meaning of "conscientization" was briefly indicated in the general introduction as the process in which people achieve a deepening awareness, both of the sociocultural reality that shapes their lives and their capacity to transform that reality. We also pointed out that conscientization implies a critical self-insertion and "praxis" understood as the dialectic relationship action-reflection.

1. Levels of Consciousness and Critical Transitivity

Freire's sociological intuition points to the lack of critical consciousness--and not to mere "ignorance" as such--as the source of cultural submersion and marginality, and the historical oppression of the popular masses. In this analysis of historical conditioning and levels of consciousness, Freire proposed the overcoming of "intransitivity" which is typical of dependent and closed societies, and the acquisition and development of critical awareness as the goal of the conscientization process at the cognitive and linguistic registers of behavior.[11]

Before we proceed with this characterization, it is important to underscore the interrelation--interdependence, in fact--of the two major foci of the conscientization process by means of the following diagram.

Conscientization

Cognitive-Linguistic		Self-Dynamics
as the acquisition and development of critical transitivity (in consistent praxis)		as the passage from oppressed consciousness to consciousness of oppression (in consistent praxis)
(semi) intransitive consciousness: develops into naive transitivity, as a result of modernization...	"Dependent - False consciousness"	it may remain "oppressed" –due to forceful suppression/ impositions; –due to "fear of freedom"...
it may regress... it may turn into a "fanatic" consciousness, apathy, etc. in social massification...		it may be transformed into oppressors' consciousness, as positive reflection of oppressors' consciousness (i.e., change of role)...
it may develop into critical transitivity, through "education for liberation"		it may develop into consciousness of oppression through "cultural action for freedom"

In Freire's view, there are several levels of how people perceive their relationship with reality. These are the historically conditioned "levels of consciousness," which must be understood in light of cultural-historical reality as a superstructure in relation to an infrastructure.[12]

a. (Semi) intransitivity is described as a mode of consciousness typical of closed societies with a "culture of silence." It is characterized by a "quasi-adherence" or "quasi-immersion" in objective reality, as a dominated conscience with no sufficient distance to objectify reality in order to know it in a critical way.[13] Because of a kind of obliteration imposed by objective conditions, the only data that this dominated consciousness grasps are the data that lie within the orbit of its lived experience. The lack of what can be called "structural perception"--i.e., understanding of problem situations in terms of institutions and other social factors, for instance--Freire adds, makes people resort to some super-reality or to something within themselves. Action is not directed towards transforming reality, but rather towards those agents falsely assumed, or their own (self-imposed) incapacity. Their social action tends to have the character of defensive or therapeutic magic.

b. The development towards a predominantly naive-transitive conscousness is assumed to be parallel to the transformation of the socio-economic patters of "modernization" (urbanization, technological development, and so on). For Freire, the main characteristics of this mode of consciousness is "simplism" in the interpretation of problematic or limit-situations. It tends to overestimate the past as a better time for living than the present. It underestimates the unsophisticated persons and tends to be seduced by massification. It is not permeable for investigation and its argumentation is fragile, with strong emotional overtones. Naive-transitive consciousness prefers arguments over dialogue, and it often resorts to quasi-magical explanations, however without the fatalistic attitude characteristic of the culture of silence. At this level, the masses can be manipulated by populist leaders and programs, even though--Freire argues--populism may become also a factor in democratic mobilization.[14]

c. The achievement of critical transitivity is not automatic. It implies the capacity to perceive reality structurally. It is a prerequisite for understanding and appropriating history as well as for explicit political commitments within authentically democratic systems. In Freire's words, this mode of consciousness corresponds to highly permeable, interrogative, restless, and dialogical forms of life.[15] It includes characteristics such as greater depth in the interpretation of problems and the substitution of magical explanations. It expresses a disposition to revise and to test opinions as well as discoveries. It assumes responsibility by rejecting quietist positions and being receptive to new approaches. Since apathy and fanaticism are the common inclinations of "naive transitivity" (indeed, fanaticism may become more illogical, alienated and enslaving than intransitive consciousness), Freire forcefully proposes that the educational task par excellence is to sponsor the achievement and exercise of critical transitivity.[16] And a basic responsibility in the developmet of critical consciousness is the discernment of what he calls the "untested feasibilities", i.e., transcending what appear to be inhibiting and paralizing limit-situations. This is the challenge to come up with creative alternatives in light of the "generative themes" of the existencial situation of the people involved in the learning and developmental process that Freire espouses.

The developmental base and structure of the Freire method may be further illumined from the perspective of cognitive psychology. This is not explicity dealt with as a distinct foundation material in Freire's works. It is rather one dimension of our own analysis and inter-pretation of Freire's contributions that calls for a separate discussion in the next section.

2. Conscientization, Self-Cognitive Development, and Liberation

Freire has demonstrated a special instance in which changes in experience are expected to correlate or even coincide with changes in cognitive structures. The literacy/conscientization method and process appears both to necessitate as well as to enhance what Jean Piaget described as the formal-operational level of cognitive development.[17] We suggest that this is veri-fiable at least in terms of the following three impor-tant expressions of the human intelligence.

a. The capacity for combinatorial thought. This is the possibility of taking many factors into account at the same time in problem posing/solving situations. To possess this capacity implies that a host of alter-natives can be perceived in the reflecting, planning and decision-making process. Structural perception of real-ity is made possible, and critical reflection and crea-tivity can be thus facilitated. Also, new existential conflicts may emerge.

b. The ability to utilize a second symbol system, or a set of symbols for symbols. When the formal-operational level of cognitive development is fostered, one's thought can be taken as an object--i.e., one can think about thinking, and the person can thus engage in introspection and refection upon his/her own mental, linguistic, personality and social situation. This is essential for uncovering dynamics pertaining to self-consciousness and alienation, for instance.

    c. The capacity to construct ideals(or "utopias"). This is the possibility of thinking or dreaming of different or contrary to fact situations, and of reasoning about contrary to fact prepositions. This capacity is essential for overcoming conformity, for confronting with confidence limit-situations, and for developing "untested feasibilities" creatively.

    To the extent that those potentialities are actualized and exercised in the conscientization process, the experience of actual liberation of thought-linguistic structures becomes possible. Adaptative and creative responses on different registers of behavior do provide actual power for the individuals and groups involved in the process.

    Free activity of spontaneous reflection starts in early adolescence usually in terms of an intellectual egocentrism according to which the whole world may be submitted to the thought systems. The cognitive processes effectively acquire a new power which involves the possibility of detachment, or disengagement, from external reality. The equilibrium previously referred to implies not only the possibility of radically contradicting reality and personal experience, but also of interpreting, predicting and transforming them.

    These processes involve a particular level of interactions between cognition and self that can be defined in terms of the adolescent phenomenon of "ominipotence of intelligence" (Piaget) which emerges with formal operations.

    Interestingly enough, we find another crucial developmental correlation between the linguistic-symbolic area and the self and social interaction in early childhood and the "play age" (3-4 years). The specific correlation at this point is between the use of grammatical speech and the dawn of "initiative," in Erik H. Erikson's framework.[18] The child now wants to find out what kind of person he is, having established already the fact that he is indeed a person. There is a need

14

for self definition and affirmation, correlated with a
perfected sense of language. His imagination is vastly
expanded, and the growing sense of initiative becomes
the basis for further manifestations of ambition and
independence.

The above-mentioned phenomena suggest that there is
in fact a developmental foundation for cognitive-self
interactions. Further, that the conscientization process
and method necessitates a developmental base. If this
is, indeed, the case, then a double conclusion is in
order. Freire does make a contribution to our understanding of cognitive behavior, and we can also get hold
of a major clue to the effectiveness of his method as
such. That method recapitulates the state transition
process: it gets the developmental process going again.
Hence, in this sense it is truly liberating.

C. Epistemological Shift

One of the central and pervasive themes in Freire
is that the cultural endeavor involved in education for
liberation is actually a socio-political struggle. In
such a situation the oppressed themselves inadvertently
contribute to the perpetuation of their own oppression.
The primordial task and responsibility is, therefore,
that of creating the conditions that facilitate the
people's liberation. This calls for redemptive enterprise for everybody, including the very oppressors.

1. A Revolutionary Pedagogy

Freire's later writings center around the relationship between politics and education, class struggle and
the problem of ideological undergirding and background
of any pedagogy. This is reflected for instance, in
the change of authorities and bibliographical sources
from Education as the Practice of Freedom (Scheler,
Ortega y Gasset, Mannheim, Wright Mills, Whitehead . .
.) to Pedagogy of the Oppressed (Marx, Lenin, Mao,
Marcuse. . .). This has significant implications in
regard to the understanding and ramifications of some
key concepts. For example, the concept of transformation recurs often in Freire's works, but in Education
as the Practice of Freedom it means participation and
integration within a democratic system--i.e., a kind of
"liberal" approach. In Pedagogy of the Oppressed and
subsequent essays, transformation includes the

possibility of subversion and revolution,--i.e., a "radical" political option. Indeed, beginning with his Pedagogy, three major themes are found at the center of Freire's concerns: conscientization, revolution, and the dialogue and cooperation between vanguard and masses in order to maintain the purity of the revolution.

From a lack of reference to the problems addressed by the sociology of knowledge, Freire moved into a position where theory, ideology and utopia suggest fundamental possibilities regarding knowledge. The observation that a "naive" understanding of conscientization may easily lead to "domestication," confirmed for him the fact that knowledge is socially conditioned.

Parallel to this change toward revolutionary radicalism in Freire's thought, a shift took place in regard to the meaning and implications of the very concept of conscientization. The educational praxis became a more revolutionary praxis and greater emphasis was placed on the subject of commitment for and with the oppressed. Freire himself refers to the alteration of his epistemological stance:

> In Education for Freedom, while considering the process of conscientization, I considered the moment when social reality is revealed to be a sufficient psychological motive for attempting to transform the reality which is discovered. Obviously, my mistake was not that I recognized the fundamental importance of knowledge of reality in the process of change, but rather, that I did not take these two different moments--the knowledge of reality and the work of transforming that reality --in their dialectic relationship. It was as if I were saying that to discover reality already meant to transform it.19

The turning point in Freire's theoretical journey lies in his reappraisal--not original, indeed, but nevertheless extremely important--of the inter-relation between education and politics in concrete historical situations.20

Freire attempted to clarify further the concept of conscientization by explaining how to avoid what he called the danger of "mythification."21 He underscores that conscientization has the following characteristics: (1) it is first of all an act of knowing and search

16

for knowledge; (2) it is a dialectic conscience-world, taking place within history, via the praxis in which transformation occurs; (3) it implies the active practice of transformation of reality; (4) it presupposes a previous ideological option towards radical social change; (5) it includes the task of organizing the practice of transformation.

2. New Epistemological Claims

Freire has adopted the Marxist interpretation of the theory of ideology as a foundation for his pedagogical approach. The technical problem of methodology as such became secondary and pedagogical theory became the main concern, including important claims in the area of sociology of knowledge.

The idea and conviction that the oppressed are bearers of truth ("pragmatic truth" à la Marx) is reflected in Freire's reiterated assertion of the need to approach people as the genuine source of knowledge and truth. This is consistent with his insistence that people are to educate themselves. Among other important implications, truth is now conditioned to a class situation.

For the "early Freire," science and education appear to be relatively neutral, whereas in the "later Freire" they become tactical weapons in the midst of the class struggle. Besides, from an emphasis on the relationship and confrontation nature-culture (the educational goal being cultural liberation of Man as a means of social liberation), Freire moved to focus on liberation from the oppressive mechanisms within the social structure at the service of the dominant classes. The educational goal is now the facilitation of radical transformation of the social structure. There are several epistemological claims in Freire's first phase, particularly in connection with the concept of critical transitivity: (1) the development and exercise of critical consciousness is the product of "critical educational work;" (2) the task of education as instrument of the process of developmetn of consciousness depends on two basic attitudes and activities--criticism and dialogue; (3) critical consciousness is typical of societies with a truly democratic structure. These claims undoubtedly depend on a deeper assumption according to which "human reason" is fully enabled for the discovery of "truth."

The "later Freire" emphasizes more the Hegelian
motif of the incorporated oppressor22 (rather than mere
"culture of silence") within capitalistic socio-economic
structures (rather than the ideal of liberty in terms
of Western democracy). He also underlines the politi-
zation of science and education. Of course, Freire was
from the beginning well aware of the political cost and
difficulties involved in his pedagogical program. However, his epistemological postulates led him to interpret such resistence as something rather accidental and
bound to be removed by means of tactical opposition to
a given dictatorship and its allied interests. With the
explicit adoption of a new political-ideological perspective, his theoretical postuales regarding ideology and
knowledge changed. From "tactics," Freire would concentrate on "strategy." Conscientization became open social
struggle. Cultural integration changed into political
revolution. This is reflected specially in Freire's
concept of critical transitivity: in the early writings,
it has much in common with the notion of the scientific
attitude (Dewey). Later, critical transitive consciousness became revolutionary consciousness.

The postulate of the social conditioning of science
was a turning point for Freire who had not previously
taken explicitly into account the agenda of sociology
of knowledge. In connection with this perspective he
affirms two opposite and total ideologies (in Mannheim
terms23): the reactionary and the revolutionary, or the
"right" and "left." There is a self-evident need for
change and for overcoming the alienating social situation which leads to the conclusion that the "pragmatic
truth" of revolutionary praxis is more reliable than
the interpretive truth of observation. A series of
epistemological claims are derived from the basic formulation about the conditioning of science:24 (1)neu-
trality on the part of science or the scientist or
educator, does not exist; (2) the science of education
is epistemologically pregnant with political meaning;
(3) knowledge is mediated through the dialectic involving opposing socio-political classes, and authentic
education is conditioned to class struggle. The oppressed
are the only possible agents of liberation, of themselves as well as the oppressors; (4) class struggle
involves a total concept of ideology; (5) conscientization is a socio-political process that requires revolutionary commitment and the organization of the oppressed.
It helps them to move from being a "class-in-itself" to
becoming a "class-for-itself," from class needs to class
interests (becoming class-for-itself is not merely a new

psychological sensitivity, but class knowledge and practice); (6) revolutionary praxis implies not only the act of knowing but also a theory of knowledge; (7) knowledge, praxis, revolution, as epistemological postulates, are always unfinished productive processes.

This reflection on the epistemological change in Freire's thought leads us now to furhter considerations pertaining to his philosophical foundations. In the next section, we will discuss his approach with the suggestion that Freire presents a kind of reconstructionist educational perspective.

D. On Freire's "Reconstructionism"

Method and philosophy[25] are difficult to separate in Paulo Freire who in his later contributions, tends to appear not only as an educator and social critic, but also as an ideologue of revolution. In the discussion above we referred to a significant shift in his epistemological perspective. We propose that the difference between the "early" and the "later" Freire would amount --in terms of American philosophy of education--to a distinction between "progressivism" and "reconstructionism."[26]

Freire has adopted as his task the defense of the oppressed by developing a pedagogy of liberation which includes cultural and political revolution and social reconstruction as valid and consistent alternatives.

In spite of the evolution perceivable in Freire's work and the inclusion of a new perspective, it is also possible and necessary to appreciate the continuity of his basic existential thrust. That continuity may be indicated by pointing to a central two-fold conception in Freire's thought: (1) modern society does not encourage the masses of population to achieve freedom and to develop critical consciousness, but it rather fosters their alienation and enslavement; (2) people must liberate themselves in order to fulfill their human potential in light of their ontological vocation as history makers.[27]

Thus, Freire insists on the proclamation of the people's need to assume and to reconstruct their own history. He develops a philosophical theoretical device concerning the people's being in history starting with the basic claim about the humanness of the people and the modern social condition which threatens with dehumanization. Along with this strong conviction, Freire also underscores, consistently enough, that a necessary and fundamental condition for any genuine pedagogy is plain faith in the people. For him, this is an a priori datum, the verification of which requires a kind of educational manifesto.[28]

The previous discussion concerning the shift in the epistemological perspective suggests that Freire's approach may be characterized in terms of "reconstructionism," provided that its peculiarities are kept in mind.[29]

In this context, the relationship between John Dewey's thought and Freire's is particularly interesting. It has been carefully established by Danilo R. Streck,[30] by focusing on their contribution to an education that recognizes the relevance of its political function. His analysis shows that the educational view of Dewey and Freire are rooted in the utopian vision and that they complement each other in their contribution towards an education which makes liberation its aim. Streck demonstrates that Freire's "problem posing" in the context of conscientization represents a significant step forward beyond Dewey's position, particularly in that it fosters the development of perception in a structural perspective.

The later Freire would probably stress more sharply than Streck does the differences and points of contrast between the two positions, in a way quite similar to a Marxist critique of Deweyism.[31]

E. A Critical Appraisal

Having analyzed and interpreted Freire's works and thought in the previous pages, in this final section we will critique that contribution concentrating on three major areas. The following comments should be considered as interrelated in the face of Freire's view of education as knowing or epistemology.

1. On Consciousness Raising and Humanization

We need to point out first of all some difficulties regarding the way in which the conception of the levels of consciousness is handled by Freire. Here it is possible to fall into the common blunder of ethnocentrism when characterizing the groups of people assumed to require special efforts towards conscientization. At this point, Freire's approach becomes vulnerable to the kind of criticism raised by Peter L. Berger in terms of "philosophical error" and "political irony." The philosophical error lies in the assumption of the hierarchical view of consciousness. The cognitively superior individual is, by virtue of his consciousness, at a higher level of freedom, and thus of humanity. An ontological hierarchy is thus implied for which there is no evidence whatever. Elitism and messianic paternalism are to be rejected in terms of political irony.[32] In addition to this, the assertion that naive-transitive consciousness develops spontaneously in the context of modernization, for example, is far from self-evident. A careful consideration of social anthropological studies, as well as those of cognitive psychology and related disciplines is needed to further ground, evaluate and supplement Freire's work and assumptions regarding the quest for critical transitivity.

"Humanization," awareness and realization of "full humanity," and related expressions, appear often in Freire's writings. The assumption is that there is an underlying human nature--or a "lost humanity"--that is to be actualized, recaptured, or restored. Further, there is the implication that some enlightened persons possess the clue to that understanding, including the necessary strategy to implement the desired actualization or restoration.

It needs to be indicated also that in his analysis of conscientization, Freire does not stress enough the inclusion of the whole person in social interaction. In other words, the development of critical transitivity appears to be per se a sufficient condition for "humanization."[33] It is apparent, however, that the acquisition and the exercise of critical consciousness is a necessary condition for humanization and liberation, but by no means sufficient. Thus the approach tends to be mainly reason-and awareness-oriented and to underestimate non-cognitive registers of behavior.[34]

2. An Uncritical Assimilation of Marxism

Starting with Pedagogy of the Oppresed it is possible to perceive that Freire has found in Marxian thought a clear epistemological foundation.[35] He

considers and affirms that base as convincing as well
as sufficient and fails to evaluate it critically.
This lack of critical discernment is precisely the kind
of attitude that Freire denounces so strongly in the
case of the "learner" who becomes the victim of the
"banking" instructional model. Furthermore, the danger
of falling into fatalistic sectarianism becomes thus
evident. Interestingly enough Freire himself refers to
this very problem:

> Not infrequently revolutionaries themselves
> becomes reactionary by falling into sectari-
> anism in the process of responding to the
> sectarianism of the Right . . . For the
> rightist sectarian, "today", linked to the
> past, is something given and immutable; for
> the leftist sectarian, "tomorrow" is decreed
> beforehand, is inexorably pre-ordained. This
> rightist and this leftist are both reactionary
> because, starting from their respectively
> false views of history, both develop forms of
> action which negate freedom . . . end up with-
> out the people--which is another way of being
> against them.36

3. Potential Dogmatism and Indoctrination

Freire appears to adopt a dogmatic position by
demanding a previous ideological option which seemingly
would be justified and validated a posteriori in the
conscientization process. It is hard to avoid indoctrination when operating from this perspective. One
can seriously raise the question about the actual goal
of education/conscientization: to what an extent is
human freedom indeed facilitated or people conditioned
to "freely" assume the political option of the educators/
"catalizers"? The educational process may be distorted
seriously by insisting on the assumption and the conviction that some kind of revolution is the only true and
trustworthy alternative freely chosen as soon as reality
is perceived demythified. Since Freire also states that
the commitment to radical, revolutionary change is prior
to conscientization as such, the question arises as to
the integrity of this approach on logical and ethical
grounds. There is the belief that the dynamics of
alienation are so strong and the oppressors' resources
so powerful, that it is only logical that conscientization should lead most people to a revolutionary commitment, defined in terms of basically Marxist lines.

However, there is no reason to infer that this in fact is the case. That conclusion about revolution may not be automatically reached through the application of Freire's methodology.

What Freire believed to be the solution for the "mythologizing" of conscientization, actually could become a manifestation of mythical thinking. As far as the content of the myth is concerned, there is a moralistic picture of good and evil depicted in terms of the struggle between the oppressed and the oppressors. Further, this is considered almost as a revealed truth, as something that everybody should be able and willing to perceive sooner or later. And once the awareness has taken place, the only alternative left is to participate in the struggle. In this case, participation should take the form of revolutionary praxis on the side of the oppressed. It is assumed that this conception is actually consistent with the tide of history. and--in Freire's liberation theology--with the manifestation of the Kingdom of God. This is part of the compelling vision that needs to be communicated and conscienticized in order to accelerate and facilitate the defeat of evil.[37]

Therefore, a conflict and contradition is present between the denunciation of manipulation and maintaining that the goal of education must be the realization of a certain kind of revolutionary option. Further, it is obvious that messianism and authoritarianism of any kind frustrate violently the creative and liberating process which Freire's praxis approach is expected to foster.

Another related area for critical evaluation along those lines refers to the oversimplications and generalizations inherent in the dichotomizing--e.g., oppressed - oppressors--analytical process.[38] Here again we have to underscore a major obstacle for the manifestation of creativity, which requires appreciation of complexity and tolerance for ambivalence and ambiguity. Freire rightly criticizes those who suffer from "absence of doubt," the prisoners of a "circle of certainty."[39] However, he himself does not always do justice to the very conscientization thrust by overlooking the variety and nuances, richness and precariousness, of social reality.

We search for consistency with Freire's all-time premises of faith in and faithfulness to the people, of the alienating character of indoctrination and domestication, and of the "untested feasibility" of dialogical communion. Freirean thought can be appreciated anew by means of a fundamental revision of its ideological assumptions. At the point of frustration in the epistemological base we rediscover a promising alternative in terms of the potential for human creativity. This is by no means alien to Paulo Freire. On the contrary, the essential orientation of his educational approach should be perceived in terms of liberation for creativity and creativity for liberation. This perspective --which we will develop below-- provides the most fruitful appreciation of the dynamics and basic integrity of Freire's contribution. It also makes it possible to relate the epistemological foundation to the theological concerns which are explicity present in Freire's thought. In the following chapter we thus proceed to describe and analyze conscientization in light of creativity.

CHAPTER 2

CONSCIENTIZATION AS CREATIVITY

In the previous chapter the challenge of Freire's pedagogy for revolutionary change was exposed and analyzed. Our critical reflection underscored some limitations and contradictions inherent in that approach. Our task now consists of unveiling the epistemology of the creative process which, we claim, is implicit in Freire's contribution. Therefore, the argument to be advanced is that the process Freire sponsors is, essentially, the creative process.

In this chapter we will develop an alternative statement of the conscientization method. Our reformulation of Freire's approach accounts for its effectiveness, and it also makes it possible to correct potential shortcomings and distortions. Seen in light of creativity the conscientization method and process maintains its integrity and its basic orientation as "cultural action for freedom" and "education for liberation."

A. Conscientization and the Study of Creativity

The possibility of illuminating conscientization from this perspective arose with the realization that we can thus perceive a very special case of human development consistent with the pattern of creativity which has a structural integrity of its own.

We claimed before that the conception of creativity as such is not alien to Freire's thought. The emphasis on a problem-posing, conflict-facing educational context and process is both persistent and consistent in itself as well as the critique of the transmission of information outlook in educational communication. Essentially, as a keen educational critic, Freire reacts against the repression of creativity. That is implicit in his rejection of conformity and of rigid patterns of teaching-learning which prevent personal initiative. Consequently, he emphasizes the search and discovery of humanizing alternatives, and the challenge towards the "untested feasibility" when facing so-called limit-situations. Besides pointing to that general orientation, we have suggested looking more closely and specifically at the literacy method which is paradigmatic of Freire's conception of education as the practice of freedom and

social change. There are at least two further observations to make regarding Freire's approach that point in
the direction of our chosen line of inquiry.

Cognitive behavior and structures. For Freire,
education is a certain theory of knowing put into practice. Thus, his work and thought focuses on cognitive
behavior and structures. It is in this epistemological
context that, as Freire states, the conscientization
program "would be an act of creation, capable of realis-
ing other creative acts."

> There is a creative drive in every man. . .
> that stems from man's inconclusive nature.
> The more education develops this ontologic
> drive to create, the more authentic educa-
> tion is. Education must be uninhibiting
> and not restrictive . . . The development
> of a critical consciousness that allows man
> to transform society is more and more urgent.
> To the extent that men respond to the chal-
> lenges of the world wihtin their society,
> they . . . are making history by starting
> from their own creative activity . . .
> The whole debate /on the democratization of
> culture 7 is highly criticist and motivating.
> The illiterate apprehends critically the
> need to learn to read and write . . . an
> attitude of creation and recreation. It also
> implies a self-affirmation from which an
> acting posture of man on his context can
> result.[1]

From story telling to history making. This second
observation has to do with Freire's implicit conception
of the "narrative quality of experience,"[2] in the context of a prophetic stance. That stance includes a
particular approach and style as sell as a consistent
emphasis on prophetic motifs. Such is the case of the
utopian denouncing (judgment) and announcing (hope) and
the identification with the prophetic church whose
mission and goal it is to proclaim and work for the
liberation of the oppressed. Thus, we can suggest that
Freire presents a particular reading of the "sacred
story," that can be translated approximately in these
terms: "Human beings are unfinished, open beings,
involved in a continuous process of representation,
interpretation and reshaping of reality. Yet, alienation has been a constant threat and a condition which
undermines and tarnishes humanity. God is engaged in

the liberating enterprise, particularly by enabling
human beings to participate in the struggle for liberation from oppression, and to shape their own lives and
destiny. The Exodus and Christ's Easter are paradigmatic
of such an enablement and orientation." This would be
the ultimate underlying and undergirding story and
"script" of the people's "mundane stories," which are
shared in the actual conscientization process and method.
In the last analysis, the thrust of conscientization
can be said to be from story telling to history making:
persons becoming "authors"--i.e., assuming "authorship,"
as writers and creators--and willing agents of social
change.

Conscientization will be shown to have a structure
which is parallel to the phases of the creative process
as commonly characterized and analyzed.[3] Indeed, we
will refer to conscientization in terms of movements and
principles discernible in the creative process. However, it will also become apparent that the conscientization method and process in turn illumines creativity.

Before we develop our argument, it will be useful
to clarify some basic assumptions related to our methodological stance, and that will be done in the next
section.

Excursus on Integrity, Non-neutrality, and Responsibility

Freire reminds us of the socio-political responsibility of the scientist, theologian and professional,
and the importance of understanding the realm of inquiry
and service within concrete historical reality. When
discussing this topic explicity, Freire underlines that
true social commitment is essentially solidarity and a
never ending search for humanization. Scientists and
professionals are always to recognize their debt to the
common cultural patrimony, and to avoid becoming alienated in the supposedly "superior world" of experts and
specialists. They are to participate in the development of a scientifically founded humanism and a structural perception of reality, and they are to assume
responsibility for continuing professional growth.[4]

Values, biases and commitments are indeed reflected
in any scientific and professional endeavor. Further,
it is impossible to isolate oneself from the socio-
cultural reality which in diverse ways demands taking

sides in the midst of political struggles at different levels. Having said that, however, it is to be acknowledged that it is possible and helpful to keep a distinction in mind--not always respected by the most politically committed scientists, scholars and theologians, including Freire--between moral responsibility and methodological integrity.[5] Furthermore, for the Christian scholar or professional in particular, that realization can be associated with participation in the life and mission of the community of faith.[6] Whereas the situations may appear to be less obvious or less directly relevant in some areas, this is certainly not the case in regards to education. There is the need today as always to discuss in very concrete terms what it means and implies to be consistent with "God's politics". To use Paul Lehmann's happy expression: "the power to will what God wills . . . what it takes to make and to keep human life human."[7] Paulo Freire is helpful in pointing sharply to this formidable challenge, as we will see later. And our own reappraisal of that contribution will hopefully show its basic integrity and its actual relevance for Christian education in particular.

B. Literacy/Conscientization and the Creative Process

In this section we will discuss the creative process vis à vis the Freire method. The asserted structural similarity of the two phenomena in regard to the dynamics of creative transformation will be tested by a functional analogy allowing for mutual enlightening. Conscientization will be shown to be a special manifestation of creativity which in turn facilities the realization of other creative acts.

In the following correlation, the movements of the creative process will be described in terms of common understandings shared by prominent creativity theorists. Freire's contribution will be discussed and reinterpreted taking mainly into account, but not only, his effective literacy method.

1. Baffled Struggle in a Context of Rapport

a. The sequence of the creative process is usually set in motion by a baffled struggle which includes both a certain need or lack, and a challenge to discover an

appropriate answer or resolution.[8] A work of art, the
meaning of a neurotic symptom, a mathematical problem,
a philosophical quest, are but a few cases in the wide
variety of occasions for the manifestation of creativity.
The essential feature is the structuration of a tensive
unit or gestalt, which works toward continuity and
completion. In other words, the lack of equilibrium
experienced as tension and conflict, will eventually
have to be resolved.

"Rapport" refers here to environmental support.
Other persons, in direct and indirect ways, are sympathetic to the conflict situation, and will somehow
encourage, facilitate, interpret, celebrate and benefit
from its resolution. Actual groups of people and diverse
language systems constitute the social and cultural
dimensions of rapport.

This necessary first stage of the creative process
involves preparation and immersion due to the challenge,
or even threat, posed to the momement of consciousness
by the problematic situation.

b. The Freire method of literacy/conscientization
begins also--and very intentionally so--with conflict
in a context of rapport. There is an obvious lack
expressed in the incapacity to read and write within a
social context where literacy is an important skill in
terms of the economic and political reality (e.g., the
possibility of better jobs, the right to vote). Therefore this lack exists in a broader framework of privation and inhibitions which includes deeper pesonal
levels such as the poor self-image of the persons
involved. From the observer's perspective, behind the
felt lacks and needs there might be a more profound
(unconscious) dimension of lack and conflict which are
eventually realized as such. This may include, for
instance, a self-depreciating perception and evaluation,
fear of learning, or ambivalence. On another level, the
"lack" may consist of the impossibility of perceiving
certain aspects of the power struggle in which one may
be a victim and an unwilling participant, or even an
accomplice. This is the case of the internalized oppressive consciousness--"oppressor within"--described
by Freire and others.

The "circles of culture" undoubtedly supply strong
environmental support and encouragement. In fact, they
provide a kind of affective climate much more appealing
than that of the traditional school setting. Both

dimensions of rapport can be appreciated: social, through the group interactions, and cultural--i.e., symbolic and linguistic. The language of a given community is in effect affirmed as such and not underestimated. The whole context--including the problems to be overcome--provide an effective motivation to proceed until the terms of the conflict are unveiled and analyzed, and the resolution is discovered.

2. Interlude for Scanning

a. The "stage of incubation" is the second phase or movement in the typical creative sequence. It appears as an interval and a pause, a seeming withdrawal. It does not mean mere passivity, however, even though some form of "capitulation" and momentary resignation may actually take place in may instances. Searching and scanning do continue even if relatively unnoticed or unconscious. The point is then a shift of concentration since the terms of the conflict are removed from local attention:

> This is indwelling the conflicted situation
> with empathy for the problem and its parts.
> In order for this to occur, one's attention
> must at least for a moment be diverted from
> the problem as such . . . Scanning is not
> only a search for answers outside the problem;
> it is also scanning and differentiating the
> terms of the problem and playing possible
> solutions against various interpretations of
> the ruptured situation. Note that it takes
> an investment of caring energy to hold the
> problem, partial solutions, and the whole
> state of irresolution together... This is
> the step of waiting, wondering, following
> hunches, and exhausting the possibilities.[9]

In Harold Rugg's terms, the period preceding the creative flash of insight is described as a state of "relaxed tension." This includes the tension produced by the conflict or problematic situation as appropriated by consciousness as well as the affirmation of the freedom from control on the part of the preconscious. For Rugg the total organism as such is preconsciously engaged in the continuous scanning or searching movement, uninterruptedly seeking completion--i.e., resolution, lack of lack.[10]

Two psychodynamic factors are to be emphasized in connection with this phase of the creative process: the structuring and motivating potential of the "incompleted acts," and conscious conflicts allowed to be dealt with more freely, "off-consciously," by the preconscious during this "incubation" stage.

> A further criterion of the creative act
> . . . that it involves several levels
> of consciousness. In problem-solving,
> pre- and extra-conscious guidance makes
> itself increasingly felt as the dif-
> ficulty increases; but in the truly
> creative act both in science and art,
> underground levels of the hierarchy
> which are normally inhibited in the wak-
> ing state play a decisive part.[11]

b. In the literacy/conscientization process an equivalent to "interlude for scanning" also takes place. It happens when the initial formualtion of the problem is set aside and the attention is directed towards representations, discussions and critical reflection. This phase occurs prior to the discovery of mechanisms pertaining to the written language, and also before alternative ways of perceiving and dealing with existential problems are unveiled. The "pause" happens basically because the educator/coordinators are not expected to provide the answers. People are encouraged to struggle together in search for fitting responses and alternatives.

At this point, then, we can underscore another major contrast between Freire's method and the traditional transmission-of-information approaches. Conscientization invites the participants to discover and complete the needed Gestalt, as a focal experience within an essentially asymmetrical communication process.[12] This accounts for facilitating the creative sequence in terms of an interlude for scanning.

3. Insight, Intuition, and Bisociation

a. The solution comes, yet it is not forced. The creative insight and discovery is called by Arthur Koestler a "bisociative act," with the prerequisite that two hitherto separate frames of reference intersect in a common element.

31

I have coined the term "bisociation" in
order to make a distinction between the
routine skills of thinking on a single
"plane," as it were, and the creative
act which . . . always operates on more
than one plane . . . a double-minded,
transitory state of unstable equilibrium
when the balance of both emotion and
thought is disturbed . . .
The bisociative act connects previously
unconnected matrices of experience; it
makes us "understand what it is to be
awake, to be living on several planes at
once."13

This is considered the fundamental property and
criterion of creativity as illustrated in scientific,
artistic, literacy creation as well as humor. Creative
insight occurs when an individual perceives that an
element pertaining to one frame of reference belongs
also to another frame of reference, and its double
membership is discovered as the relationship capable of
solving the initial struggle.

This third stage or movement of the creative process consists of the often sudden and unexpected flash
of insight generated beyond consciousness that illumines
the resolution of the conflict, and eliminates the
initial "lack." It is a constructive act of the imagination.

b. Again, we can identify the phase of creative
insight in the literacy/conscientization process. This
is the generally sudden discovery of literacy rules as
well as the realization of personal potential for learning and transformation, many times not even suspected
before. It involves also the perception of the paradigmatic character of the social interaction which takes
place in learning and working together in the circles of
culture.

The context of rapport in which conscientization
takes place provides a peculiar setting for the emergence of insights, including group phenomena of col-
lective illumination. The "codifications" presented to
the group are meant to foster critical reflection, and
to raise imaginative responses, like a projective screen.
The persons involved in the experience actually discover
and at the same time re-create and re-define those very
situations being presented in a variety of ways.

Here, "bisociation" also takes the form of the
recognition of the double membership of a given element
which is perceived as the solution to the problem. It
may have seral dimensions and expressions such as the
capacity to become literate and the potential to participate in some way in the transformation of reality
of one's self and society.

4. Release of Tension and Transformation of Energy

        a. Release of tension and discharge and transfor-
mation of energy take place simultaneously with, or
immediately after, the occurrence of insight. As we
just saw, "insight" may be described in terms such as
conflict-solving image, bisociation, or intuition. The
tension that is the by-product of the problem situation
or baffled struggle tends to disappear. If this is not
the case,

        then it is evident that the conscious con-
        flict was not the one resolved by the
        emergent image; an unconscious influence
        (a conflict concealed from the subject) has
        entered disruptively into the pattern of
        reality consciousness.14

        This fourth movement has a definite affective and
conational character in terms of energy discharge.
Psychodynamically, the successful resolution of a conflict situation which demanded self-involvement and in-
vestment allows for the release of the energy which was
sustaining that very baffled struggle. Further, that
discharge of energy is also evidence of the effort and
the process involved in the creation of the bisociative
act, or integrating insight, having taken place particularly outside the conscious mind. Says Koestler:

        The emotional manifestations of the Eureka
        act--sudden illumination followd by abreac-
        tion and catharsis--also testifies to its
        subconscious origins; they are to some
        extent comparable to the cathartic effects
        of the analyst's method of bringing 'repres-
        sed complexes' into the patient's conscious-
        ness.15

        Further, the usually pleasant and joyful release
of tension and discharge of energy functions as a reward
which reinforces the whole creative process which is

taking place. Joy is associated with the realization
that some kind of liberation and transformation is in-
indeed occurring, and that one is participating in the
reshaping of reality, however minor the creative acts
may be. After having confronted frustration and anxiety
and, perhaps, even fear and guilt, the feeling of
gratification and satisfaction becomes predominant.
There is a major question that emerges in light of this
discussion and in regard to the destination of the
energy that is released, because--in principle--that
energy can be utilized for anything.

Still another point to be underscored in connection
with the affect-value dimension of creativity--especially
apparent in this fourth movement of the creative process
--is singled out by Eric Klinger in his respondent- process
theory of fantasy as one of the conditions of creativity:
hospitable reception of one's "respondent" experiences.

> Individuals vary widely in their reception
> of their own impulses, affects, and ideas.
> Reception is a complex matter, however, that
> includes at least two largely independent
> dimensions . . . the inclination to attend
> to or report them and the disposition to
> exploit them fully in thought and social
> interaction . . . The dimension of attend-
> ing to inner events therefore represents
> tolerance for them and perhaps the learned
> capacity to utilize them.
> The state of receptivity to one's respondent
> experiences has never been experimentally
> related to creative activity, but a consider-
> able body of correlational data supports the
> validity of the theory that relates them. . .
> creative individuals not only attend to their
> respondent processes but value, trust, and
> actively exploit them.[16]

Creativity assumes and necessitates a considerable
degree of self-confidence and affirmation. There must
be some form of trust and anticipation of the creative
response, even if that response then seems to appear
rather suddenly or unexpectedly.

b. When we turn once again to the literacy/
conscientization process, we can detect varied expressions of that basically affective "Eureka!"effect. It
means release of tension, discharge of energy and joy
due to the discovery of new existential possibilities:

self-reaffirmation, acquisition of skills such as literacy, critical reflection, taking distance to "ad-mire" and evaluate problems and alternative solutions, and so on. The overwhelming realization of worth and new power is expressed in simple testimonies such as that of a man who told the group "last night I could not sleep because I could write my name." Freire refers to visible changes in the illiterate's former attitudes, by discovering themselves as makers of the world of culture and that they as well as the schooled persons have a creative and re-creative potential:

> Many participants . . . affirm happily and self-confidently that they are not being shown "anything new, just remembering". "I make shoes" said one, "and now I see that I am worth as much as the Ph.D. who writes books.". . . "Tomorrow", said a street-sweeper in Brasilia, "I'm going to go to work with my head high." He had discovered the value of his person . . . [17]

There are also dramatic examples of released energy being re-directed in favor of further learning and practice. Freire wonders how one can explain the fact that a man who was illiterate several days earlier could write words with complex phonemes before he had even studied them. After the mechanism of phonemic combinations has been discovered, he attempts and manages to express himself graphically in the way he speaks. As a rule, Freire points out, the illiterates wrote confidently and legibly, largely overcoming the natural indecisiveness of beginners. We agree with the hypothesis suggested by Elza Freire on this point: these persons have "discovered themselves to be more fully human, thereby acquiring and increasing emotional confidence in their learning which was reflected in their motor activity."[18] To perceive the whole process in light of the creativity sequence, allows for a comprehensive understanding including that type of phenomenon. There is no question that the insights are received hospitably and that this is facilitated by the special context of rapport of the circles of culture which enhance strong self-affirmation and confidence. Thus, conscientization clearly includes the fourth movement of the creativity paradigm with a two-fold sign: Release of energy and personal openness to further experiences of liberating expansion of awareness. This is a peculiar sample of conscious effort to foster the experience of creativity, not as a rare or unusual

phenomenon, but as a special manifestation of freedom
for transformation, that can be made available to any-
body and sponsored for all.

5. Interpretation and Verification

a. By definition, creativity involves the process
of making or bringing somehting new into being. In
many occasions, a whole new perspective and major transformation takes place. Hence, the discovery and inspirational dimension of creativity must be accompanied and
supplemented by proper verification, elaboration or
articulation.

The final necessary phase in the creative sequence
is characterized mainly but not only by discerning
activity. The person is to recognize and understand the
connection between conflict and insight. Major questions
to be dealt with here are: what struggle was addressed
and resolved, how and why the resolution was achieved,
whether or to what extent the "discovery" or insight is
appropriate to that particular conflict of baffled
struggle. Interpretation is to work in two directions,
backward and forward:

> Working backward I will call congruence; this
> makes explicit, congruent connections from
> the essential structures of the imaginative
> construct back into the original conditions
> of the puzzle. Working forward I will call
> correspondence: this makes the apparent
> congruence public and a matter of consensus.
> Thus, the imaginative construct is examined
> for its correspondence to a consensual view
> of the world.[19]

The social dimension of creativity is thus further
underscored. Creative insight moves beyond subjective
immediacy through symbol process, and public language.
The sequence is completed and its structure effectively
captured and appropriated. Interpretation socializes
the privatistic experience of creative conflict resolution. In addition, the discovery or insight is shared
and put to test for verification and scrutiny within
the larger "context of rapport." Therefore, here we
can visualize new opportunities for socially validated
reward and reinforcement. In other words, interpretation involves more than cognitive registers of behavior.
Participants are thus freed and motivated for further

engagement in creative problem posing and conflict resolution.

Lack of interpretation truncates the creative process and causes the kind of repetitive patterns that, for instance, psychoanalytic interpretation is supposed to dissolve in the therapeutic setting by facilitating the reception and integration of the "healing" images.

Misinterpretation is another serious problem. It leaves the basic conflicts unsolved (including now the "false consciousness" of apparent resolution and--perhaps--further repression and alienation) and causes disruption. The process has to be carefully related to a context of interpretation so that it does not contribute to alienation. In discussing Kierkegaard on this very point, Loder concludes:

> The principle implied is that a misinterpretation of revelation--or of any creative image which enlivens the empirical world according to the four preceding steps --may be disruptive to reality consciousness if it fails to keep the "meaning" of the image entirely indigenous to the context of the conflict in which it emerged.[20]

b. In the literacy/conscientization method and process, interpretation is seen basically in terms of the concept of "praxis" understood as reflection and action. It implies making sense out of the whole experience, and the connection of emerging phenomena with actual problems and conflicts in everyday life. Confirmation and demonstration are considered together. A major change in the life of the persons involved has taken place and it can be appropriated and further developed as such.

Literacy dramatizes learning and the practice of writing and reading one's own story. Interpretation in this context includes affirmation and celebration of the fact that--by telling one's story--it has become possible to realize the vocation to "make history." It is by indwelling this story that people actually acquire "authorship." As mentioned before, this is the main thrust of conscientization as education for liberation.

Examples from different settings where the Freire method has been used, show a certain danger in regard to this state of the literacy/conscientization process.

It consists of the abrupt inclusion of political-
ideological analysis--especially in terms of the Marxist
understanding of class struggle, provided by the
"experts." The attempt to promote the development of
"political consciousness"[21] in such a way actually
produces a deleterious effect because violence is done
to the very educational process supposed to be liberating. Besides, from a purely pragmatic perspective,
ideological teachings (Marxist or otherwise) unneces-
sarily elicit or exacerbate opposition to the conscientization project from different sources. Interpretation
and appropriate action must refer to the very conflict
situations engaged by the people who participate in the
process (e.g., improvement of specific living conditions,
devising new educational plans, organizing for some sort
of political action).

C. Conscientization and Creativity Principles

Not only can we perceive the structural similarity
between the Freire approach and the basic pattern of
creativity, as described above, but the case for conscientization as creativity can also be discussed with
the focus on fundamental principles involved that account for creativity. We refer to certain principles
that run through the phases or movements of the creative
process and are intertwined through the proces as a
whole. They can also be identified as operative in
conscientization.

1. Orthogenesis

This term means "development in a straigh course."
It refers to the fact that the organism--including all
registers of behavior--tends to develop proceeding from
(1) a state of relative globality and lack of differentiation, to (2) increasing differentiation and articulation, and (3) hierarchic integration that yields
greater operational complexity. This basic sequential
gestalt of the model of orthogenesis is proposed as the
organic core or biolocial base of the creative process[22]
The pattern of straight-line development inherent in
human beings provides the organizing principle for the
associations involved in creativity.

The three basic phases of the model or orthogenesis
are apparent in the literacy/conscientization method and
process. The learning sequence and the development of

critical awareness clearly reflect a movement from a
global state to increased differentiation and articulation and hierarchical integration. This process is in
fact intentionally and explicitly fostered through
consideration of "generative themes" and "generative
words". Participants learn to operate with families
of syllables, words, sentences and utterances, in a
reversible pattern. Likewise in regard to development
of levels of consciousness, including the analysis of
social interaction, self-image, patterns of behavior
and relationships. Orthogenic structures can be thus
identified in the facilitating group process of the
circles of culture.

2. Transposition

The human mind can transpose information from one
register of behavior to another by means of its "semiotic
function"--i.e., the process by which signs, symbols
and signals are recognized and utilized. The creative
process can maintain an identifiable continuity because
of a number of states of transposition that take place.
It occurs, for instance, in the movement between the
felt sense of a baffled struggle or conflict situation
--e.g., trying to solve a puzzle, facing an existential
dilemma, etc.--and its verbal articulation (phase 1);
between the statement of the problem and its submission
to a "deeper" or alternative chamber of the mind (phase
2); and similarly with the rest of the sequence.

This principle of transportation, which accounts
for the continuity of the process, needs to be post-
ulated also in the case of conscientization. Its occurrence through the different stages can be inferred
both in the case of the literacy method as well as in
the wider conscientization process in other educational
programs.

"Bisociation," the concept coined by Koestler and
discussed above, involves in this light a special
instance of transposition. When insight occurs, the
recognition of the double membership of a given element
is perceived as the solution to the problem situation.
Creative "bisociations" do take place in the process of
learning to read and write as well as in the development
of a structural perception of reality in the conscientization process. The overcoming of illiteracy is in turn
bisociated with the confrontation of oppressive socio-
economic situations, and so on.

3. Annihilation

Creative expressions always involve an element of negation and aggression. Creativity, like growth itself, has in it elements of pain and does violence to ordinary patterns of expectation. Every creative act, therefore, bears the marks of annihilation transcended but not obliterated.

This principle of annihilation is also particularly manifest in the Freire method as such as well as in the creative "products" of literary and conscientization. The explicit rejection of traditional patterns of education and leadership, and the denunciation aspect--i.e., "judgment"--of the utopian perspective with regard to education and society, are but two general manifestations. On a deeper level, annihilation is the meaning of the aggressive thrust to overcome inertia, apathy, conformity, and internal opposition and resistance (e.g., the "oppressor within" that needs to be dislodged together with certain dependency habits, etc.).

This aggressive thrust should not be confused with destructive violence, however, a common temptation apparently justified by the intrinsic violence of oppressive living conditions. In fact, annihilation in terms of the creative process may include the reversal of the "natural" tendency to retaliate. Retaliation is a manifestation of the old order that needs to be transformed and liberated. Therefore, to "kill" oppression necessitates the "salvation" of the oppressors in some creative fashion.

The affective and subjective dimension of this phenomenon is also noteworthy. Creativity as such is often accompanied by a certain degree of anxiety and guilt feelings, and this is also the case in the conscientization process. The source of these personal experiences lies in the fact that creative acts are at the same time acts of annihilation or destruction: insights and discoveries, new ideas and different ways of perceiving reality always destroy something such as beliefs, prejudices or understandings about what is "real," "natural" or "true." They may actually shake the existential foundations of many people, including those who appear to be the main beneficiaries of the creative transformation. As Rollo May states:

. . . anxiety is understandably a concomitant
of the shaking of the self-world relationship
that occurs in the encounter. Our sense of
identity is threatened. The world is not as
we experienced it before, and since self and
world are always correlated, we no longer are
what we were before.23

Not only does creativity shatter previous hypotheses and assumptions, but it also changes the terms of
the relationships between oneself and reality. The more
intensively this situation is lived, the more likely are
manifestations of anxiety and guilt to appear. Fear of
retaliation and punishment, and even fear of freedom
itself, may be the unconscious meaning of those personal
expressions. In the case of conscientization projects,
this is obviously reinforced whenever there is external
suspicion or outright hostility to the educational
program.

4. Structuralism[24]

The basic pattern of creativity has been described
with remarkable consistency by a variety of theorists.
Besides, the essential continuity among creative acts
has been established in regard to diverse manifestations
of creativity in areas such as art, science, and literature, as well as in other expressions of human life and
endeavors--e.g., resolution of problem situations,
humor, and religious experiences. In other words,
creativity has its peculiar structure. It has an integrity in its linear movement which leads us with compelling force to complete the sequence and to resolve the
lack of equilibrum originated in a given conflict situation.

We have underscored that the process of conscientization, and the literacy method in particular, essentially involves a manifestation of human growth and
development with its own structure. The initial lack
must be resolved and the task has to be performed with
a particular learning sequence in the group setting of
the circles of culture. Interestingly enough, the
Freire method has maintained an essential continuity,
and proven effectiveness, in a variety of cultural settings. This is to be accounted for in ligh of the
peculiar grammar and syntax of the syllabic languages,
and a learning process which is patterned in terms of
creativity.

41

The relevance of this principle of structuralism actually allows us to look at conscientization from the standpoint of this perspective, including Claude Lévi-Strauss' design for cultural transformation.25 Even though we are not dealing with myths of the kind Lévi-Strauss analyzed, we do have many records of stories and reflections shared by the people involved in the conscientization process.26

In Freire's work and thought there are a number of different and reiterated polarities which he explicitly deals with: life-death, human beings-social situations, oppressor-oppressed, oppression-liberation. Freire emphasizes the liberating potential of the community context in which learning and teaching, objectivity and subjectivity, are seen dialectically and whose social interaction becomes paradigmatic. This emphasis is important in light of the mediating process required for the resolution of the opposites, Freire suggests that the liberating agent is neither the vanguard nor the ideology--although both are indispensable--but the group of people mutually committed to learn and to work together for social transformation.

Dialectically speaking then, conscientization is expected to foster a "double negation" or cancellation analogous to the one suggested in Lévi-Strauss' design.27 The "annihilation of that which annihilates"--structures of domination and oppression--includes an internal dimension that needs to be acknowledged both in regard to the self as well as in the relationships within the group. As Freire points out, this implies that the oppressed themselves assume responsibility for the perpetuation of the alienating situation due to their interiorization of the "oppressors' ways." This is a phenomenon for the analysis of which Hegel and Freud together provide very valuable and complementary clues.28

D. Recapitulation

Our observations lead us to underscore that Freire's great intuition is to have perceived the structural continuity between his literacy method on the linguistic-symbolic dimension and the conscientization process on the level of self and social interaction. In one of the few explicit references in this regard, Freire, quoting Noam Chomsky, states:

Conscientization occurs simultaneously with the literacy or post-literacy process. It must be so. In our educational method, the word is not something static or disconnected from men's existential experience, but a dimension of their thought-language about the world. That is why, when they participate critically in analyzing the first generative words linked with their existential experience; when they focus on the syllabic families which result from that analysis; when they perceive the mechanism of the syllabic combinations of their language, the learners finally discover, in the various possibilities of combination, their own words. Little by little, as these possibilities multiply, the learners, through mastery of new generative words, expand both their vocabulary and their capacity for expression by the development of their creative imagination.[29]

Therefore, it is in that context that he can properly refer to his approach in terms of cultural action for freedom.

In the first chapter we pointed out that the method recapitulates the stage transition process. The developmental process is stimulated by enhancing the formal-operational level of cognitive development at least in terms of the following: capacity for combinatorial thought, ability to use a second symbol system, and capacity to construct ideals. We proposed that to the extent that those potentialities are developed in the conscientization process, the experience of actual liberation of thought-linguistic structures becomes possible, and that adaptative and creative responses on different registers of behavior do provide actual power for individuals and groups involved in the process.

Two brief additional comments pertaining to language, freedom and limitations may now be included.

On Language and Freedom. The Freire literacy method--especially in the case of Spanish and Portuguese --provides an interesting occasion for illustrating the fundamental role that two major operations and principles play in language: combination and selection. They are discussed in Roman Jakobson's essay "The Cardinal Dichotomy in Language."[30] The Freire method encourages the experience of actual freedom in the multiple choices

43

and substitutions possible (<u>selectivity</u> principle) of
word and sentence formation. It is also possible to
observe a peculiar and pleasant expression of freedom
facilitated by the method in terms of playful invention
("new words," "funny words," or "bad words," over against
"thinking words" as conventional vocabulary). This is
a concrete expression of the enablement to "own one's
word," as Freire states, within the rules of the game
of the syllabic languages (combinatorial principle).
The discovery of the mechanism of phonetic combinations
is precisely crucial in this sense. As Jakobson points
out, freedom reamins small in the combining of phonemes
into words, but "in the combination of linguistic units,
there is an ascending scale of freedom."[31]

Likewise, freedom is experienced in the context of
formulation of problematic situations, alternatives,
decisions, and action, within the enduring existential
"syntax" which calls for some resolution out of the
lacks and conflicts. In both dimensions of the process
(linguistic-symbolic/self) we find learning as growth
and development and the release of energy ("power") for
further experience and action. Both are expressions of
human creativity to the extent that the "grammar" is
completed. The Freire method demonstrates the insepa-
rability of thought processes and self transformation.
The capacity for self-recreation based upon the freedom
to shape one's own destiny is associated with consciousness and self-awareness.[32]

On Freedom and Limitations. The dialectical tension
between freedom and limits/limitations can now be made
more explicit and spelled out. Freire stresses the
possibility of challenging the very understanding of
so-called "limit situations" in order to move beyond
resignation and conformity. His work and approach
illustrate very well the creative endeavors to overcome
"limitations" (e.g., illiteracy, overdependency, prejudices about oneself) while--in the same process--
structural "limits" (e.g., a given form of grammar,
certain structures of the human mind, a given historical
context) are acknowledged.[33] Actually, the creative
process always starts with a struggle that involves the
recognition of different kinds of "limitations" in terms
of barriers, needs, or lacks, together with the challenge to discover an appropriate answer or resolution.
In this sense, limitations are not only necessary but
valuable because, by creatively confronting them,
learning and development can take place.

It might well happen as in Freire's experiences, that persons realize that previously considered limits or "givens" are in fact "limitations" which can be overcome. And the opposite case--"limitations" becoming "limits"--may also be a creative and liberating insight in many instances --e.g., the recognition of unchangeable situations in the past. Both cases illustrate the exercise of freedom--e.g., freedom from deceptive, simplistic appreciations of reality; and freedom to acknowledge and appropriate intrinsic, structural limits, and the expansion of awareness.

Our argument has been that the literacy/conscientization process that Freire advocates is essentially analogous to the pattern of the creative process. Further, we have also perceived that conscientization and creativity are mutually enlightening, as summarized below.

Creativity illuminates conscientization. It provides a fundamental freamework for understanding different dimensions (linguistic-symbolic, self) and levels (ego, group process, socio-cultural structures) involved in the process which can thus be seen as a variation of the creativity model. A special developmental sequence is raised to the level of critical awareness. An arrested state of development is resolved cooperatively. Creativity is esessential in order to explain why the Freire mehtod works and also how it works. Likewise, it is necessary in order to understand and avoid possible contradictions and distortions that may take place in the conscientization program. In light of creativity, conscientization is perceived as a very powerful process, potentially liberating although ambiguous in principle. Indeed, it can be utilized in such a way that it contributes to further alienation, even by those committed to overcome specific oppresive situations. Therefore, the focus on creativity actually liberates conscientization itself in order for it to maintan its integrity on both epistemological and ethical grounds.

Conscientization illuminates creativity. It presents a peculiar setting meant to become a creative group.[34] Thus it helps to appreciate the social dimensions and expressions of creativity, for instance in terms of certain prerequisites such as trust in the people and respect for their own situation and their popular language.

The scope of creativity in the special event of consientization is also noteworthy. Participation in this version of education for creativity becomes available to "common" persons, particularly those usually considered "underprivileged," "underachieved," and "underdeveloped." The very fact that such an experience can be facilitated is remarkable. Freire demonstrates that creative insights are not the exclusive privilege of enlightened minds, or special groups of people such as artists, poets and scientists, and that the experience and practice of the creative potential is tantamount to freedom and health. The liberating potential of creativity as recognizable in conscientization sheds light on how to operationalize a creative thrust in terms of an educational approach and methodology.

The creative process is perceived here as taking place simultaneously on different levels and dimensions. For individual participants, it is the ego and the coping consciousness that are subject to creative transformation. The circles of culture function as "hermeneutic communities," and the structures of the social milieu become also subject to radical change. This last special aspect of conscientization's creative-liberating potential just underscored can now be discussed in some detail from a different perspective. This will help us to further illumine and expand our main argument concerning conscientization and creativity.

E. Conscientization, Creativity and Revitalization

The scope and goal of the conscientization process clearly go beyond the levels of individual selves and small group interaction. They are understood in terms of "cultural action for freedom" and meant to facilitate the transformation of inhibiting and oppresssive social structures. "Cultural revolution" is usually referred to as the long-range aim of the program. The educational approach as such in this sense fits rather well the characterization of reconstructionism, as it was suggested in the first chapter.

In light of creativity this level of the conscientization process can be analyzed as a special manifestation of "creative courage"[35]--concentrated efforts to challenge the status quo which ruling interests are devoted to protecting. It consists of an intentional, organized endeavor to construct a more satisfying culture.

46

Anthony F. C. Wallace's programmatic paper "Revitalization Movements"[36] provides further light for this discussion. He formulates the general features of major cultural-system innovations--"nativistic movements," "messianic movements," "revolutions," and so on--that typically involve religious patterns. They are characterized by a uniform process--"revitalization"--with a structure that has five somewhat overlapping stages: steady stage; period of individual stress; period of cultural distoriton; period of revitalization; and new steady stage. The term revitalization implies an organismic analogy, and the movement is defined as a deliberate, organized conscious effort of cultural rebuilding by members of a given society. The revitalization process essentially involves visions of a new way of life by individuals under extreme stress. The movement is usually conceived in a prophet's revelatory vision, and social transformation often takes place with comparative suddenness.

Wallace calls "the mazeway" the psycho-historical premise upon which revitalization is based. It is the mental image of society and its culture as well as of one's own body and patterned behavior. It is maintained by each individual in order to act in ways which reduce stress at all levels of the system. The presence of stress confronts individuals with a choice between tolerating the tension with the available mazeway, or changing the mazeway. The endeavor to work a change both in the mazeway and the "real" system so as to permit more effective stress management, is the effort at revitalization. The collaboration of a number of persons in such an effort is called a revitalization movement.[37]

In discussing the period of revitalization as such, Wallace argues that religious revitalization movements must perform at least six major tasks: (1) Mazeway reformulation, abrupt and dramatic, usually occurring as a moment of insight, a brief period of realization of relationships and opportunities; (2) communication, when the dreamer becomes a prophet who tells his vision; (3) organization established through converts who relate to that kind of charismatic leadership; (4) adaptation through strategies of compromise, force, doctrinal modifications, diplomatic maneuvering; (5) cultural transformation, when the whole or a controlling portion of the population comes to accept the new vision and its interpretations through ideology, internal organization, and wider corporate influence; (6) routinization, the transformation patterns and the stress-management patterns of the new movement become normative. A new steady stage is thus created by means of revitalization in a given society.

A few additional considerations by Wallace are also very suggestive for our own study of conscientization as creativity. One has to do with the choice of identification on the part of the revitalization movement. Freire's approach is strongly Utopia-oriented in a way analogous to other utopian movements and programs aimed at establishing a truly new culture some time in the future. Another interesting observation is the tendency for movements to become more political in emphasis as problems of organization, adaptation and routinization become more pressing. Political polarization in the face of mounting opposition is a common phenomenon in this regard and conscientization experiences in Latin America and elsewhere seem to point exactly in the same direction. A third point, closely connected to the other two has to do with success and failure of revitalization movements. Says Wallace:

> Two major but not unrelated variables seem to be very important in determining the fate of any given movement: the relative "realism" of the doctrine; and the amount of force exerted against the organization by its opponents . . . probability of failure would seem to be negatively correlated with degree of realism in conflict situations, and directly correlated with amount of resistance.[38]

The connection between revitalization and creativity has been established by James loder,[39] who distinguishes different levels of human existence on which the creative process may be seen as conjointly operative. He discusses the transposition of the paradigm of the creative process into revitalization of a social milieu. That is, the creative sequence can be replicated for a particular social setting, and social transformation may take place through revitalization. This is discussed as the fashion in which a social sequence unfolds coordinating with personal development: revitalization as mirror image of its chief advocate.[40]

In the conscientization process, no less than a change of "mazeway" is sought--a major transformation in the understanding and the image of nature, society, culture, self, the body, relationships and behavior.

The people themselves are to discover and spell out a new "code" to --literally--re-write their story and reshape their life and destiny. Existing social conditions which--in "necrophilic" fashion--inhibit or repress and violate human development, are to be transformed and "revitalized" (a "biophilic" orientation).

In this context, and in light of our reformulations, the conscientization method and process could be seen as operative in specific ways. For one thing, it is a special instance of an intentional use of the creative process in order to correct certain cases of arrested development, as discussed above. Secondly, conscientization would function also--even if partially and in particular circumstances--on the level of historical and social revitalization. In this last sense, it becomes a manifestation of the will and power of the human spirit that can erupt with dramatic power to redress the balance of forces for the health of the social organism.

The next comment on "proximate" and "ultimate" mediation will further help us to make the transition from the epistemological to the theological dimension of our study.

Paulo Freire is aware of the tendency to absolutize the value and effectiveness of conscientization. He has referred to this kind of methodological and ideological problem in terms of "mythification of conscientization." Put in other words, this is the case whenever this primarily corrective method--devised in order to alter a given oppressive and alienating situation--is idealized or becomes an end in itself, over-estimated either by social planners and educators or by participants themselves.[41] Actually, this situation should not be perceived merely as a frustrated human endeavor, but as pointing simultaneously to the power of the mediating-liberating agents in light of their proximate character.[42] As indicated a t the beginning of this chapter, Freire suggests a particular reading of the "sacred story" in terms of God who is engaged in the enterprise of liberation, especially by enabling human beings to participate in the struggle for liberation from oppression, and to shape their own lives and destiny. In spite of Freire's explicitly Christian commitment, however, the ultimate character of Christ's mediating-liberating work (rather than the avant-garde's and the oppressed's) is not clearly established in his thought. This distinction between

49

ultimate and proximate mediation and liberation is important in light of what appears to be some confusion on the part of the most enthusiastic admirers of Freire.43

Our attention must be turned now to the theological dimension, in order to develop necessary analytical, critical and constructive considerations. We will attempt to establish a legitimate and effective theological frame of reference for Freire's thought and contribution. Finally, we will bring our discussion within the theoretical concerns of Christian education together with the epistemological foundation established in this first part of our study.

SECOND PART -- THE THEOLOGICAL FOUNDATION:

EDUCATION AND THE KINGDOM

In the final analysis, the Word of God is inviting me to re-create the world, not for my brothers' and sisters' domination, but for their liberation. I am not really able to hear that Word then, unless I am fired up to live it fully . . .

. . . because it saves, that Word also liberates, but human beings have to accept it historically. They must make themselves subjects, agents of their salvation and liberation . . .

A utopian and prophetic theology leads naturally to a cultural action for liberation, and hence to conscientization.

Paulo Freire
Letter to a Young Theologian

Thus far in our discussion we have underscored, firstly, that the conscientization method and process, as presented by Freire, involve serious limitations and contradictions of the basic thrust of "education for liberation." This is due mainly to the ideological components and assumptions which stem from an explicit Marxist orientation. Secondly, we were able to perceive also that conscientization and creativity are mutually enlightening. We have demonstrated that the literacy/conscientization process that Freire advocates is to be understood in the light of creativity. In other words, that there is an implicit and latent epistemology of the creative process in his contribution.

We now concentrate on the theological dimension of Freire's thought and work. We will follow the same procedure developed in terms of the epistemological formulations. Chapter 3 will state, analyze, and critique Freire's contribution, and it will then be followed by a more constructive presentation. By utilizing the same method employed in the first part of this essay, we expect to achieve results parallel and complementary to those derived from our study of his view of education as knowing. We shall have delineated, then, a base which is both epistemologically and theologically sound, from which implications for Christian education theory can be drawn.

CHAPTER 3

FREIRE AND LIBERATION THEOLOGY

In this chapter we shall begin by presenting briefly the religious and theological background of Freire's thought and work. We shall then focus on several important reflections in connection with major areas of theological concern. In so doing, the relationship and integration of epistemological and theological dimensions of conscientization will become more apparent. The perspective of liberation theology partially articulated in Freire's approach will be spelled out in terms of his basic understanding of God, Christ, and the church and its mission. Finally, a critical appraisal will point out specific shortcomings and anticipate needed correctives or alternative formulations. This will be done on the basis of our view of creativity and from the vantage point of our theological perspective in dialogue with Freire's position.

A. On Freire's Intellectual Background

Freire's works and thought reveal a variety of sources which, nevertheless, appear integrated in a peculiar fashion and at the service of his educational enterprise. We shall refer to those most directly related to his religious and theological outlook.

From a personal perspective, Freire has to be perceived as a Brazilian Catholic whose mother directed him in the first steps of faith. He refers to this experience as well as to the fact that he once left the church, precisely at the point when he started to become acquainted with existentialist and personalist thought. He was particularly sensitive to the contradiction between the pious words spoken at Sunday services and the lack of commitment in everyday life.[1] According to Freire's testimony he has since then attempted to realize in concrete form the biblical imperatives. Conscientization would be the means to overcome oppressive silence in order to pronounce the word of liberation ("denouncing" and "announcing") as a reflection of the very face of God.

Explicit personal references as confessions of Christian faith can be found in different writings and speeches:

Christianity is for me a wonderful doctrine.
Even though it is said that I am a Communist
leader...I have never been tempted to cease
being a Catholic (because I am not yet completely a Catholic, I must keep on trying to
be one more completely day after day). Up to
now I have not felt the need to leave the
Church, to abandon my Christian convictions
in order to say what I am saying, or to go or
not to go to jail or to exile. I just feel
passionately, corporately, physically, with
all my being, that my stance is a Christian
one because it is 100 percent revolutionary
and human and liberating, and hence committed
and utopian...2

According to Freire's own account, his intellectual
formation began to crystallize at the age of twenty,
when he started the study of philosophy and psychology
of languge. At that time he was teaching Portuguese in
secondary school and, together with the reading of
Brazilian and Portuguese grammaticians, he was becoming
acquainted with Tristao de Atayde, Jacques Maritain and
Emmanuel Mounier among other religious thinkers. We
shall consider briefly the major influences that have
shaped Freire's thought and which inform his writings
in diverse ways and degrees.

In the first state--from 1947, when he became
engaged with adult literacy education, until 1965 the
exile in Chile--the predominant orientation combines a
humanist perspective with clear personalist influence,
and existentialist ingredients as interpreted mainly by
Gabriel Marcel. Freire represents in this sense a specific case of Christian humanistic perception of and
concern for the underprivileged people in northeastern
Brazil. It is a reaction against a system and a
condition of existence that prevents human beings from
developing personhood because they are conceived of
almost as a mere part of nature and entirely dependent
on the will of the lords of the land.

An emphatic humanistic stance is actually present
in all of Freire's writings.3 It assumes a vision of
life with man at the center. (That is why he will
insist that a relevant theology has to take its starting
point form anthropology). Within this humanistic view
Freire has been influenced by Herbert Marcuse and Erich
Fromm particularly. From them he gets further inspiration for the reaction against capitalistic alienation

and the smothering power of the supposedly omnipotent modern state. Already in this dimension of his thought, the reference to Marxian humanism is obvious.

The personalist current (Mounier) is present and apparent even after the Marxist influence becomes increasingly greater. The person cannot become an object but is a complex and dynamic reality essentially open to dialogue in a broad an interpersonal context. At this point, Martin Buber's own approach is explicity affirmed in terms of dialgue and freedom, as well as Marcel's, in the religious existentialist tradition. Karl Jasper's seminal concept of "limit situations" is in this context incorporated and reinterpreted by Freire. We discussed that reinterpretation in Chapter 2, in the light of the potential for human creativity.

As indicated in the first chapter, since 1970 (Pedagogy of the Oppressed) the theoretical instruments of historical materialism determine Freire's analysis of reality as well as the major propositions concerning the process and the program of conscientization. Marx presented a concrete phenomenology of economic relations in his time, underscored the dialectical character of reality and the meaning and purpose of philosophy vis à vis the praxis for social transformation.

Freire's assimilation of Marxism is closely correlated with recent theological developments in Latin America, especially among Catholics (Liberation Theology) whose methodology consistently presents a twofold character: the use of what is called "the mediations of sociopolitical analysis" and the primacy of critically reflected political praxis.

Besides the currents of thought in the background and also included in Freire's approach that we have mentioned, we can still refer to the particular influence of a distinctly Catholic heritage. Thus, there are elements of Thomistic philosophy and theology such as those portrayed in Freire's rather static view of man and nature, already referred to. However, Freire also reflects to some extent the thought of Teilhard de Chardin in regard to the evolutionary character of the humanization process and even the reason of human evolution.4

Finally, religious and theological trends in Latin America in the last two decades, which emphasize the liberating vocation of the church in the midst of socio-economic, political and cultural conditions of oppression have made a major impact on Freire and his work.

We are in agreement with John L. Elias who has demonstrated that the religious dimension of Paulo Freire's thought (as well as Ivan Illich's) is a most important factor in understanding his social and educational approach and contribution. At all major points of this thought, the religious dimension becomes indeed most apparent and influential.[5] In Freire's case, the outstanding features of his religious and theological foundation are:

-A conception of God in the Judeo-Christian tradition, that is, God actively engaged in the development of humanity and in the course of historical events.

-Jesus Christ is perceived as a radical transformer or the liberator who calls people to realize human life in a community of freedom and love, in the light of the coming Kingdom of God.

-The church is called to be an effective living witness of liberation, an agent of hope actually involved in the struggle against all manifestations of oppression and alienation. The Christian Gospel is essentially prophetic, utopian and revolutionary.

It is on the basis of these considerations that we have chosen to concentrate also on the theological foundations of Freire's approach.

B. Theological Formulations

Paulo Freire has not developed a carefully analytical, rigorous approach. He rather follows the flow and movement of his own thought, including a number of intuitive assertions. This fact makes it sometimes difficult to assess his theological propositions directly. The risk of misinterpreting or forcing upon his thought alien categorizations and concepts is indeed great. We will try to solve this problem by respecting Freire's own way of presenting his material. Our analysis will take into account both the explicit theological considerations and those instances in which theological material appears less focused, or implicit, in the overall scope of Freire's educational work. We look more for the inspirational or motivational meaning of

that learning, in this context, is the process by
which one moves from one level of consciousness to
another. Language, worldview, self-concept, and
present living conditions, manifest themselves more or
less consistently and point to a given level. The
actual content of each of those levels of consciousness
includes essentially two closely related phenomena:
self-understanding as the view that one has of one's
existence in the social world, and the power that one
possesses to determine one's future. The educational
task par excellence is, for Freire, to facilitate the
achievement and development of critical-political
consciousness or critical transitivity. In our own
analysis, we have already underlined the two foci of
the conscientization process in terms of cognitive-
linguistic and self-dynamics.[15]

   At the risk of oversimplifying the discussion, it
is possible to summarize these considerations in a
suggestive diagram such as the following. The levels
of consciousness were discussed in Chapter 1. The
correlations are here indicated for three areas in
general terms and not necessarily for specific items
within each column. (See pages 62-63).

Excursus on Marx, Freire, and the "Opium of the People"

   Freire's critique of church and religion essentially reasserts Marx's judgment on the subject which
has been popularized with the phrase "opium of the
people." Before discussing Freire's theological foundations more fully, we will present a dialectical reformulation of his implicit proposal which affirms a
distinctly Christian and prophetic confession and
commitment.

   That famous phrase of Marx appeared first in his
critique of Hegel's Philosophy of Right (1843). This
reveals the "young Marx"--at 25 years of age--strongly
influenced by Feuerbach, who had published his classic
The Essence of Christianity in 1841. Marx followed Feuerbach's general proposition that it is Man who created
god, and that Man thus becomes alien to his own essence
because it is projected onto "God." Religious alienation is seen by the young Marx already closely related
to the political critique of the state, and economic
alienation rooted in alienated and alienating labor.
Also already at this early stage, economic alienation
was for Marx the most basic kind of estrangement, religion and

I. SOCIO-CULTURAL STRUCTURE	LEVEL OF CONSCIOUSNESS	... Colonia...
A relatively closed process	Semi-intransitive or "magical" consciousness	closed dogmatism
closed society and "culture of silence"	limited historical consciousness and relative immersion in a one-dimensional oppressive present	biblical and patristic literalism
rigid, authoritarian political organization	facts of socio-cultural situation taken as "givens"	dichotomizing (heaven-hell, church-world, body-soul, etc.)
extreme dependency and marginality	fatalistic mentality (life related to destiny, fortune forces beyond control)	general "necrophilic" orientation:
passivity, apparent lack of interest in change and development	self-depreciation due to internalization of negative image values from dominant culture and class	—the world as place of evil and sin
illiteracy and cultural deprivation	emotional dependency and compensatory magical thinking	—life as temptation and spirituality of flight
. . .	. . .	—depreciation of the "material" and salvation or "conquest" of "souls"
		—etc.
		spiritualizing and privatization of sin
		ritualistic sacramentalism
		cult of saints
		refuge of the masses
		. . .

II. SOCIO-CULTURAL STRUCTURE	LEVEL OF CONSCIOUSNESS	CHURCH – RELIGION
Transition	"Naive" or semi-transitive consciousness	Modernizing or Reformist Church
Relative technological development and economic growth	superficial vision, nonstructural questioning and appraisal of reality and search for solutions	superficial changes in organization, liturgy, theological formulations, educational materials and techniques, etc.
emergence of the masses	tendency to accommodate to the given situation via available socialization means	lack of risk and commitment in prophetic witness and service
"cultural invasion"		
assitentialism on the part of elites		
mobility	limited place for dialogue	external reforms in search for greater efficiency
interest in participation, change and education	seduction and manipulation by populist leaders	assistentialist approach
. . .	. . .	. . .

politics being dependent variables. The question that bothered Marx was how it is that religion can play its alienating role. This is the crux of the matter. For him, religious alienation is only one among other forms of man's estrangement. Besides, that alienation is but a reflection of the more basic phenomenon of socio-economic reality. Marx's sociological approach, then, portrays religion as the reflection of the people's oppression.

"Opium of the people," therefore, needs to be read in the context of Marx's analysis. That analysis underscores what he perceives as oppressive social and economic conditions in a situation where, ideologically, the ruling classes determine what is to be believed and taught. There is a correlation of material and intellectual power. Religion thus expresses and represses the people's suffering. (Had Marx been more consistent in his dialectical method, he would have paid more attention to the elements of protest included even in "alienating religion," and the ambivalence and irony involved in that). Against this background it is easy to understand Marx's insistence on the priority of the criticism of religion. He did not change his position in later years but attempted to be consistent with his "demythologizing" program by focusing more on the critique of political economy--notably in Das Kapital (1867). Interestingly enough, a pivotal analysis there--actually identifiable as the continuation of Marx's theory of alienation--is that of the "fetichism" of commodities. This affirmation, together with the recognition that the targets of Marx's atheism were Hegel's "God" and the deity associated with European industrial capitalism and colonialism,16 takes us right to the next point.

The question of Marx's atheism is actually misleading until we ask what kind of "god" is being negated, and why. Our hypothesis then is that Jesus' God is not negated in Marx simply because He is not know. (By the same token, the great prophets of Israel, for instance, were "atheists" to a certain extent, i.e., insofar as they violently negated several gods). Further, it can be argued with Freire that Marx's atheism amounts to a pre-requisite in order that the Christian God might be radically affirmed. The prophets had to exercise a kind of dialectical movement whose first moment is a negative one, namely "atheism" regarding idolatry. The affirmative moment was, of course, the proclamation in hope of the creating-liberating-gracious God. It can be said then that Marx's (and Freire's) negation is analogous to the negative moment of the prophetic dialectic to the extent that the presiding modern idols (money, "fetichism of commodities") are negated. But Marx fails to produce the affirmative moment, except as radical anthropology. Although both Feuerbach and Marx confused the Hegelian Christendom god with any possible "god," from a politico-theological perspective it is important to perceive the value of Marx's critique of Hegel's sacralization of the establishment.[17] Together with this fatal generalization, it is obvious that neither Feuerbach nor Marx could realize that the oppressive structures they criticized--insofar as oppressive and religiously sanctioned--were themselves already the implicit negation of the creative-liberating God. Hence, Marx's potentially prophetic affirmation was collapsed and exhausted in his peculiar anthropology.[18]

In sum, together with Freire, we can first affirm partially Marx's critique of religion and his brand of atheism as the negation of alienating idolatry.[19] He became a secular prophet, a "master of suspicion"-- like Freud, as Paul Ricoeur says--whose vision and proclamation may help us understand and purify our own faith. And yet, immediately we have to state our own criticism of Marx from this Christian perspective. He was not able to perceive that his negation had positive Christian value. It actually amounted to the negation of the negation of the creative-liberating God. Further, that his critique was merely the first step towards affirming the God who provides, among other things, the necessary frame of reference within which any critique and any vision can have real power for transformation and promise of hope.

C.   Theological Formualtions (II)

1. On God and Theology

Freire is careful to indicate that he is not a professional theologian but a committed Christian who also considers that theology has a vital function to perform.[20] He sees the history of mankind as the starting point for the theological reflection: "Just as the Word became flesh, so the Word can be approached only through man. Theology has to take its starting point from anthropology."[21] Further, Freire considers that it is in the context of the Third World--not third in the

geographical sense, but in the sense of the world that
is dominated, dependent, voiceless--where a creative
utopian and faithfull theology can emerge. The rationale
for this idea is that only in that kind of human condition can there be openness and capacity to hear the Word
of God. In contrast, a theology that serves the bourgeoisie cannot be utopian and prophetic and hopeful; it
tends to create a passive, adjusted personality who
waits for a better life in the hereafter and is bound to
dichotomize the world.22

It is in this context that we can understand
Freire's idea that a prophetic theology leads naturally
to a "cultural action for freedom," to conscientization.
Therefore, theological training iteself in this light
should be a kind of cultural action for liberation
starting with a rejection of an alienating conception
of God.

freire sees God as a Presence in history who also
encourages man and woman to "history making," i.e., to
participate in the history of their liberation and
salvation. The certainty that "God does not go back on
his promises" does not warrant inaction or neutrality
on the part of the Christian whenever people are being
prevented from being human:

> My waiting (espera) makes sense only if I
> struggle and seek with hope (esperanza).
> A theology in which hope would be a wait-
> ing but not a searching would be profoundly
> alienating, because it would presume that
> the average person abdicates his/her praxis
> in this world . . . our salvation has to be
> achieved, if it is to be hoped for . . .
> and I deny the very act of love by which God,
> the Absolute, limits Godself by seeing some
> value in mankind--limited, unfinished and
> incomplete as they are--as beings that choose,
> as sharers in God's creative work.23

It is clear in Freire's thought, then, that a basic
religious and theological issue has to do with the
relationship between God and human beings. That relationship sets the foundation and the pattern for human
relationships in any society:

(Man's Transcendence for us is also based
on the root of his finitude and the awareness of this finitude, of the fact of being
an incomplete being whose fulness is achieved
in union with his Creator. This is a relationship which, by its very nature, can never be
a relationship of domination or domestication,
but is always a relationship of liberation.
Thus religion--"religare"--which embodies this
transcendent meaning of man's relationships
with others, should never become an instrument
for his alienation. Precisely because he is a
finite and indigent being, man finds in trans-
cendendence-through love--the possibility to
return to his source, who liberates him.[24]

Normatively speaking, oppression should not take
place because it negates the very nature of human beings
in terms of their relationship with God the Creator and
Liberator. What it means to be human and the concept
of God are intimately related propositions. Human
beings have been given self-consciousness, rationality,
freedom, transcendence. They are to develop as the
persons they were created to be (and, essentially
already are) in relationship with God and among themselves. Hence, human nature is incomplete, and the
striving for completeness is the occasion for realizing
the "ontological and historical vocation" to attain
full humanity on both individual and corporate levels.
This is an often quoted concept: ontological vocation
to be subjects who can separate themselves from the
world in their own consciousness, be critical of it, act
on it and transform it to suit their purposes. It makes
possible history-making, creation, self-assertion and
community. The emphasis on liberation form oppression
is not restricted to the external or objective conditions such as poverty, ignorance, or hunger, but it
refers also to the oppressor within, i.e. internalized
self-depreciating stereotypes and myths about oneself.

Freire reveals in this manner the religious nature
of his intuition and his metaphysical assumption about
what it means to be human vis à vis a creating-liberating
God. It is on this basis that he speaks prophetically
by denouncing oppression and announcing liberation with
radical and optimistic hope. His emphatic criticism
of a distorted view of God is particularly noteworthy
in this context.

Conformity and fatalism on the part of the oppressed are to be interpreted in view of a false image and concept of God. God is there first of all a distant, insensitive, inaccessible and domineering being. God appears to be utlimately responsible for the given situation and, therefore, nothing or very little remains to be expected or done. God becomes the sustainer of oppression. Further, this fatalistic attitude and outlook,

> ...in the guise of docility is the fruit of an historical and sociological situation, rather than an essential characteristic of a people's behavior. It almost always is related to the power of destiny or fate or fortune or to a distorted view of God. Under the sway of magic and myth, the oppressed ...see their suffering, the fruit of exploitation, as the will of God--as if God were the creator of this organized disorder.[25]

Attempts to subvert the oppressive reality are taught and felt to be rebellious acts against God's sovereign will. This situation becomes, then, the negation that needs to be negated as we stated before, in the name of the creating-liberating God of Jesus Christ, to whom we now turn our attention.

2. Towards a Liberating Christology[26]

Freire's explicit if fragmentary references to Jesus Christ affirm Him as the image and symbol of the radical transformer and true liberator. He is the One who calls people to realize human "ontological vocation" in the light of the Kingdom of God.

The example of Christ, as Freire perceives it, is a major encouragement for the revolutionary transformation of the existing oppressive structures. The prevailing image of Jesus is that of non-conformity with the status quo, radical disruption of the social order and willingness to die in order to produce the fruit of new life.

The Exodus motif is coupled with the Easter symbol: liberation and redemption are to be seen as two dimensions of the same process towards full humanity. Easter involves what Freire calls "class suicide"[27] on the part of those who would contribute to the cause of liberation:

willingness to die to (or renounce) any ideology,
privilege, or attitude which contradicts the interests
of the oppressed who "will have to die as an oppressed
class, in order to be reborn as a class that libeates
itself."28

In this manner Freire identifies in principle
"incarnation" and "Easter" in his implicit Christology.
They are operationalized in terms of the utopian-
prophetic stance of denouncing-announcing discussed before. The references to Christian teachings in Freire's
educational theory--love, hope, trust, freedom, equality
and so on--are less directly related to his view of the
Christ and the Kingdom Gospel. Nevertheless, their
theological and religious inspiration is apparent.

The prophetic line is clear also in regard to the
style of Freire's formulations: appeals and exhortations
abound in sermonlike fashion with prescriptive force.
There is the certainty, conviction, and fervor typical
of the religious crusader. Further, in this context,
Freire's gospel of liberation is by far more precise
and clear in terms of the critique ("denouncing") than
in the constructive proposal ("announcing") concerning
education and the contours of the utopian society.

3. The Prophetic Church

Freire characterizes the type of church that com-
municates and teaches those theological views in terms
of an alternative approach to the "traditionalist" and
"modernizing" models. The "prophetic" church rejects
the assitentialist approach of the other two perspectives
and has an utopian hopeful orientation. It is the
church committed to the oppressed in order to transform
society radically. It assumes a critical thought and
it does not conceive of itself as neutral nor does it
hide its political and revolutionary option. It does
not dichotomize (this)-worldliness-otherworldliness,
salvation-liberation, and so on. It is community
oriented ("we" liberate ourselves, "we" know) and it has
a dialectic view of reality, among other features.

This is a church where the politico-social sciences
are seriously taken into account because the scientific
knowledge of reality is a necessary condition for being
prophetic.29 The church is meant to be continually
traveling, at work, always dying and being reborn, like
Jesus Christ.

This conception of the Christian community has pointed to a context for a fruitful theological reflection particularly in Latin America. Its subject matter comes from objective conditions of dependent, exploited, invaded societies.

The educational enterprise in the prophetic church consists of a method of transforming action, political praxis at the service of the permanent liberation of the human beings. It is very much concerned with the development of the critical consciousness of reality.

The following diagram (III) suggests the correlation between socio-cultural structure and dynamics, level of consciousness and the character and mission of the prophetic church, in Freirean thought. It should be compared with diagrams I and II above   (pages 62-63).

4.   The Christian and Revolution

In the first part of this essay, we discussed Freire's pedagogy of liberation, which includes the assumption of political and cultural revolution. We focused then on the epistemological foundations of conscientization: revolutionary praxis is integral to this view of education as the process of knowing, and to the theory of knowledge espoused. Freire's approach was then characterized in terms of social reconstructionism: education is considered as an indispensible means for achieving and expanding a radical transformation. This reconstructionist view began to be reinterpreted in the light of creativity in the second chapter. We add now further considerations undergirding Freire's approach to socio-political revolution. They are basically the corollary of his view of Christ's Gospel as the call to radical removal of oppressive structures and the affirmation of utopian hope for a classless society where full humanity is possible.

When it comes to specifying the theological task in relation to the mission of the prophetic church and the individual Christian, Freire stresses again the imperative of siding with the oppressed and "wretched of the earth." Once this basic choice has been consciously made, the call is to act consistently in love. The loving action requires firstly tearing away the veils that hide the facts, and the exposure of the causes underlying misery and oppression in a dialectic vision of reality.

70

| III. SOCIO-CULTURAL STRUCTURE | LEVEL OF CONSCIOUSNESS | CHURCH - RELIGION |
Open Society	Critical transitivity (critical-political consciousness)	Prophetic Church
responsible participation fostered	depth in perception and understanding ("structural" perception and appraisal of reality)	utopian and hopeful
democratic mentality		committed to the dominated classes and in search for radical social transformation
cultural synthesis and permanent cultural revolution	receptiveness and dialogical discurse	rejects dogmatisms and static religious thought
utopic formulations and creativity fostered	interdependence and self-confidence	
commitment to solve common problems	flexibility	theology based on and authenticated in praxis
liberation of the oppressed	. . .	liturgy as celebration and commitment
. . .		encourages critical thinking and adult responsibility
		service oriented
		. . .

That loving activity implies at the same time the
challenge of the powerful. For Freire, the main proof
of true love that the oppressed can show their oppressors is not to bend masochistically to their oppression
but to radically take away from them those objective
conditions that make oppression possible. It is a
political and revolutionary task.30 In regard to the
means of accomplishing this task, Freire claims that
the right to rebellion has to be recognized far beyond
the thought of St. Thomas, in light of the "institu-
tionalized" or "structural" violence of the systems.

How can violent revolution be justified according
to Christian principles is an issue that lies in the
backgroung of Freire's proposal for radical change.
By 1970, he definitely joined the ranks of Latin American Christians who believe that the revolutionary
option is the only effective means available to produce
the transformation required. Therefore, in this view,
violent revolution against oppressive regimes may become
not only permissible but also an imperative in the name
of love. Freire in fact declares to be convinced that
true revolutionaries must perceive the revolution,
"because of its creative and liberating nature," as an
act of love.31

Freire has in mind specific revolutionary figures
such as the Argentine-Cuban Ernesto (Che) Guevara and
the Colombian priest Camilo Torres, who expressed this
very idea of the moral responsibility to participate
in the revolution, and the belief that this is ultimately an act of love.

The church is to work in favor of radical change
in society including involvement in liberation movements.
This may obviously assume the direct political and even
armed challenge of the ruling regime.32 It appears
that Freire as well as other liberation theologians
present in this regard a new edition of the old and
popular "just war" theory and the "right to rebellion"
rationale: manifest or objective social injustice,
economic and political oppression--i.e., structural
or institutional violence--make it necessary, and therefore, they justify the Christian's participation in
armed confrontation in order to right the situation.

In this discussion, Freire and others have to labor
hard in order to stretch the Exodus and Easter biblical
motifs so as to provide inspiration for the call to
revolution as "an act of love." Their attempt is to

inject religious sanction to a "revolutionary love" that
necessitates the extermination and/or the subsequent
repression of the "oppressors."

Hopefully, it became clear that Friere is very
much interested in developing and communicating a
theological understanding of his educational method and
strategy. His theological stance in general, and
specially the approach to the participation of the
church in liberation movements to bring about revolutionary change, are to be seen against the background
of his personal, religious and professional experiences
in Latin America. They reflect the way in which
Freire's thought and work has been decisively shaped
by Roman Catholic Christianity in the light of that
historical and social context.[33]

Structurally speaking, Freire's theological foundation can be appraised in terms of a "millenialist"
perspective that he shares with the wider movement for
liberation in Latin America and elsewhere. As Malcolm
Warford rightly states, this is a theology which understands revelation as an ongoing event in the history of
man and sees the just ordering of society as the unfold-
ing history of the Kingdom of God.[34] This is precisely
an essential assumption in Latin American liberation
theology that Freire has contributed to inspire and
which, in turn, has influenced his own approach and
contribution.[35]

D. A Critical Evaluation[36]

1. On the Biblical Basis and the Nature and
    Mission of the Church

In this theological perspective, the task of the
church appears to exhaust itself in the struggle for
the vindication of the economically oppressed. Obviously,
exploitation and domination--both foreign and internal
--is a major apparent trait in the picture of social
injustice, particularly in Latin America. But the sole
affirmation of the rights of the poor in terms of the
crusade for the "just revolution" seems to lose sight
of a more comprehensive biblical picture. God does
side with the weak and oppressed, but they too are
under judgment. Besides, the "wretched of the earth"
are not to be equated simply with the "people of God"
in the tradition of Abraham and Jesus Christ. If indeed
the biblical documents are to be taken seriously, it

would appear that the "people of God" are not any or every nation or any oppressed class of any nation, but those within the historical context of the Old and New Convenants, where God takes the initiative and sets the terms and direction.

The ecclesiological issue is crucial in any discussion of liberation theology because it poses sharp questions regarding the church's identity, nature and mission. To the extent that God sides with the dispossessed, in the midst of whom Christ is present, do not they become somehow constitutive of the mystery of the church? Does not the "revolutionary fellowship" which includes non-Christians, possess a certain missionary ecclesial character? There are diverse ways of dealing with those and related questions within the group of liberation theologians, but a common thrust is the prophetic call for renewal in the light of obedience to Jesus Christ in the actual historical context. The problem that immediately arises, however, is how to decide what kind of manifestations are really consistent with the Gospel of the Kingdom, especially concerning service and social witness. This question takes us to the issue of biblical interpretation.

In Freire and others, the biblical notions of liberation, love, reconciliation, new humanity and so on are often taken outside the context of the history of Israel, the teachings of Jesus and the apostles. Thus, the historical faith becomes more and more secondary and the categories for understanding the references to God, the Kingdom, or the meaning and goal of history start to be borrowed and "Christianized" from elsewhere. The tendency to confuse the cause of Jesus Christ with socio-political revolution does not seem to do justice to either one of them.

There is in fact a curious hermeneutical selectivity in making Jesus normative as a prophet who confronts and dislocates the socialorder and overlooking at the same time, or minimizing, his call to discipleship in the light of the "way of the cross."37 Further, even though we find an appeal to the revolutionary political character of Jesus Christ, the references tend to be mere slogan-like generalizations. That is, there is no serious or in-depth attempt to consider the substance of Jesus Christ's unique position as portrayed in the Gospels and in the light of the whole context of the biblical documents. The "radical Jesus" is called on then, in order to legitimate certain contemporary visions. Yet, the uniqueness of his vision is usually disregarded, including the original rejection of the Zealot alternative.38

There is also selectivity in picking up Old Testament motifs, notably the Exodus story as a privileged hermeneutical clue.39 The particular problem of the relationship between the Testaments is extremely important for the present discussion because of the practical implications arising from the way that relationship is understood.

2. On the Hope for History and the Nature of Human Beings

It has been suggested that one way to characterize social ethical thinking in our time is to say that Christians are obsessed with the meaning and direction of history and that social concern is motivated by a deep desire to make things move in the right direction.40 This proposition is particularly fitting for liberation theology in Latin America and for Freire's "practical theolgoy" especially. An indispensable handle by which to get hold of the course of history is here "education for liberation," the conscientization process and program. There are several assumptions included in this perspective, such as: that relationships of cause and effect are visible, understandable and manageable, so that if we make our choices on the basis of how we hope society will move, it will be moved in that direction; that we are adequately informed to be able to set for ourselves and for all society the goal toward which we seek to move it; that effectiveness in moving towards these goals which we have set is itself a moral yardstick. All these assumptions are based, of course, on the axiom that it is a high good to make history move in the "right" direction. In the case of "education for liberation" the strategy involves, as we have indicated, the political organization of the oppressed to achieve power so that the new society may be built.

Freire and other liberation theologians are not critical of the Marxist foundation which is often utilized unilaterally and, therefore, naively. Yet the eschatological stance has to be demythified. Marxism betrays an essentially utopian thrust in which hope plays a fundamental role: proletarian messianism and the vision of a kingdom of peace to be established

after the revolution, nurture the passion of radical
militancy. There is something of a caricature of
Christian hope secularized which, nevertheless, carries
the mark of the Judeo-Christian heritage. There is a
declaration of faith in the future of mankind; a manifestation of hope in the enjoyment of a future that makes
possible the sacrifies of the present; the claim of love
expressed somewhat paradoxically in the revolutionary
enterprise. It has been indicated already that Marxism,
like other social radical movements, borrows a Christian
eschatological perspective which is provided a new content. This is a point at which it is possible to
perceive the potential for idolatry in the radical movements: the "kingdom" is in fact given a divine-like
character, a certain doctrine and ideology is considered
practically infallible and even the sacrifice of human
lives (especially the oppressors' and their allies') is
plainly justified in the name of the coming era. The
pseudo-eschatological[41] dimension is present in the
vision of a new order--a "new creation"--which is the
product of revolution. The only way of coming to grips
with the present evil is by acknowledging the fact of
class-struggle and becoming involved in the search for
power on the side of the proletariat. In Freire's work
and thought we find an example of the classic juxta-
position of a method and the content of a program set
to achieve radical social change.

The basic problem here resides in the Marxist confusion of a historical analysis with the assumed discovery
of certain iron laws of history believed to be universal
and immutable. The fact is that global historical reality is always more complex than the limited understanding
obtained with just one analytic tool or method. reduc-
tionism is a formidable foe of any truly "incarnational"
approach. Incarnation for the purpose of service, such
as conscientization, necessitates an adequate interpretation of the setting within which that service is going
to take place. The danger of historical determinism and
the dogmatic character of an ideology are indeed serious
issues to be reckoned with.[42] Further, the blending of
determinism, dogmatism and revolutionary optimism,
contradicts and collapses Christian eschatology.

One particular dimension of this problem is an
anthropology that fails to realize the enormous human
potential for evil while affiring class-assertion and
vindication.[43] It is possible to argue that there is a
significant parallel between a biblical and a Marxist
anthropology, as Míguez Bonino puts it for example.[44]

While the righting of the idealist misunderstandings in traditional theology can allow us to recover a biblical anthropological perspective, we are forced to move beyond such an approach in the recognition of deeper roots of alienation than the distortions of capitalism[45]

In close connection with that issue, and particularly fitting in regard to Freire's emphasis on praxis, we can add the biblical epistemological parallel.[46] There is no truth outside or beyond the concrete historical events in which people are involved as agents. There is no knowledge except in action itself, in the process of transforming the world through participation in history. Analogously, the biblical witness points to faith as a way rather than gnosis, as something to be done. Correct knowledge is contingent upon right doing, and knowledge is disclosed in doing. This undoubtedly involves a progress, again, in relation to any "idealistic" or "spiritualistic" conception. However, this is not to be identified with an "epistemology of obedience"[47] in terms of the confessed lordship of Jesus Christ, unless his person is seriously taken into account. The identification of a revolutionary anthropology --including the references to "humanization" and "liberation"--with that of the Christian faith is often taken for granted. It is not clear, however, what the relationship, if any, is between Jesus Christ--the New Testament Christ--and the New Man of the revolutionary vision. Are not the ministry, teaching, death and resurrection indispensable for "humanization"? When it comes to the question of human wholeness, is it indeed a finite possibility or an eschatological vision revealed in the wholeness of Jesus Christ?

In spite of Freire's recognition of basic ambivalence and conflicts in people's selves, it is also clear that he is too optimistic regarding their potential (the oppressed's potential) to realize the ideal of humanization once the oppressive structures and relationships begin to be confronted and transformed.[48] At this point it is also proper to remember that Freire and other Latin American theologians represent a Catholic tradition which--apart from any "humanistic" ideology--tends to offer a more optimistic anthropology than that of Protestantism in general.[49]

3. Another Look at the "Prophetic" Church

There is no question about the view of a church
incarnate and in constant mission in the light of God's
politics ("the power to will what God will . . . what
is takes to make and to keep human life human", in
Lehmann's expression). Yet, precisely in order to
maintain the prophetic orientation it would seem that a
relative "dualism" has to be affirmed in terms of the
radically unique "Christian revolution." This revolutionary character is to be perceived by looking at the
church's insertion as an original kind of community,
different from the alternatives that Jesus faced and
rejected and of which we seem to find contemporary models
(Essenes: escape via isolation; Herodians and Saddu-
cees: social political compromise; Pharisees: escape
through purity within the system; Zealots: violent
confrontation).50 Jesus adopted a peculiar model in
the formation of a community with a distinctive frame
of reference, consistent with incarnation itself.51 At
the center of that experiment service is included over
against the tendency to use power for domination.

In this view, the foretaste of the Kingdom is to
be searched for primarily within a faithful community of
people committed to Jesus Christ and his "little brothers
and sisters" whose involvement in society and the world
is claimed to be comprehensive enough to go even beyond
the ministry to the economically oppressed. This
"prophetic Church" does not seek to get hold of the
power structure and to repeat or mirror the strategy
and tactics of the "old order." The Cross becomes here
the central paradigm of both power and obedience, not
merely as a better strategy but as a way of life.
Actually, does not the very existence of such a social
reality constitute a major threatening change and
creative inspiration for transformation? To the extent
that these communities remain prophetic, cannot they
become instruments of the creative-liberating Spirit of
God? It is clear that the history of Christian communities has not reflected necessarily this calling. This
is precisely why the conscientization method and process
needs to be examined carefully in terms of the challenges of the church and its mission.

4. Reconciling the Irreconciliable

Much of the discussion just included in the picture
of the Christian koinonia--particularly the reference to

domination and mutual service--is also part of what we described in the second chapter as the mediating and liberating agent in conscientization. And that is the case even more with regard to the vision of a just society after the political revolution. Several decisive differences need to be indicated however.

For one thing, in the Christian koinonia the ultimate mediation of Christ is affirmed and the creative power of the Spirit is acknowledged and celebrated. Negatively, this implies a radical critique and rejection of the absolutizing of any proximate mediations (including the church's own inclinations in this regard!). On the other hand, as the "body of Christ" it is called to participate in the experience of spiritual creativity at diverse levels and fronts. It is enabled to become both a hermeneutic community for discernment--and especially demythifying--of reality, and a messianic community as a living witness to the cross and resurrection of Jesus Christ. This apparent tension is in itself creative.

The other major point of departure form the pattern of "revolutionary fellowships" lies in the daring contradiction of the dictum, which Freire often quotes, "it is impossible to reconcile the irreconciliable." This is precisely the core of the Christian story: the impossible reconciliation has taken place through Jesus Christ. The fellowship creating reality of Jesus Christ can now include the "untested feasibility" that "there is neither Jew nor Greek . . . slave nor free . . . male nor female."

In this light, it would appear not that other formulations are too radical, but that they are not radical enough.

CHAPTER 4

KINGDOM GOSPEL AND CREATIVITY

In the previous chapter we considered an analysis and a critique of Freire's theological foundation and perspective. As we now turn our attention to a constructive reformulation, we need to move beyond Freire's liberation theology without losing contact with his thought and contribution. Therefore, we shall start with an affirmation of the need and the possibility of integrating much of that theological stance into our own approach.

A. Introduction: Further Dialogue and Reformulation

In the light of our theological analysis and critique, it seems that some of the weakness of liberation theology can be corrected. It must also be acknowledged that the recent revival of Evangelical[1] thought in Latin America and United States has been stimulated to a certain extent by liberation theology. The stimulus comes not only in terms of a reaction against problems perceived in that theology, but also because of its major insights and reminders, such as the release of resources for social justice in the biblical faith. In other words, theological views and undergirding such as Freire's also challenge, correct, and illumine much of our own perspective and commitment. Further, it is a major dimension of serious inquiry to allow the position under analysis to speak to us and even to enlighten us. Actually, if that were not the case, there would not be any space left for further dialogue and integration. In our situation, no constructive reformulation with significant connection with Freire's theological foundation would thus be possible.

We can now make explicit reference to two important areas in which the interaction with Freire and liberation theology is specifically rewarding: one has to do mostly with the content of theological reflection, and the other refers basically to theological-exegetical method. Let us discuss them briefly.

We are challenged by liberation theology first of all to take very seriously the concrete historical situation in which the church and the Christian are committed to serve. And that service--even if defined

81

in conventional terms such as "mission outreach,"
pastoral and social work, or Christian education--must
be an actual expression of the love of God with specific
means to face current existential problems and specific
power to transform alienating conditions. By taking
seriously the historical situation, the Christian faith
is compelled both to act and to hope in the light of
diverse oppressive situations that afflict so many human
beings around us. This is another way of underscoring
the sociopolitical dimension of the Kingdom Gospel of
Jesus Christ. "Salvation" is here perceived not merely
as an individual, private possession, but also as
including the aspects of solidarity and liberation.
This emphasis on the diaconate function of salvation
implies a more hopeful appraisal of the human predicament and its potential for recreation and creativity
than that of other Christian traditions.

    Secondly, we need to point out the reiterated
insight about the non-neutrality of theological analysis
or biblical exegesis. Freire and liberation theologians
rightly remind us of the socioeconomic constraints on
education and other areas of knowledge and reflection.
As indicated in the first chapter, Mannheim's sociology
of knowledge and Marx's epistemology provide an important basis for this kind of realization: not only is
human knowledge conditioned by one's cultural, historical
context, but it is especially structured by a frame of
reference essential to organize personal experience.
Stephen C. Knapp has wisely pointed out several needed
correctives to traditional evangelical hermeneutics and
theological method in the light of that contribution[2]:
The myth of pure, objective exegesis and the inevitable
interference of ideological, socio-political values and
commitments of the interpreter/theologian need to be
exposed. Theological reflection can benefit from the
criticism of ideology, and it should include a serious
analysis of the historical and contemporary functioning
of the believer and the church in relation to society.
Theological reflection thus becomes a multi-directional
endeavor. Furthermore, this task needs to be perceived
and carried out in the light and in the midst of actual,
historical power struggles. The "truth" of theology or
its correspondence to revelation has to be verified
partially in terms of concrete practical expressions.
Faithful theologizing as reflection on praxis is hereby
seen as an integral part of human and social transformation, which is the essence of praxis: Transforming
reflection, as radically new obedience, should be the
end goal and actual result of all theology.[3]

B. Liberation, Resurrection, and Creativity

Having acknowledged those contributions, however, we must again qualify the emphasis on the liberation motif in the sense that liberation is not an end in itself. A more comprehensive understanding is called for. Emancipation, freedom from bondage or oppression as described by Freire, is a major dimension repeatedly underscored. Freire's concept of ontological vocation illumines still another aspect of the quest for freedom: freedom to choose and to be a subject or a willing agent for self-determination and self-realization.

There is however another, even more positive understanding of freedom, alluded to in Freire's thought but not developed in his theological reflection: freedom to create and to care, freedom for creative service beyond self-assertion and vindication. It seems that the reference to Easter in his explicit formulations concerning the Christian faith is to be interpreted also as pointing to the new creation and to resurrection especially. It can be argued that the definite biblical model of salvation is resurrection rather than liberation as such.[4]

By expanding and spelling out the meaning of Freire's reference to the Easter motif, fuller justice can be done to the biblical concepts and symbols otherwise partially or selectively appropriated. Simultaneously, the theological foundations involved become more meaningful. Moreover, resurrection, new creation and new humanity, are essentially biblical motifs that can be consistently perceived in the light of creativity in theological perspective, which points further in the direction of our thesis.

1. Resurrection as Total Liberation

In liberation theology there has been a tendency to present an open, unqualified escatology which arises out of the present and concrete historical struggles or praxis. Christian hope is based on incarnation rather than on resurrection. A prophetic future is affirmed rather than an apocalyptic future (which irrupts from the future to the present).[5]

Christological studies in Latin America, however, place a greater emphasis on the resurrection. Leonardo Boff, Franciscan priest an theologian from Brazil, and discusses resurrection under the heading of "realization of a human utopia." [6] Resurrection is seen as an eschatologization of human reality, an introduction of the total human person into the Kingdom of God, a complete realization of the capacities God placed within human existence. Therefore all the alienating elements that lacerated and disfigured life have been annihilated such as death, void , pain, hatred, and sin. Human hope was accomplished in Jesus' resurrection and is already being realized in each person. Boff adds that to the question: What is to become of humankind? Christian faith joyfully responds: resurrection, as complete transformation of the human reality, corporal as well as spiritual.[7] The resurrection of Jesus is to be seen intimately bound up with his life, death and proclamation of the Kingdom. The connection between resurrection, liberation and the gospel of the Kingdom of God is thus stated:

> If "kingdom of God" is the semantic term
> connoting total liberation, if Jesus' life
> was a liberated and liberating life, and
> if his death was his completely free offer-
> ing up of that life, then his resurrection
> realizes and fulfills his program in its
> eschatological form.[8]

Resurrection reveals God's ultimate intention for his creation. It is the victory of life and making explicit all its latent potentialities as a gracious gift from God. The resurrection points to the goal and fulfillment sought by every genuine liberation process: achievement of complete freedom. It is because of his resurrection that Jesus continues to minister among human beings, especially through the Spirit and the church. In this light, instances of real human development, increase in the potential for creativity, enhancement of justice--i.e., expansion and growth in life, represent ways in which the resurrection is actualized in the present while its future fulfillment is being expected and prepared.[9]

Jesuit Basque-Latin American theologican Jon Sobrino further illumines the import of the resurrection motif as it relates to humanity's destiny and history:

> Humanity has been offered a new kind of life
> based on hope and love...Because the resurrec-
> tion also confirms the life of Jesus himself,

we are now offered the possibility of living
a particular way of life in the footsteps of
Jesus. We can and should live as new, risen
human beings here and now in history.[10]

In other words, Jesus' resurrection is essential
for an effective and hopeful Christian challenge of the
present order. It is because God raised Jesus from the
dead that we can affirm that the Messianic Age of peace,
justice and reconciliation ("shalom") has indeed invaded
the old age. Because of the resurrection, the gospel
of the Kingdom of God is not naive utopianism but rather
the reliable promise of God incarnate.

From a hermeneutical standpoint, Sobrino firstly
suggests that the expression "resurrection of the dead"
points to the total transformation of people and history,
which involves the biblical model of hope against death
and injustice.[11]

In the second place, in order to grasp the meaning
of the resurrection, one needs to possess a historical
consciousness that perceives history both as promise
and as mission to be performed. Thirdly, the experience
of the resurrected empowers us to become engaged in the
praxis of discipleship, the following of Jesus. Something new has entered the world with Jesus' resurrection.
Like Jesus, the disciples must serve the cause of establishing a new creation and making things new under the
auspices of the Spirit's creative process. Finally,
Sobrino points out that knowing the resurrection of
Jesus--like knowing God--is not a one-time event. The
horizon of understanding must be constantly fashioned
anew. The Christian hope and praxis of love are to be
kept alive and operational at all times. That is the
way to grasp Jesus' resurrection as the resurrection of
the "firstborn" and as the promise that history will
find fulfillment.[12]

Those are the kinds of insights which make the
Christian disciple confess together with the apostle
Paul: "All I care for is to know Christ, to experience
the power of his resurrection. . ."[13] This is the power
to discern, be transformed by, and participate in the
Spirit's liberating and creative work. Dialectically
speaking, the power of the resurrection lies in the
fact that resurrection negates the negation of life.[14]
It is the power which can historicize itself also in the
context of conscientization as creative process.

2. Another Look at Conscientization

We need to remind ourselves that Paulo Freire is not a theologian in the traditional sense of the concept and that he is not interested in presenting a systematic theological statement about education. Indeed the genius of what Freire has done theologically is to work out the meaning and implications of his own faith in relation to education and the way he has accomplished it. He has entered into the problem and allowed his religious and theological orientation exercise a decisive influence on his whole pedagogical perspective. Freire has thus provided a paradigm of what it means to reflect theologically in the midst of concrete historical situations today and allow that theology to affect both the content and the process of thought.

Before we move on the discuss further the theological foundations in Christological terms, it is useful to reconsider briefly Freire's contribution in light of our present reflections. The point is that already in Freire's epistemology and educational approach as such, we can appreciate a religious and theological dimension which is in fact an inseparable, integral part of his work and thought. That dimension involves both religious-theological content and method--doing theology in a praxis fashion.

In different ways we have underscored that Freire's educational thrust concentrates on the human potential for creativity in the midst of political-economic and cultural oppression. It points to the discovery and implementation of liberating alternatives in social interaction and to transformation through the conscientization process.

First of all, the developmental nature of conscientization was demonstrated by means of a critical analysis. The process indeed enhances the formal-operational level of cognitive development and makes it possible to experience actual liberation of thought-linguistic structures. An arrested state of personal growth is thereby overcome and new possibilities and power become available for individuals and groups engaged in the conscientization process. By moving beyond the limitations and contradictions in Freire's perspective, we were able to illumine its enormous potential to facilitate greater freedom and wholeness, i.e., ways in which the resurrection is actualized here and now. Conscientization involves a special case of human development consistent with the pattern of creativity, having a structural integrity of its own. It confronts people's systematic and massive frustration of the drive towards freedom and wholeness by powerful forces of socialization which impose adaptation and conformity upon the creative spirit of persons.

As stated before, different dimensions and levels can be affected by conscientization: the linguistic-symbolic area, the self and group interaction, institutional and social structures. Conscientization is the focal concept in "education for liberation" and "cultural action for freedom." The philosophy of education represented by Freire's approach was discussed in terms of reconstructionism. In socio-political perspective, his stance is meant to foster a cultural revolution. Anthropologically, it fits the revitalization pattern of social and cultural transformation. These liberating ideas and endeavors were reinterpreted in terms of creativity, within Freire's Christian prophetic and utopian vision. Theologically, our constructive reformulation involves a reappraisal of the liberation thrust, including incarnation and nonconformity. It emphasizes the resurrection motif and it necessitates spelling out the gift and the promise of the Kingdom of God.

It seems that Freire's theological foundations and understanding are enhanced in the light of our reconsideration. His thought does not appear to be distorted in the process but, on the contrary, it becomes more coherent and illuminating. The implicit "sacred story" alluded to in the second chapter, which informs and inspires Freire's thought and work throughout, becomes indeed more transparent. Further, his self-understanding as a prophetic figure could probably be augmented in the light of these theological reflections.

C. The Centrality of the Kingdom of God

Our claim, together with that of several theologians taken into consideration, is that the pertinence of the Kingdom message and the expectation of the coming Kingdom are essential to help us recapture the whole biblical thrust. We will state our own position in constructive terms in this section, prior to focusing on the question of Christian education.

At the present time we will not engage in a thorough study of the symbol of God's Kingdom in the biblical

documents and in Christian theology[15] but we will assume
that it is in fact a key symbol on the basis of the
treatment of which different theological approaches can
be considered. If our concern is to understand, to
live, to share and to proclaim the Gospel of the Kingdom,
the question is, then, how we can interpret the implications of the acknowledged centrality of the Kingdom
motif and the expectation of the Kingdom. On the basis
of the previous discussion, the following considerations
are in order.

Kingdom is Central: Formal Implications[16]

We interpret "Kingdom of God" as a symbol for God's
liberating and re-creating action, will and promise, as
we perceive them first of all in the Scriptures and,
mainly, in the light of Jesus' ministry. He promised
and demonstrated the fulfillment of that utopia of total
liberation as a reality introduced by God: The overcoming of alienation and evil, the destruction of the
consequences of sin--violence, pain, death. The Kingdom of God would be the manifestation of God's sovereignty
and lordship over all. As Boff indicates, the Kingdom
of God is a total, global and structural transformation
of the human reality. It is also the cosmos completely
and full of the reality of God. The Kingdom of God is
actually the old world transformed into a new one. The
Kingdom that Christ announces is not merely a liberation
from political oppression, from the economic hardships of
the people from other specific evils, or from sin alone.
The Kingdom cannot be narrowed down to any particular
dimension or aspect. The whole of life and reality are
to be transformed by God. In this light, Jesus' words
"The kingdom of God is among you" (Luke 17:21), mean
that we already have access to the new order introduced
by God.[17]

The eschatological character of the Kingdom and its
implications have been aptly discussed by Sobrino.
First of all, eschatology means "crisis" because God
passes judgment on the present reality in order to re-
create it. The eschaton, as the last and ultimate
reality creates a crisis for people and history. It
reveals what is of definitive relevance. Therefore,
the concept of eschatology is consistent with Jesus'
fundamental demand for a conversion (metanoia). Jesus
offers the possibility of attaining true identity and
peoplehood by facing up to a crisis and undergoing a
conversion. Secondly, Jesus' eschatology has a historico-

temporal character. The present situation is not the ultimate possibility for us. The future is not simply an extrapolation based on the present; it is an as yet unrealized utopia. Third, the matter of the relationship between God and human beings can now be posed in terms of a tension between fashioning the Kingdom on the one hand and asserting that God is drawing near in grace on the other. Fourth, eschatology presents the problem of God in a new light, pointing up his relationship to the future as a mode of his own being.[18]

1. The Person of Jesus

The reference to the Kingdom involves taking seriously the person of the "King". Any adequate hermeneutics has to include concretely the person of Jesus Christ as a man related to time and to people. He cannot be translated into a subjective or ideological equivalent but he should be seen as possessing an eschatological conviction that it was his task to assist in the next stage of the in-breaking reality of God's Kingdom.

Jesus did not begin preaching about himself or about the church but about the Kingdom of God. The center and the object of his message is this biblical symbol, the longing of Israel. Jesus promises that it will no longer be an utopian dream and expectation, but a reality introduced by God. Jesus' total ministry is to be perceived and interpreted in the light of the coming Kingdom. Thus, the miracles performed are precisely signs that the Kingdom is already breaking in and fermenting within the old world. Other deeds of Jesus such as the forgiveness of sins, are also signs of the Kingdom as transformation and overcoming of oppressive situations. They bear witness to God's liberating and re-creating will and action. The presence of Jesus negates the negation of life: diseases are healed (Mt. 8:16-17), struggle is changed into victory and joy (Lk. 7:11-17, Mk. 5:41-43), death is transfigured into sleep (Mk. 5:39), sins are forgiven (Mk. 2:5), impure demons are dislodged by the Spirit of God (Mt. 12:28).

"Kingdom of God" means total liberation brought about by God's grace and power. It is indeed a kingdom of God in a subjective and objective sense, as Boff notes:

Christ understood himself not only as a
preacher and prophet of this good news
(gospel) but as an element of the new
transformed situation. He is the new
human person, the Kingdom already present though veiled in weakness. Adher-
ence to Christ is an indispensable condition of participation in the new order
to be introduced by God.[19]

Jesus is not merely the one who proclaims and
anticipates the Kingdom. He is also the new way to
enter the Kingdom. In deducing the nature of Jesus'
distinctive consciousness from his attitudes and actions,
Jon Sobrino suggests the following:[20]

a. Jesus is aware of the fact that in and through
his own person the Kingdom of God is drawing near as
reflected in connection with the "signs" referred to
above (Lk. 11:20), the parables of the Kingdom (Mk.
4:30f), and his teachings (Mk. 10:4f, Mt. 5:22, 28, 32,
34, 39, 44).

b. Jesus is bold enough to assert that eschatological salvation is determined by the stance a person
adopts towards Jesus' own person (Mk. 8:30, Lk. 12:8f).

Jesus is aware of the fact that people's ultimate
salvation is functionally related to his own person.
In Jesus' teaching, discipleship has a salvific function
as service to the Kingdom and it is associated with his
own concrete person (MK. 8:34 f, Mt. 8:19-22). Further,
it is clear in the gospels that Jesus was not only
aware of a mission on behalf of the Kingdom but also
conscious of a special relationship to God as the
Heavenly Father. Unconditional trust and obedience to
the Father's will are two respects in which that kind
of consciousness is made explicit.

As the paradigm of new humanity, Jesus proclaims
a message of radical liberation from all alienation.
Further, he himself appears as the new man, as of a new
creation reconciled with itself and with God. Boff
points to the person of Jesus as someone with extraor-
dinary good sense, creative imagination and originality:

Imagination is a form of liberty. It is born in
confrontation with reality and established
order; it emerges from nonconformity in the
face of completed and established situations

. . .We can say that imagination, understood
in this manner, was one of the fundamental
qualities of Jesus . . . Imagination postulates
creativity, spontaneity, and liberty.[21]

2. History and Community

a. History

The reference to the Kingdom involves history
(over against a Neoplatonic dualism manifested, for
example, in a unilateral emphasis on inwardness).
Jesus Christ's message and ministry confirm God's
purpose of being active among people, through people,
with concrete objectives and processes.

The Kingdom of God is not something purely "spiritual" or outside of this world. Rather, it is the
totality of this "physical" world that is being introduced into God's order. It is the manifestation of the
liberation and new life (Rom. 8). This symbol of the
Kingdom signifies that God is the ultimate meaning of
the world and that God will intervene to bring restoration and to establish "a new heaven and a new earth."
The utopia (that which does not exist anywhere) becomes
topia (that which exists somewhere). However, the
Kingdom is not to be regionalized--e.g. in the church
or a given social system--because no liberation process
within history can define the ultimate shape of the
Kingdom which is an eschatological gift from God.[22]

There is but one history, and one process of
liberation that culminates in Jesus Christ. Therefore
the Kingdom is essentially a historical reality to be
perceived and valued (proclaimed, searched for, shared,
celebrated) eschatologically.[23] And the core of the
eschatological dimension lies in this tension of what
is to come, expectation of a new action of God which
facilitates a fresh look at and participation in the
present. The conflict and complementarity between
present and future is thus affirmed.

b. Community

The reference to the Kingdom involves community: the "new man" (Eph. 2:15) or the "new creation"
(2 Cor. 5:17) means new humanity and does not have anything to do
with modern individualism. Actually, it rather confronts
individualism and mere "self-realization." The

appropriation of the Gospel of the Kingdom implies the
formation of a people.

"Kingdom" symbolizes a new and definite way of
being and relating. It involves total renewal: in
human selves, in societal relationships, in all creation.
Viewed in terms of its end results, states Sobrino,
the final goal is one of universal reconciliation,
which stands in opposition to existing realtiy:

> To effect reconciliation is to do justice. . .
> Jesus does not propose to leave people as they
> are and simply console them in their plight;
> he proposes to re-create their present situa-
> tion and thus do "justice" to them . . .24

In our critical discussion in the previous chapter, there
is a reference to the creative model of the community
of people committed to Jesus Christ who are called to
participate in a concrete foretaste of the Kingdom.25

3. Political Obedience

a. Radical Discipleship

Theology and ethics, faith and obedience cannot
be separated. The announcement of the Kingdom (e.g.,
Mt. 4:17, 23) is followed by the new ethical model
(Mt. 5). Ethical challenges and appeals are to be considered   at least as deep and "theological" as those
pertaining to "doctrine" or Christian orthodoxy.

The reference to the kingdom involves obedience.
We can repeat here the old Anabaptist saying now often
stated in Latin American Christological reflections:
"The only way to know Jesus is to follow after him in
one's own life." Only through Christian praxis is it
possible for us to identify with Jesus and draw close
to him. Following Jesus is the precondition for knowing Jesus.26

There exists an interesting correlation between
ontology, epistemology and ethics in the biblical
documents. "God is" and "God exists" really mean and
imply "God reigns." The divine "rule" is part of God's
very reality. Or, the essential reality of God is
inseparably united with the operative reality of the
reign of God. And to know God or, to have faith, means
and implies that one obeys (or one is faithful to) God,

or that one is attuned with God's will or with "the Kingdom of God." Sobrino rightly states:

> Our relationship with Jesus must embody this same relational character. . . Jesus' intrinsic relationship to the Kingdom means that our contact with him will not come primarily through cultic acclamation or adoration but through following Jesus in the service of God's Kingdom.[27]

The Kingdom of God presupposes radical transformation in patterns of life and relationships. There is a new creation (2 Cor. 5:17). The Sermon on the Mount spells out programatically the new life style of the disciple of Jesus Christ. It implies love with no limits human beings truly liberated for greater and creative accomplishments.[28]

The heart and essence of the Sermon is the affirmation that love, service and truth constitute the only kind of power capable of anticipating the Kingdom. From this perspective, Jesus' command to love one's enemies expresses the complete radicalness of discipleship in the context of the Kingdom.[29]

b. Kingdom Politics

The reference to the Kingdom implies politics: together with "history" and "community," the issue of structures, interests, socio-economic and political projects and power,has to be included. The wrongly assumed neutrality on the part of many Christians involves not only a conservative stance (contradictory to the broad social dimension of love for the neighbor) but a hermeneutical mistake: The political pertinence of Jesus Christ is overlooked.[30]

By the very nature of its content, the symbol of the Kingdom is essentially a political symbol. Historically, the theme of the Kingdom of God is central in post-exilic literature and the inter-Testament time. For the Jews it obviously possessed a political connotation since politics and religion were so much interrelated. For them the effective symbol[31] "Kingdom of God" designated liberation from opppression and life at its fullest potential. God's lordship over all had also to be demonstrated politically. The Messiah would inaugurate the Kingdom.

Jesus corrected the messianic and apocalyptic expectations of the people, however. He negated nationalistic dreams and strategies, even though classical political messianism seems to have been a major temptation for Jesus (Mk. 1:12 ff, 11:10; Lk. 15:26, 24:21).

> The great drama of the life of Christ was to try to take the ideological content out of the word "Kingdom of God" and make the people and his disciples comprehend that he signified something much more profound, namely, that he demands a conversion of persons and a radical transformation of the human world...32

The political character of the Kingdom involves a much more radical and comprehensive reality both as negating (i.e. subversive) of current establishment and as creating of alternatives for life enhancing and community building.

The biblical concept of shalom, which includes justice, wholeness, wellbeing, righteousness, peace, salvation itself,33 needs to be seen in close connection with the symbol of the Kingdom. The Kingdom of God is really the Kingdom of Shalom, which points to the process and the content of the politics of God.

Kingdom is Central: Critical Material Implications

1. Only one Kingdom

The reference to the Kingdom involves a distinction regarding other kingdoms. If Jesus is Lord (kirios),34 others are not. If he is radically obeyed, then other loyalties and commitments cannot claim any precedence or absolute priority. Thus, the conflictive, exclusive and confrontational character of the Kingdom Gospel should be properly appraised.

The disciples of Jesus feel themselves to be in a considerable degree like aliens in the midst of smaller "kingdoms" which tend to present manifold contradictions of the Kingdom of God. Discomfort, conflict and ambivalence are normal experiences for the citizen of the Kingdom en route to a more human (i.e., closer to God's will) society.35

God's Kingdom always challenges and calls into crisis more immediate and partial interests whether they be political, religious, economic or social. It retains its characteristic features of totality and universality.[36] The radicalness of the demand for discipleship in fact needs to be seen in terms of the mutually exclusive alternatives that the Kingdom of God poses to the present world:

> The alternatives can be described in theological terms (God or wealth), Christological terms ("He who is not with me is against me"), or anthropological terms ("Whoever would preserve his life will lose it, but whoever loses his life for my sake and the gospel's will preserve it").[37]

2. An "upside-down Kingdom"[38]

"Kingdom of God" involves radical social transformation, including profound changes in one's personal existence. "Conversion" (metanoia) is the biblical term for that kind of process, which we interpret as one dimension of the total, structural revolution of the old order which the Kingdom presupposes. As Boff puts its, Christ makes two fundamental demands: He demands personal conversion and postulates a restructuring of the human world.[39]

The revolution of the human world, the establishment of signs and beach-heads of the Kingdom also affects the "normal" order and social conventions as well as all the forces, interests and powers that oppress and alienate human beings. However, "conversion" is not only needed in the first stage of this development process. The disciple will have to remain open and attuned to the creative work of the Spirit of Christ, which may become manifest in seemingly scandalous, illogical, impractical, and ineffective ways (e.g., loving the "unlovable," suffering without seeking retaliation). Hence the need to keep affirming also an "abnormal epistemology."

The reference of the Kingdom coming as a gift requires in fact an abnormal epistemology,[40] i.e., a new and different way of conceiving knowledge and truth. Those who need to receive God's "revelation" cannot determine or dictate the form salvation-liberation will take. There is plenty of space for surprises and

disappointments. Thus, Jesus affirmed the fulfillment
of the messianic expectation but with a radical change
of definition of kingship. An inversion of values is
involved: the new context for the Kingdom symbol is
service. Jesus Christ is a Lord Servant (Mt. 20:25-30;
Lk. 22:25-30; Jn. 13:13 ff). Royalty is defined in
terms of service, and the Kingdom is shared by sharing
the cross and walking in the power of resurrection.

3. Power and Service

The "King-Servant" does not impose himself by force.
A consequence from the previous formulation regarding
the peculiar nature of the Kingdom is that it is offered
in love while affirming human freedom. Also, to
proclaim the Kingdom means to acknowledge the central
place of the problem of power. The temptations of
power (or, to become a "normal" king) seems to have
been crucial and always rejected by Jesus. This calls
for the exercise of suspicion regarding the claims by
those who practice that kind of authority. On the other
hand, this implies an invitation to participate in the
creation of viable alternatives in social transformation,
the "untested feasibility" (Freire's term) of the
contours of life in the Kingdom of God.

The relationship between the essence of sin and
the essence of power is an important aspect of Jesus'
teachings. Further, he discusses the personal characteristics of sin as well as the social and structural
dimensions of sin and evil.

> For Jesus, sin is the rejection of God's
> Kingdom . . .and the anthropological
> essence of sin is people's self-affirmation
> which leads them to assert their own power
> in negative ways. . . Only one kind of
> power is proper if one seeks to anticipate
> the Kingdom. It is the power of love, of
> sacrifice, of service, of truth.[41]

Kingdom is Central: Constructive Material
Implications

1. Creative Power

The reference to the Kingdom involves creative
power for transformation. To proclaim the Kingdom in

96

hope presupposes new sensitivity and concern for human suffering, the critique of the present order as well as the promise of the renewing power of love, forgiveness, and service. The very presence and experience of a nonconformist community creating models for service is already an agent of change. Further, the Kingdom refers to the totality of human experience and not only the global or structural dimensions. That is, the whole arena of human life and relationships is involved: the different dimensions of daily life as much as the political or economic institutional orders.

Salvation--or ultimate liberation or resurrection-- and the coming of the Kingdom is a gracious gift of God in Jesus Christ. However, actual historical realizations presuppose human participation. There is space for hope, then, and for an optimism which is not grounded on a faulty anthropology.[42] Brazilian Protestant theologian Rubem Alves has criticized classical Protestantism because, in his view, "it concluded that there was no room for human creativity in history. Grace, instead of making man free for creativity, makes creativity superfluous or impossible."[43] He states the need to affirm both grace and creativity: "God's grace, instead of making human creativity superfluous or impossible, is therefore the politics that makes it possible and necessary."[44] The idea is not that God is dependent upon man for establishing the future, the Kingdom. Rather, that a part and parcel of the Kingdom gift is the invitation and the enablement to co-participate in God's liberating and recreating endeavors. God's grace and the Spirit of the resurrected Christ will always be a necessary, indispensable dimension in any truly liberating and re-creating process.

It is in this light that we perceive the challenge of the church to participate in the building of the new order. This is the meaning of fulfillment of the human vocation--Freire's "ontological vocation": to be subjects in history-making.

2. Critical Discernment

To proclaim the Gospel of the Kingdom involves the affirmation that its ethical thrust can be the criterion for discerning "what God is doing to make human life more human. The Kingdom message describes a new quality of life which is impossible if the Kingdom has not come (Mt. 3:2 ff, Lk. 3:11-14, 4:18-21, the Lord's prayer, etc.).

The "already" of the Kingdom is discerned whenever and wherever there is forgiveness, sharing with the needy, discovering more humanizing alternatives. Discernment points to those historical events, whenever they happen, insofar as they correspond to that definition of "making human life more human." The claim here is that the reference to the actual ethical thrust of the Kingdom Gospel is less ideological and less subjective than other criteria which involve formulations such as "order" or "revolution," or the mere "reading" of history in terms of the relative failure or success of a given movement.[45]

In regard to the quality of life corresponding to the Kingdom--and therefore possessing eschatological meaning--our proposition is that the biblical documents point in the direction of shalom and resurrection: justice, solidarity, access to God's creation, freedom to participate in community-building on the basis of love and work, and so on. In order to analyze and critique the present order, a major criterion to be used is precisely the Kingdom of God.[46]

The Kingdom is to be the ultimate fulfillment of all creation, the final completion of salvation and liberation. Therefore, the question arises as to what an extent our present situation and praxis are consistent with the politics of God concerning the building of justice, solidarity and the other signs of the Kingdom. The Kingdom provides criteria for discerning both the negation and the affirmation of the new creation, within the church and in society at large. It also presupposes dreams, hopes, and goals for future realizations. The idea is that the moral content of the Kingdom proclaimed and expected is the criterion for discernment. Thus, for instance, the Sermon on the Mount outlines the basic elements of the ethical originality of the Kingdom: a new quality of life which corresponds to the coming of the Kingdom. Therefore, the affirmation of the pertinence of this vision means the proclamation of the Kingdom. God's reign is discerned (even if God is not mentioned) if events fit that definition of what it means "to make human life more human."[47]

3. The Messianic Community

Together with the pertinence of the Kingdom Gospel
there is the confession of the pertinence of the presence
of the people who assume the paradigm of the Kingdom or
the "sacrament" of history. The church's vocation--but
not necessarily its history--is that what emerged and
was expressed in Jesus ought to emerge and be expressed
in his followers:

> . . . complete openness to God and others;
> indiscriminate love without limits . . .
> a critical spirit that cultivates creative
> imagination, which in the name of love and
> the liberty of the children of God chal-
> lenges cultural structures . . .[48]

In its existence and mission the church proclaims
and shares the Kingdom in the heart of human history,
by preaching the Gospel of shalom, by the experience of
koinonia, worship, a nonconformist lifestyle and models
of social service. A healing community of reconciliation where discipleship, the following of Jesus, is
"contextualized" in terms of actual historical situations. Further, as a "sacramental community," to use
Gutiérrez's term--that is, as a sign or revelation--
the church finds its meaning in its potential to
signify the reality in function of which it exists.
And it is towards the fulfillment of this reality that
the church is oriented: the reality of the Kingdom of
God which has already begun in history.[49]

The coming Kingdom is necessarily a historical,
temporal, and social reality. The prophetic announcement of the Kingdom of shalom involves the establishment
of structures for justice, freedom, and community.
These social realities are expected to be manifested
primarily within the community of people who confess
the lordship of the risen Lord. The announcement of
that Kingdom in words and deeds reveals to society itself the aspiration for a just society by leading in
the discovery of unexpected dimensions and unexplored
paths in human interaction and development. Partial
and imperfect realizations, to be sure, that in turn
open up the promise and the hope of complete reconciliation and liberation.

D. Formulating the Guiding Principle

We have discussed the main features of current
theological reflections in light of Freire's foundations.
Analysis and critique led us to a constructive reformulation with focus on the Gospel of the Kingdom whose
centrality for a relevant hermeneutic was underlined.
The core of those biblico-theological basis and
dimensions was thus summarized and articulated in the
course of our reinterpretation. The discussion was
facilitated by the implicit understanding of theology
in terms of a threefold commitment: to the Word and
the Spirit, to the historico-cultural context, and to
the church. This suggests a set of interrelated
"agendas" for theolgical reflection to which we shall
return later on:

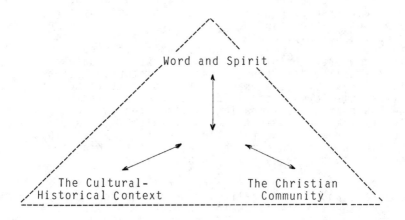

Word and Spirit

The Cultural-
Historical Context

The Christian
Community

Our proposition at this point is that the Kingdom
motif (understood as pointing to God's gift, promise,
and demand of the in-breaking reality of the new
creation under the lordship of Christ) inspires an
adequate guiding principle[50] for the mission of the
church and for Christian education specifically. On the
basis of this principle, the theory and the task of
Christian education can be illumined, oriented, and
evaluated.

There is no question as to the priority represented
in this beginning point. In order to start operating
consistently, we need to be clear about the heart of the
matter of Christian education expressed in such a guiding principle which, simultaneously, will lead our
educational endeavors and will provide the clue for
communicating and implementing them. We need to clarify
and spell out together with the "lay people" the
essentials, as they emerge from the interpretation of
Scripture and the Spirit's work, the understanding of
our historical context, and our view of the nature and
mission of the church.

Latin American theological reflection is illuminating in this regard precisely because of the attempted
articulation of these three vectors--referred to above
in terms of a threefold commitment--which converge or
intersect in the direction of God's Kingdom. The
intrinsic limitations and contradictions--most of which
we pointed out before--should not be overlooked, nor the
indebtedness to western theological traditions. The
conviction and the decision is, nevertheless, to affirm
the possibility of new syntheses and creations taking
seriously into account the historico-cultural situation.
This is obviously something that other approaches cannot
do alone, even if they are assumed to be normative in
some manner or degree.

The rediscovery of the centrality of the Kingdom
and the Gospel as Gospel of the Kingdom, calls for a
guiding principle centered in this vision. The Kingdom
is not merely "in the mind of God" or in a transcendent
other-worldly reality. It is God's will and gift of the
new creation in Christ. It is not just pictured or
clearly defined in the Scriptures, and yet the Bible
does provide indispensable clues and "windows" of God's
manifestations through the symbols, narratives, declara-
tions, pointing to the freedom to live in peace (shalom)
even in the midst of death.

The church is not to be identified with the Kingdom,
and yet its calling is to be a foretaste and a sign, a
beachhead of the Kingdom values, life, and projections.
The Kingdom is not to be equated with a given socio-
cultural structure, and yet it is to be discerned and
realized in its midst. In fact, this proposition
involves a challenge for further theological reflection
about the intrinsic relationship between the Spirit's
creative work inside and outside the Christian

communities, since it is confessed that the Spirit is freely involved in the world at large.

That is why the integrity and the interrelations of the threefold commitment and the three vectors must be maintained. The following diagram is but an attempt to picture those interrelations with the inclusion of the "agendas" as both raw material and product of biblico-theological reflection, oriented towards the Christian education task and process (next page).

The agenda of the Word and the Spirit involves discerning God's action in promoting the Kingdom, on the basis of the biblical documents. The agenda of the church refers to the history and tradition of "God's people," and especially to the nature, life and ministry of the concrete Christian community in which educational endeavors take place (that is, along with and also a dimension of worship, koinonia, social service, prophetic announcing-denouncing, discipling, and so on). The

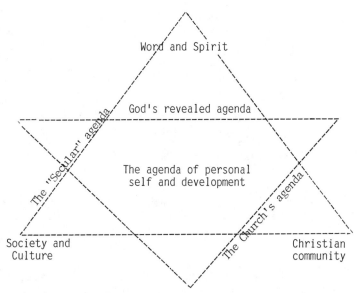

Biblico-theological Reflection for
Christian Education Task and Process

"secular" agenda (perhaps an unfortunate choice of words, given the negative connotations in some circles) involves the political and economical situation, prevailing cultural values, traditions, mores, as well as alternative movements and experiences that affect in some degree the life of the people. All of these need to be perceived interrelatedly in diverse ways and in tension with each other as well.

At the core of the process of Christian education we perceive the persons actually involved in learning in community. The agenda of their lives, particularly in terms of growth and development and personal experience, conditions the way in which the others operate in a given situation.

There are several criteria for considering the guiding principle as a dependable guide to practice and genuinely the focus for theory and communicable to all. Such a principle must be adequate, both theologically (central and convincing) and educationally (informed by, and its implications developed in terms of, the educational disciplines). It must be simple and clear.[51] To the question whether there is an element that will be the soul of theology, and yet so dynamically personal and transforming that is indispensably educational, the answer for us is the Gospel of the Kingdom of God. Our choice concerning the content of the guiding principle is due primarily to the fact that the Kingdom of God is the central scope of Jesus Christ's own preaching and ministry, whose eschatological vision and perspective we desire to underscore. Secondly, the very person of Jesus Christ is also at the center in this approach in which we do not maintain a sharp distinction between "the message about the event" and "the Christ event itself." By the same token, we stress a close connection between, say, "communicating the good news of the Kingdom." Thirdly, we underscore the Kingdom motif because this is consistent with current theological foundations under consideration. The political and eschatological dimensions of the Gospel in our historico-cultural situation, thus become more explicit. The principle dramatizes tensions such as between "already" and "not yet," and the experience of alienation in the midst of present bankrupt structures. It embodies a corrective to mere "teaching of the sound doctrine," characteristic of much of the present educational situation. Indeed it includes also a critical dimension with regard to society's educational institutions, assumptions, goals and methods.

On the basis of the previous discussion, it should be obvious that it is not only the confrontational or "nonconformist" character of the Kingdom Gospel that is underlined here. However, the omission of the critical dimension makes any Christian educational theory and enterprise suspect of helping to support the present order of things, that is, lesser or evil "kingdoms." The message and the reality of God's Kingdom is the main focus of concern and the driving force of the life of the Christian community wihin the historical situation. Therefore, the educational ministry of the church should be oriented, conceived and evaluated in the light of the Gospel of the Kingdom of God. This is the guiding principle. This is the essential element and the center on the basis of which all the dimensions and levels of the Christian education process and enterprise can be meaningfully arranged.

We have thus completed the discusson of the theological foundations of Freire's educational work and thought.52 Having previously focused on the epistemological foundations, we can now proceed to the last part of this study by pointing out implications for Christian education.

THIRD PART -- RAMIFICATIONS

FOR THEORY AND PRACTICE

To discuss the question of the Church and
education in general is to discuss, inevitably, the relation between the church and
the world . . .

I would judge the teaching witness of a
church in the light of the question whether
it is a witness of the courage to love,
which is expressed in the search for the
means by which man will be liberated.

                        Paulo Freire
                        Witness of Liberation

CHAPTER 5

IMPLICATIONS FOR CHRISTIAN EDUCATION

Introduction

As we considered the epistemological and theological
foundations of Paulo Freire's work and thought, we
employed the same method and we followed a similar
procedure. Critical analyses and constructive reformulations were presented in each case and the structure
of the study was thereby maintained.

As far as the content of the essay is concerned,
the discussion underscored creativity as anticipated in
our main hypothesis: the method and process of conscientization include an implicit epistemology of the
creative process. The articulation of such an epistemology is essential for understanding the connection
between the linguistic and self-dynamics involved, and
for overcoming the limitations in Freire's contribution.
Further, that being the case, the educational and
theological perspectives can be integrated thus providing an adequate base for Christian education theory.
The last part of this formulation is the theme of the
present chapter.

We will demonstrate how the previous considerations
provide needed resources, especially in light of the
following three tasks:

a. To look at the socio-cultural situation in
historical perspective and its relationship to Christian
education particularly. The phenomenon of colonization
and some of its implications will be underlined as we
consider briefly the Latin American case.

b. To discuss and engage in Christian education
theory building, with emphasis on the interrelationship
of practice and theory.

c. To indicate content material for Christian
education theory, that is, to propose specific principles
as dependable guides to practice, on the basis of our
reappraisal of Freire.

A.   The Latin   American Case

Two foci will occupy our attention in this section:
a reference to the cultural background and setting, and
to Christian education within that context.

1.   On the Cultural Background

This is an indispensable starting point because the
church (and Christian education in particular) always
reflects and responds to the culture in which it lives.[1]
The life and the program of the church, and even its
theology, cannot help but take on cultural features of
its day. At the same time, the church seeks to deal
with the historico-cultural situation in a creative
fashion given its call to be a "hermeneutic," "prophetic,"
and "messianic" community that announces the Gospel of
the Kingdom of God. Hence, the witness and the mission
of the church to society and culture are critical,
constructive and reconstructive in character. As
Wyckoff states:

> The church always reflects and remakes the
> culture in which it lives . . . The church is
> a social institution, and as such always
> tends to reflect its culture . . . At the
> same time the church is that body of Christ,
> and as such tends to resist cultural inroads
> and to work for the redemption of culture
> . . .The church is the human instrumentality
> brought into being by God in Christ to con-
> tinue the ministry of redemption to the
> world. It is the New Israel, sustained and
> guided in its work by the Holy Spirit.[2]

On the basis we can now take a brief look at the historical conditioning of the Latin American situation in
terms of the establishment of the Christian religion.
We will pay special attention to the illuminating thought
of John A. Mackay. His major intuitions--in spite of
his different cultural background and religios tradition
--are strikingly consistent with recent anthropological,
historical, and theological reflections on this matter,
including Freire's thought. Mackay has provided an
important clue for an adequate understanding of the
religious situation in that context, in terms of both
his approach to the problem and the content of his
contribution.[3] Those insights concerning the "portraits"
of Christ, their meaning and implications, must be taken

into account in the attempt to evaluate and develop
Christian education contextually. And this is particularly the case for an approach whose guiding principle
is the Gospel of the Kingdom of God.

The Conqueror's Christ

Mackay's central argument is that the Christ
brought by the Spaniards--the "Christophers" = "Christ-
bearers," beginning of course with Christopher Columbus
--was not the "authentic" one:

> A Christ came to South America who has put
> men in agreement with life, who has told
> them to accept it as it is, and things as
> they are, and truth as it appears to be.
> But the other?
> He who makes men dissatisfied with life as
> it is, and things as they are, and tells
> them that, through Him, life shall be trans-
> formed, and the world overcome, and His
> followers put in agreement with reality,
> God and truth? He wanted to come, but His
> way was barred . . .[4]

With regard to the characteristics of this prevailing Spanish Christ, Mackay provides a clue. In Latin
America, Christ represented the tragic victim and the
focus of a cult of death as an expiatory creature with
neither personality nor power, i.e. the one who shows
people how to die rather than how to live. Says Mackay:

> A Christ known in life as an infant and in
> death as a corpse, over whose helpless
> childhood and tragic fate the Virgin Mother
> presides . . . Full-blooded men with a
> passion for life and liberty found their
> religious inspiration in the figure of the
> Virgin who had never died.[5]

Several years after Mackay suggested that appreciation, anthropologist Eric Wolf picked it up explicitly
and was able to confirm it in his interesting study
"The Virgin of Guadalupe: A Mexican National Symbol."[6]

Not only does Mackay describe this Spanish Christ,
but he also traces his steps from the time of Spain's
own subjection to the Moors, to the conquest and colonization of America and beyond. The reference to the

mystic motive of the conquest and Spain's sense of
mission carried out in the clear fashion of a succesful
--"Constantinian" style--crusade, is particularly
helpful. Together with the description of the colonial
theocracy, it clarifies much of the background and
actual meaning of the whole colonizing enterprise and
especially the task of evangelization and religious
instruction. Mackay underscores the lack of intellectual content and ethical thrust of that religion.
And with regard to personal dynamics involved, there is
another observation expressed as follows:

> The contemplation of His passion produces a
> sort of catharsis, as Aristotle would say,
> in the soul of the worshipper. . . The total
> sensation intensifies his sense of the real-
> ity and terribleness of death; it increases
> his passion for life and, in the religious
> realm, makes him cling desperately and trag-
> ically to the dead Victim that died to give
> him immortality.7

Mackay also produces testimonies of the magical
character of the relationship to that Christ in the
Eucharist where "He is taken for the mortal vigour and
immortal life He can give, but not as the Lord of Life
to whose influence the soul submits. The Sacrament
increases life without transforming it . . . Having
no necessary connection with either right reason or
right conduct, this religion has best been propagated
by awakening fear."8 Further description of the
"Creole" Christ includes such negative features as a
lack of humanity and manhood which has made little
appeal to South American worshippers, whose "exclusive
interest in Christ's meaning for death and immortality
has led them to ignore the One who by the lake-side
told men how to live."9 We suggest that this could be
a "neocrophilous" Christ.10

Mackay concludes that the lordship of Christ has
not been acknowledged and that He remains to be known
as Jesus, the Savior and the Lord of all life.

The "Other" Spanish Christ

The spiritual history being researched also shows
a long and subterranean tradition which, in Mackay's
view, no constructive religious policy for South America
can ignore. To this tradition belong several figures,

particularly the great mystics of the sixteenth century
(Fray Luis de Granada, Juan de la Cruz, Santa Teresa de
Jesús, Fray Luis de León), and other "rebels" and
prophets down to the present. The picture of this
("biophilic") Christ is presented in terms of characteristics associated with life, work and thought of a
number of those figures. There is in general a twofold
emphasis on inward spiritual experience and outward,
social ethical expression.

In connection with contemporary figures Mackay
includes other features of this other Spanish Christ
and particularly a strong prophetic stance together with
a conflict-affirming religious experience and perspective.[11] Cross and resurrection, new life and Jesus
Christ as actual mediator of death and life, are other
central features inherent in the portrait of the "other
Spanish Christ," the one that needs to be rediscovered.
We would put it this way: over against a Christ that
promotes adjustment and resignation, this one invites
us to follow Him in order to be free and responsive
by becoming engaged in the creative-liberating vocation
for the Kingdom of God. This is precisely the new
understanding articulated more recently by Paulo Freire
and Latin American theologians, as we discussed in
chapters 3 and 4.

2.   On Christian Education

Because Christian education is one of the
chief functions of the church, the educational ministry being in and of the church,
it too is influenced by the culture. In
fact, as the cultural situation affects the
church and through it its educational work,
so also the cultural situation affects educational procedures and institutions, which
are in turn mirrored in the church's educational work.[12]

John A. Mackay perceived and described the kind of
religious instruction consistent with colonization in
the name of the conquerors' Christ. The imprinting of
a "neocrophilous" and alienating Christ on the thought
and the imagination of the people was the product of an
easily characterizable pedagogical method distinguished
by two main features-"catechetical" and "sensuous".[13]

111

The indoctrinating and domesticating character of religious instruction in most areas and most of the time has been in fact apparent. Most authors agree with Mackay in this negative evaluation and in regard to the fact that since the conquest Latin America has been basically, in Freire's words, a subjugated land: "Its colonization consisted of transplantation by the invaders."[14] The role of religion and education in the colonial relationship could be further documented and analyzed for example in terms of Albert Memmi's "por-traits" of the colonized and the colonizer.[15] What Mackay describes concerning the prevailing situation in the history of religious education in Latin America corresponds very much to the traditionalist and mis-sionary type of church criticized by Paulo Freire dis-cussed above. It involves a religious view that is instrumental in maintaining and sacralizing the status quo. This ideology concerning the world, human beings and destiny, promotes an education inevitably quietist, alienated and alienating.[16]

There are signs suggesting that meaningful changes are taking place among both Catholics and Protestants. That is, changes in the direction of greater relevance in regard to the historical-cultural context and more consistent with the Gospel of the Kingdom of God. Let us examine briefly some of these developments.

Christian education among Catholics reflects well the background of several approaches to the mission of the church in society. The most traditional one--still dominant in many areas--is associated with the old (medieval) "Christendom" motif, which identifies Christianity with culture, and national citizenship in particular, has a strong sacramental stance, and aims at creating a more or less uniform "Christian" mentality in conjunction with the civil (or military) power. It is directed basically to the masses and has had an indoctrinating and repressive character as manifest in the old catechetic procedures, so well criticized for example, by Hubertus Halbfas.[17]

Within a modernizing category we find the "new Christendom" approach which is inspired in Jacques Maritain's influence, particularly since the early 30's. The basic idea here is the creation of Christian insti-tutions such as political parties, Christian labor unions, revitalization of schools, and so on. It attempts to be less obviously "religious" than the previous alternative and it has attracted a considerable

intellectual and political élite in Latin America who
are preoccupied with socio-political change. Efficacy
is a major focus of concern in this case and religious
education is steered to provide both foundation and
support for those endeavors, and to be actually "effective" Christian education for the nurture of exemplary
democratic citizens and institutions.

A Major renewal movement has been apparent since
1968 (the occasion of the Catholic Episcopal Conference
in Medellín, Colombia). The main trends of this thrust
have been characterized as follows:[18]

--An anthropological catechetics as the starting
point in the sense of "situational catechetics."

--A Christocentric emphasis in which Jesus Christ
is proclaimed as liberator beyond the many forms of
"pietistic" deformation.

--A communitarian approach centered on grass-
roots congregations and "base communities."

--A more consistent focus on the Bible, recently
translated into popular language and widely distributed.

--A religious education oriented towards the pro-
motion of social transformation in the face of poverty
and injustice.

A stated priority of these efforts is the "re-evangeli-
zation" of adults among the majority of "nominal"
Catholics. Thegeneral emphasis tends to reflect a
"reconstructionist" approach to Christian education
among those actively involved in working towards transforming and adapting the church's educational task.
The special case of the "basic ecclesial communities"
offers a significant paradigm in this regard.[19] Still
in many instances a real polarization exists between
conception and practice of more or less "traditionalist"
or "modernist," and "prophetic" stances. This is also
the case in other denominations. The coexistence of
different and even conflicting approaches often creates
tensions at the level of denominational and interdenominational policy-making.

The overall situation of Christian education in
Latin America among Protestants is not encouraging. It
presents a poor reflection of the predominant "banking
model" in the public school system so sharply criticized

by Paulo Freire, and an uncritical incorporation of
methods, curricula and organization flowing mainly from
foreign missionary agencies and publishing houses.
Much of Protestant Christianity in these countries
reveals consistently the influence of the missionary
enterprise in planting and nurturing the churches.
Thus, for more than a century Christian education in
the congregations has reflected heavily a traditional
theological approach, essentially concerned with the
transmission of a divine and authoritative message of
salvation, in consistency with the theological stance
of the sending "mother churches" and mission boards.
There are still many "transplanted" congregations of
immigrants and descendants and many missionary churches
closely associated or even under economic and administra-
tive dependence of foreign mission agencies. The
peculiar and fast development of some indigenous,
pentecostal-like movements, is another predominantly
Protestant characteristic. In the last case, Christian
education either follows the main line patterns, or
else it is minimal as far as deliberate educational
endeavors are concerned.

It is possible that a thorough survey of the situation of the church and Christian education, would suggest a picture similar to some observations registered
on worship and liturgy. They indicate that the church
in general does not foster an encounter with the Gospel
in its structural and cosmic dimensions, nor commitment
with Latin American reality.[20]

Gerson A. Meyer, former Secretary for Christian
Education--Program Unit Education and Renewal (WCC),
has identified some consistent patters in the Third
World. He notes first that those nations have very
much in common, with strikingly similar educational
programs in many instances. He adds that this probably
due to the fact that the so called Third World has
inherited the same church structures transplanted from
the same countries, usually the United States and
Europe.

Even today . . . the patterns of church education in the Third World are the ones that
missionaries brought to Africa, Asia, Latin
America, the Middle East, the Caribbean Islands
and the Pacific regions . . . the importation
of programs which were prepared to fit another
culture and social setting . . . Everything was
imported: structures, content with different

materials, and methodology. Needless to say, all this brought with it cultural elements, consciously or unconsciously imposed on the nationals, disregarding their social and cultural heritages.[21]

After indicating how patterns were established in terms of specific problems with educational agencies such as the Sunday school, and methodological shortcomings in particular, Meyer pinpoints the main characteristics of those patterns that need to be replaced:

. . . the conservative approach to the Bible and doctrine; the disassociation form the social reality; the ghetto mentality; the narrowness of the objectives for Christian education; and the fragmentation of the educational programs. All these together have been impediments to the development of a creative and realistic educational program meeting the needs of today.[22]

Recent improvements in Christian education still betray a lack of sound educational and theological construction. Increasing cooperative interdenominational projects begin to provide resources and opportunities for filling those gaps in a creative way. Here we can mention the Latin American Evangelical Committee for Christian Education (CELADEC) which was formed in 1962, with the purpose of assisting the churches in fulfilling their educational task through a number of programs. CELADEC has made important contributions to curriculum planning and design, teachers formation and, more recently, to Christian education for liberation and popular education.[23] Our own study is an attempt to sharpen educational and biblico-theological reflections for making a much needed foundation for Christian education more explicit and better formulated than before.[24]

This discussion thus far underscores two major issues. In the first place, it is clear that there is a need and a challenge to further improve and develop Christian education theory and practice. The articulation of theory must be done in light of ecclesial and theological developments as well as in response to the growing demands for relevance stemming from the sociocultural situation. This is essential in order to build and recreate whenever necessary a sound basis for effective educational practice. Besides, the task requires the participation and commitment of different groups of persons engaged in the Christian educational task rather than isolated endeavors on the part of a few individuals.

Secondly, in the context of our overall study, our discussion points further to the relevance of Freire's thought. His insights are indeed important for the educational ministry of the church in several ways. Analysis and critique of the present situation as well as the construction of alternative approaches can both find inspiration and resources in the work of the Brazilian educator. Precisely, our task now is to indicate more specific implications and applications of Freire's contribution as reinterpreted by us.

In the next section we will present a methodological approach to theory building. Finally, this will be followed by particular considerations concerning Christian education principles, i.e. the content of theory, in light of our foundations.

B.   Methodological Approach to Theory Building

As indicated in the introduction to this book, one of the stated purposes of our study is to make a contribution to the very understanding of Christian education and particularly to the development of Christian education theory.

1.   Preliminary Considerations

We have been engaged in theorizing from the beginning of our study, from the moment we decided to examine and reinterpret the work and thought of Paulo Freire, with a focus on his epistemological and theological foundations. That approach and those points of concentration mark both the possibilities and the boundaries of our investigation. Education as a discipline has a derivative character, and this is obviously the situation of Christian education too. It has to take into consideration especially the development and contributions of the science of education as well as current theological reflections and concerns.

In our study we have been dealing with substantial resource material pertaining precisely to the fields of education and theology. By employing our constructive reformulation of Freire's contribution, we will be able to indicate more clearly our approach to Christian education theory building, and to formulate several Christian education principles. However, due to the fact that we have taken into account only a selected number of foundation materials, we shall not develop-- on that limited basis--a comprehensive theory of Christian education. Yet, our discussion attempts to indicate the direction and the shape that such a theory could assume. Furthermore, this is a special situation in which, foundations emerging partially from Latin America may be thus utilized in the development of Christian education theory.25 As we indicated above, it is indispensable to be fully aware of the close relation- ship between culture and the church and Christian education in particular. Taking seriously into account the cultural situation, reflecting the life and the thought of the church accurately, and taking full cognizance of the educational process, are essential to guarantee the usefulness and adequacy of the principles that constitute the required theory. Our foundations assist us in this regard, and they also become informative and even normative for our consideration of process and content in Christian education. The question of the theological and educational normativeness of Christian education is reiterated by Wyckoff:

> It is from these foundations that the two
> major concerns of Christian education
> theory--theology and the science of educa-
> tion--stem . . . Christian education can
> and must be theologically thorough and
> accurate, and at the same time maintain
> educational integrity and soundness . . .
> The basic question is whether it is possible
> to construct a theory of Christian education
> (a body of principles) that will be theologically
> valid and at the same time educationally sound.26

In our particular case, then, further theorizing will deal with the integration of epistemological reflections (in terms of conscientization as creativity) and theological discussions (focused on the symbolic and paradoxical motif of the Kingdom of God). The unifying factor and ultimate inspiration of Christian education principles is to be provided by the guiding principle which, at the same time, is to facilitate a clear and adequate understanding of both practice and theory.27

2. Methodological Cycle

We can now proceed to indicate the logical, sequential movements in the process of theory building in Christian education, as we approach it.

a. The starting point is the church itself in the midst of the socio-historical situation. It has an educational task in the midst of the socio-historical situation. It has an educational task and ministry to fulfill, for which it commissions some of its members. Therefore, there is a vocation or call to serve in terms of the Spirit's freely provided gifts for the building and nurture of the church. Together with this recognition of special gifts, there is the affirmation of the need for working and reflecting in close association with other persons, experts and lay people alike.

b. The Christian education enterprise in its theoretical dimension is thereby understood as involving what we have called the discernment of interrelated "agendas" with a three-fold commitment to the Word and the Spirit of God, to society, and to the church. The corresponding vectors converge or intersect in the direction of the Kingdom of God in our model. At the core of the process we perceive the persons actually involved in learning in community. (See diagram and discussion in Chapter 4, p. 102).

c. The heterogenous character of the socio-cultural environment calls for a careful scrutiny from different perspectives such as anthropological, socio-economical, political, and theological. Special attention is given to the educational situation in terms of characteristics, approaches, trends and needs. For instance, in the Latin American scene several deleterious factors are to be taken into account such as diverse degrees of economic underdevelopment, relative political instability and extensive curtailment of freedom and lack of human, civil, and political rights, and cultural deprivation. Rapid industrialization, urbanization, and modernization in certain areas, plus struggles for empowernment and liberation, are other aspects to reckon with. The church's denouncing and announcing in the midst of society is to be performed with the assistance of adequate equipment available, including the critical sciences. Possibilities of confrontation, cooperation and service are thus discovered, together with a continuous assessment of the church's own life and mission.

d. In the face of the previous discussion, the next question refers to the selection of priorities for the educational task. What are the most pressing challenges and needs to be focused in the Christian education enterprise, as the church gets involved in discerning those interrelated agendas in terms of the Kingdom Gospel? As we perceive the present situation, there is the need for a comprehensive theoretical formulation of the Christian education task and process as well as specific derivation of principles with a focus on certain target groups (youth, adults, families, teachers-leaders, especially).

e. Having stated the basic challenges, we work on tentative answers (hypotheses) and new questions, while engaging in the search for resources from a variety of fields and from our own personal and professional experience as Christian educators. From these areas of experiences and thought we endeavor to obtain information, directions, and clues to deal with the problems and questions posed by the Christian education ministry. We gradually gather material--ideas, insights, basically--that illumine our concerns and approach, and facilitate the formulation of guidelines and answers for effective educational practice.

The sound basis for effective practice? There is no assumption that we are after something that is fixed and final. There is a way to keep if fluid and flexible, and at the same time to keep it responsible and dependable. We identify carefully the principles upon which what we are doing is based. We identify carefully the theological and educational assumptions underlying these presently operative principles. We review these theological and educational assumptions, changing them as needed. We review our operative principles in light of these changed theological and educational assumptions. On the basis of this review, we draw implications for new theory and new practice. The process of analytical examination and reconstruction of theory and practice is complex. If we neglect any of the essential steps, we are likely to misunderstand Christian education and fail to deal with our task intelligently.[28]

The resources are articulated and integrated in consistency with the guiding principle, in terms of a body of principles (basic theory) and also in the fashion of operative principles concerning method, curriculum, and administration.

The whole endeavor of theory building and rebuilding in Christian education is dynamic, multidirectional, and theory is to be seen closely and continuously interrelated with practice. Actually, the integration of theory and practice is an imperative for religious education. In Margaret Webster's words:

> To be effective, religious education must continually be involved in the on-going task of developing theory which will be a guide to practice. The development of that theory must be informed and enlightened by the actual practice of religious education within the local church and school.
> What is called for is a relationship of mutual interaction of theory and practice, with neither being unduly dominated by the other . . .
> Theory which can be applied to practice must be comprehensive... / It / must continue to wrestle with the relationship between theology and religious education . . .
> Religious education theory should also consider the contributions of the social sciences . . . the insights from general education, especially the theory/practice dialogue which takes place there . . .
> still, the theory we build must be distinctly religious education theory for the religious education enterprise requires unique approaches to the defining of the discipline and the building of theory and practice . . .
> Theory/Practice integration requires the mutual acceptance and effort of "theorists" and practitioners."[29]

The following diagram represents a summary of our methodological approach just briefly discussed.[30] The arrows indicate that relationships between steps and elements are to be considered dialectically, that is, mutually influencing each other. As far as the foundation is concerned, different levels are implied both in the case of the church (history, life and work; biblico-theological, historical reflection; personal and

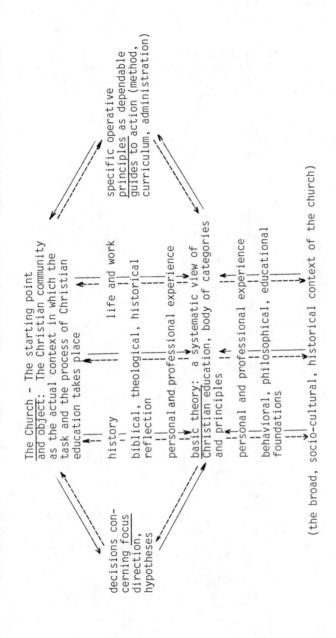

The Church - The starting point and object: The Christian community as the actual context in which the task and the process of Christian education takes place

specific operative principles as dependable guides to action (method, curriculum, administration)

life and work

history
&
biblical, theological, historical reflection

personal and professional experience

basic theory: a systematic view of Christian education, body of categories and principles

personal and professional experience

behavioral, philosophical, educational foundations

decisions concerning focus direction, hypotheses

(the broad, socio-cultural, historical context of the church)

121

professional experience) and in the case of possible
contributions stemming from the broader socio-historical
and cultural context (behavioral, philosophical, educational foundations; personal and professional experience).

C. Content Implications for Christian
Education Theory

1. Introduction

In this last section of our essay, several educational principles as dependable guides to practice will
be discussed on the basis of our dual-focused reinterpretation of Paulo Freire's work and thought. Having
proposed a general guiding principle centered on the
Gospel of the Kingdom of God (the paradoxical symbol
for God's gift, promise and demand of the in-breaking
of the new creation under the lordship of Christ), we
can proceed to state some of its implications in terms
of major educational categories. These categories are
essentially practical questions which stem from the
operational dimensions of Christian education. However,
the posing of the questions in the fashion of theoretical
categories--such as scope (what?) of process (how?)--
is to be done in the light of the guiding principle.31

The Kingdom principle suggests some specific
priorities and a particular sequence within a fairly
standard set of educational categories. The principles
thus discussed, then, which address those categories,
are actually ramifications of the guiding principle.
So now we need to point out how Christian education
might reflect and be informed by the Kingdom motif
which--as indicated in Chapter 4--further illumines
our understanding of conscientization as creativity.32

As we mentioned before, at the beginning of the
previous section (B), we will not develop a detailed,
comprehensive theory of Christian education, given the
limitation of the foundation materials considered.
This is the case not only in regard to principles for
a general constructive theory, but also because
Freire's contribution is associated solely with adult
education.33 In spite of this disclaimer, we hope to
complete our discussion in such a way that the validity
and usefulness of our study becomes apparent and provides inspiration and direction for the development of
Christian education.

2. Personnel in Context

A Christian education theory that takes into account Freire's contribution and is inspired by the Kingdom motif, calls for this starting point and for a close association between the who and where curricular questions: Who are the persons that are partners to the educational process and what are their roles? What kinds of interactions will be most conducive to the learning tasks and experience? What is the proper environment or setting for Christian education to carry on its work with integrity? Assuming as we do that Christian education partakes of the whole purpose and mission of the church, what characteristics should the church possess in order to serve as a context for Christian tranformation through conscientization, in the light of the Kingdom? The issues to be dealt with include responses to those crucial questions.

The foundations strongly affirm the participation of God's Spirit in the midst of the learning community that is called to embody the gift and the promise of the new creation under the lordship of Christ. This affirmation involves a critical assessment and rejection of prevailing models which make too rigid distinctions between "teachers" and "learners" on the basis of age, schooling, or appointment. The Kingdom Gospel challenges the assumptions and values involved in that situation as well as the occasion for indoctrination and manipulative educational styles. Even though particular teaching-leading gifts and vocations are recognized, the major emphasis is on learning together and from each other, in mutual service and celebration.

Freire's description of the coordinator of the circles of culture, provides some clues that illumine both the personnel and context categories, with clear implications also in regard to the Christian education process. The relationship between teachers and students is one of equality. Teachers are to have a deep respect for all the persons involved and they are to be committed to dialogical learning. The teacher's role is that of a facilitator, avoiding imposition of ideas as well as noncritical transmission of information. That is, the authoritative (and often authoritarian) magisterial function is questioned: educational goals and contents are not to be defined, and determined from the top, or dictated in an unquestioned and static manner. In other words, there must be a major change in regard to the "schooling-instruction paradigm," to use Westerhoff's concept. The context of education has been functionally equated with schooling, and the means of education with formal instruction. A more comprehensive understanding of the context is needed[34] in order to overcome the limitations and contradictions of the traditional educational endeavors of the church. It is needed also in order to make room for conditions which foster, support and develop transformation through conscientization, in light of the Kingdom of God. The following principles indicate some of those conditions[35] which refer to both personnel and context educational categories.

a. <u>The church is to facilitate the experience of mutual support</u> in order to provide the necessary "context of rapport" when individuals and groups confront baffled struggles and conflict situations. By "rapport" we mean that other persons are sympathetic to the situation and that they will somehow encourage, facilitate, interpret, celebrate and benefit from its resolution. When this is the case, the social and cultural dimensions of rapport are clearly represented in group participation in both the whole congregation, and in smaller groups, and in the Christian language system that is utilized and which--simultaneously--has the potential creative power to generate its social context (koinonia).

We are referring to a special manifestation of the Pauline metaphor of the body of Christ in which "each member belongs to all the others" (or, "serving individually as limbs and organs to one another"[36]), and "if one member suffers, all suffer together and if one is honored, all rejoice together with it."[37] If this kind of setting does not exist, persons will lack the trust and the freedom to engage themselves in the sort of existential struggles that become the subject of conscientization. The confidence to explore and to change will be curtailed, and the utilization of avoidance and denial mechanisms will probably be augmented.

The following three criteria[38] for the church as an appropriate learning and educational context in the face of our study, constitute principles in their own right but they also qualify further what is meant by "context of rapport."

b. The church is to foster a sense of self-worth
and affirmation. "A positive self-regard is to be
prized as a major personal premise for embracing and
sustaining existential conflicts with persistence and
expectance."39 It is also essential for a hospitable
reception of the person's own insights and intuitions.
In terms of Freire's approach, a sense of self-worth
is a necessary subjective dimension of the experience
of being subjects with an ontological vocation to make
history and to shape one's own destiny. Christian
educators should relate to the learners in consistency
with that affirmation.

Negatively speaking, this means that authoritarian
and paternalistic instructional approaches and methods,
so common in religious education, are to be rejected.
In the first case, the personal interaction involved
and the kinds of content usually taught--narow-focused,
simplistic, stereotyped, or traditionalist--are designed
to maintain given established frames of reference by
means of a rigid, oppressive control. In the case of
paternalistic stances, in general as well as in regard
to specific groups such as women, youth, or the
handicapped, there are similar basic assumptions: some
persons need to be continually provided for, and pro-
tected, otherwise they are not able to develop their
potential.

That is not to say that authority as such is to be
negated. Rather, that there must be a delicate balance
between trusting the authority of one's judgment and the
recognition of established patterns and practices
within the community of faith which also includes experts
and teachers.40 This statement takes us directly to the
next point.

c. Together with the affirmation of unity and
equality, personal differences must be recognized and
accepted. This is a closely related to the criterion
and principle just discussed and together they can also
be perceived in terms of the reference to the body of
Christ.41

In the face of our overall concern, maintaining
the integrity of each member happens to be a basic
authority principle. This is implied in the recognition
and acceptance of personal differences between persons,
between persons and groups, and between groups of
people. Uniformity and conformity simply compromise
and contradict our creative potential, and they distort

and negate the very peace (shalom) which they supposedly preserve. The alternative is to promote inter-
actional integrity, including respect for the other
person's choices. The consideration of persons and
groups beyond the membership lists and the church's
boundaries, points to the next criterion.

d. The church as the educational context needs to
remain open to and increase its interaction with the
social milieu. The experience of mutual support and
security provided in the community of believers is not
an end in itself. In fact, the church is not to become
merely a refuge or a ghetto for pious people. On the
contrary, our foundations emphatically point to the
openness, outwardness, and service-orientation of the
Christian vocation. The corresponding educational
ramifications of this stance pertain not only to the
content of Christian education--e.g., identification of
social needs as occasion for involvement and cooperation
--but especially to the process.42

The previous reference to the church as a proper
educational context focused mainly on attitudes and
approaches concerning persons and some of their needs.
The following two criteria and principles have to do
with the community of believers and its stance regarding
the complex nature of human reality and the privileged
status of conflict situations in particular. They are
necessary in order for the educational ministry to fulfill its questioning, problematizing function so well
illumined by Freire and our epistemological and theological foundations.

e. Complexity, rather than simplistic and pre-
fabricated answers, is to be underscored when dealing
with persons and problems. This is a special challenge
given our basic search for meaning, for direction and
purpose, and for coping with ethical dilemmas or understanding the seemingly senselessness of suffering.
Religion as such provides needed answers but quite often
in a very simplistic, authoritarian, and dogmatic
fashion. The alternative required in order to foster
conscientization and creativity calls for the development of tolerance for ambiguity (cognitive dimension)
and ambivalence (affective-personal dimension). This is
implicit in our proposition of four interrelated agendas
to deal with the question of the church's mission and
its educational program and process. That is, the
discernment of problems, perspectives and new alternatives, involves not merely the isolated focus on "what

126

the Bible says," or "the church's doctrine on the matter," or "what persons really want," but a more careful, complex, dialectical-hermeneutical process, often not yielding an easy resolution.

Closely related to this emphasis on complexity and conflict engagement, we have to point out the "price" of bearing tension, anxiety, and lack of comfort during at least part of the educational process.[43] We might suggest that, in terms of the overall mission of the church, this is probably an educational corollary and dimension of "bearing the cross."

f. Existential conflicts are to be embraced and engaged as normal and even necessary situations within the life of the church, and especially in the educational process. In the second chapter we discussed some conditions needed to facilitate the initiation of the creative process with the movement called "conflict (or lack) in the context of rapport." This "context" is to help individuals and groups to discern the contours and causes of their concerns, and to provide a communal and linguistic -conceptual framework into which a creative movement can develop and liberating transformation can take place.

The church is called to be a non-conformist, prophetic community, and is bound to encounter conflict --intrapersonal as well as interpersonal, and especially social and cultural--in response to its vision of the Kingdom. Otherwise, the Christian community succumbs to the powerful socialization forces in favor or harmony with life as it is. In Westerhoff's words:

> The converted life is a revolutionary existence
> over against the status quo, a life committed
> to a vision of God's coming community of liber-
> ation, justice, peace, whole community, and
> the well-being of all people . . . God calls
> his people to be signs of Shalom, the vanguard
> of God's coming community, a community of
> cultural change . . .
> The people of God are called to live for this
> vision and the church's educational ministry
> is given the responsibility of transmitting
> and sustaining that vision and enhancing its
> understanding.[44]

Now we can proceed to consider other major educational questions in the fashion of categories of Christian education theory. In each case, we will emplore other educational principles as dependable guides to practice, beginning with the subject of the purpose of Christian education in the next section.

3. Purpose of Christian Education

By purpose of Christian education we mean the fundamental question of why and what for, or the basic objective: Why engage in Christian education? What is the end toward which we shall involve ourselves in the educational ministry of the church? This purpose may be stated essentially in terms of the persons, the process and the scope included in this special educational task and experience. It is "the objective which should provide the direction for all the educational experience in a program; act as a criterion for planning and negotiating with participants short-term goals, learning activities, and resources; and serve as a means of evaluating a program."[45] So we need to indicate now how our foundations enlighten the question of the purpose of Christian education.

Freire's educational approach emphatically refers to the question of the aims of education in terms of the quest for freedom. He underscores the social and political dimensions of the educational enterprise. The radical transformation of oppressive socio-cultural, economic, political structures for the increase of freedom is for Freire the ultimate purpose of education. Human liberation is made accessible by the exercise of critical consciousness in the conscientization method. And the prophetic religion that Freire espouses has a clear educational dimension--as Christian education, theological education, or any church-sponsored educational program. In those instances, the basic objective is also radical transformation. However, on the basis of our reinterpretation of Paulo Freire, we can now discuss the matter of Christian education purpose more specifically.

In the face of the guiding principle of the Kingdom of God we can state very broadly the response to the twofold question that we posed at the beginning of this section. We engage ourselves in Christian education in order to enable people to appropriate the Gospel of the Kingdom of God. "Appropriation" (i.e., making one's own) of the Kingdom Gospel, in this context implies conversion as well as development and nurture of a Christian life style, in the sense of lived Christian faith in response to the gift,the promise, and the demands of the Kingdom.

That way of stating the overall purpose of Christian education underscores first of all the need for a comprehensive approach to the question of the basic objective: comprehensive in regard to the persons, because the whole Christian community is to be involved; comprehensive as far as the process is concerned, because Christian education is to engage different dimensions of the life of faith (believing, trusting, and doing[46]) and social interaction; comprehensive also in terms of the scope, since all of life is subject to be perceived and acted upon in light of the Kingdom of God.

Secondly, it is clear that the overall purpose of Christian education is to be consistent with the mission of the church as announcing and being a sign of the good news of the Kingdom. Christian education as such includes the deliberate educational endeavors of the church. This is the main reason to establish a relative distinction between church mission in general, and Christian education purpose in particular.

In the third place, it is also apparent that we need to translate that broad statement of purpose into more specific references to objectives that can be considered and utilized as educational principles. Our biblico-theological reflections with focus on the Kingdom motif led us to the consideration of four interrelated areas to which we can now return in order to spell out the ramifications of the general objective. The following formulations are meant to indicate four dimensions of the same overall essential purpose of Christian education.

a. "Appropriation of the Kingdom Gospel" implies to follow Jesus Christ and to fulfill the call to discipleship. The Christian claim is that God has taken the initiative in Jesus Christ, with whom God's Kingdom is in fact inaugurated. His person, teachings, ministry, cross and resurrection, become normative for human life in response to the gift, the promise and the demands of the Kingdom of God. Therefore, from the standpoint of the church, the call to discipleship and the affirmation of the lordship of Jesus Christ--which necessitates participation in the community of believers--is essential.

b.   "Appropriation of the Kingdom Gospel" implies promoting social transformation for the increase of freedom. This means to participate in God's recreating and liberating activity in the midst of society and history. The purpose of Christian education, as perceived in light of the "secular agenda," then, is to sponsor Christian responsibility and involvement in the world. Social transformation for the increase of freedom is realized in different ways: by discerning and critiquing oppressive, unjust structures and their sustaining values and practices; by becoming involved in diverse kinds of service projects; by guiding and assisting Christians--individuals and groups--in their own vocational engagement in society; by discovering more humanizing alternatives and becoming a paradigm ("a city set on a hill..." or--in Catholic terms--a "sacrament" of the Kingdom: an efficacious sign that encourages the realization of what if signifies).

c.   "Appropriation of the Kingdom Gospel" implies to know and to love God as Creator, Redeemer and Sustainer of life. This means to know and to love God whose will is shalom, and who makes accessible the freedom from bondage and alienation as well as the freedom to create and to care, through Jesus Christ. This corrects both oppressive and alienating under-standings about God's character, and defective ideas about the process by which communion with God (i.e., "to know and to love God") is developed and nurtured. Our epistemological and biblico-theological bases are clearly and strongly praxis-oriented. They suggest that this dimension of the objective is to be seen mainly in terms of commitment, obedience and faithfulness. This realization, therefore, takes us back to the two pre-vious formulations of objectives in terms of disciple-ship and service.

d.   "Appropriation of the Kingdom Gospel" implies --to use Freire's words--to become more human, or "to be more." Conversion (metanoia) and nurture of the service-oriented Christian life style provide content for those otherwise vague and abstract expressions. On the personal level, the gift of salvation (essentially another way of referring to the gift of the Kingdom) involves self-affirmation and integration as well as the freedom for creativity and care as expressions of Christian identity and vocation. "To be more human" is to be closer to Jesus Christ as a member of the messianic community, and to grow in the knowledge and the love of God.

These ramifications of the purpose of Christian education broadly stated in terms of the appropriation of the Kingdom Gospel, are to be seen as closely inter-related. In fact, they should be considered together lest we miss the comprehensive character of the basic objective or distort its content. Practically speaking, any improvement appraised in any one of those four dimensions, will necessarily point to some progress in relation to the rest. A summary statement would then be: <u>The purpose of Christian education is to enable people to appropriate the Gospel of the Kingdom of God by responding to the call to conversion and discipleship in the midst of the community of Jesus Christ, which is to promote social transformation for the increase of freedom, make accessible the knowledge and the love of God, and foster human wholeness and personal development and fulfillment</u>.

The truly liberating thrust of that fourfold purpose lies in the face that <u>human transformation</u> is thereby sponsored in terms of <u>the Kingdom of God</u>. In light of Freire's inspiration and our reinterpretation of his contribution, not only can we underscore the liberation motif but also specific processes consistent with the pattern of creativity that should be utilized in order that the purpose may by fulfilled. That is precisely the focus of our discussion in the next section.

4. Process and Scope

Our foundations indicate a very close association between the educational questions that refer to the approach (<u>how</u>) and to the content (<u>what</u>). The rich and complex dynamics of learning and teaching are to be perceived as intimately related to the scope of Christian education, that is, what is to be dealt with by way of subject matter and experience. Further, these two major educational questions are to be related closely to the other categories already discussed--personnel in context and the purpose of Christian educa-tion--and with that of timing (<u>when</u>) which will follow immediately after this section.

In the discussion of Freire's conscientization
method and process, it was indicated that human learning is perceived as the process by which one moves from
one level of consciousness to another. We also pointed
out that the content of consciousness includes the view
persons have of their own existence in the social world
and the power they have to determine their future.
Learning takes place starting with the present level of
consciousness as this is manifest in current living
conditions as well as the language, self-concept and
world view of the people involved. In this context,
learning implies becoming aware of the contingency of
social reality which--precisely in the face of this
contingency--lies within the human power to create and
transform. Freire's work and thought challenges much
of the church's educational enterprise, particularly
in regard to the questions of method and content. For
one thing, diverse problems with prevailing practices,
already alluded to, can be identified more pointedly.
Also, we can indicate several alternatives, especially
in line with Freire's insistence on considering the
learners as subjects who are called to participate in
the recreation of their world. His contribution
inspires an approach to Christian education that is
strongly hermeneutical in character, praxis oriented,
and prophetic-eschatological in vision. Now, such an
inspiration--like in the case of the other educational
questions--needs to be made explicit on the basis of
our appraisal of his thought. Several principles can
be suggested in connection with Christian educators,
specific learning sequence and tasks, and the subject
of scope or content.

a. Some Teaching Principles

Christian educators whose task is illumined by our
foundations and constructive reformulations will take
seriously into account the following general guidelines.

First of all, there is the need for educators to
engage themselves in a thorough search into the life
situation of learners, with acceptance, respect and
hope. The content of Christian education is to be
focused in terms of the real life challenges and conflicts of the people: their concerns, needs, longings
and dreams. Educators should be willing to consider
and choose, together with the learners, outstanding
themes for reflection, selected from the existential
situation of the persons who share in the church's

educational program and process. Further reflection and action will then take place with reference to that context.

A special teaching concern and objective will be the facilitation of dialogue as an encounter of subject with subject. This includes the possibilities of sharing personal stories and visions as well as reflecting critically and acting upon these. Rather than a method or an educational strategy, this dialogue is to be fostered as an attitude that wil decisively shape and inspire the learning context. Freire has carefully indicated the requirements for such a dialogical stance: profound love, humility, an intense faith in the human power to create and recreate, hope, and the will to question critically reality as it appears to be.[47]

Appropriate resources and activities that will facilitate the discussion of the themes may be adapted or created, such as printed materials, graphic representations, drama, and so on. Different methods and techniques can be utilized in a manner roughly similar to that of the "codification" phase in the conscientization process. That is, far from being passive observers, teachers are to develop their ingenuity in order to enhance the learning process and consciousness raising in particular.

Educators will also search for ways in which the Word and the Spirit will be allowed to inform and transform the discussion, the subject matter under consideration and the very lives of the participants. Scriptural input as well as the church's teachings and understandings are to be made available. However, this will not happen necessarily--or, not only--by direct and "directive" involvement on the part of the teachers. The learners themselves, and other persons such as visitors to the group or class, can also take part in this regard, although teachers will maintain their leadership in the process.

The educational approach involves a definite praxis orientation in which educators are directly involved too. Therefore, commitment to action on the part of all is to be elicited as consistent responses to the gift, the promise and the demands of the Kingdom.

As indicated before in the discussion of personnel in context, the role of the Christian education teacher is at least partially informed by that of the

coordinators of "culture circles" as described by
Freire. We thus place a major emphasis on how communication occurs and the relationship among communicators,
given our concern with the process--not as isolated
from the content, but as part and parcel of the same
creative-liberating educational dynamics.

b.   Learning Sequence and Learning Tasks

Ideally, the Christian education process inspired
by conscientization will show the kind of learning
sequence that reproduces the patter of the creative
process or "grammar of transformation" in Loder's terms.
Further, we can also identify specific learning tasks
in connection with different steps of that transformational pattern. Those intentionally fostered forms
of learning must be seen as interrelated, completing
and supplementing each other. As special learning
"products," learning tasks become, then, an integral
part of the scope of Christian education that can be
focused in diverse time frames. In general terms,
therefore, the question of a typical learning sequence
and specific learning tasks can be indicated briefly
as follows.

1.   The process starts with the identification and
focus on actual existential conflict situations. We
pointed out before that the church as a Christian education context will tend to regard complexity and conflict
engagement positively; and we further suggested that
Christian educators will be especially sensitive to the
real life challenges of the people. "Generative themes"
and seemingly "limit situations" of Christian life will
thus be isolated and worked through as problems to be
solved in the group setting although personally borne.
This corresponds roughly to the movement of "baffled
struggle in a context of rapport."[48] In our experience
and setting, one example of a theme that represents a
limit situation for many is family economy, and finances
specifically. This theme is promptly associated with
critical issues such as work and employment, consu-
merism, values and priorities, and stewardship. The
type of learning immediately associated with this step
in the transfromational sequence is precisely learning
to discern, face and embrace conflict with care and
perseverance. As Loder points out, however, learners
are to move beyond the sole concern with human struggles
on different levels, so that the consciousness of God's
action in the world may be heightened.[49] This

realization will then decisively inform the rest of the learning sequence in a distinctly Christian educational setting.

2. Interlude for Scanning. "Problematizing," in contrast to traditional transmission-of-information approaches, has been underscored. In actual educational practice, the formulation of critical problems and conflicts is followed by dialogue and discussion in search for the discovery of new associations and meanings. This may take a variety of forms in terms of methodological procedures and group dynamics, with the inclusion of the Christian message--"Story" and "Vision" as Groome indicates--explicitly made available to the learners. In the case of our example, the group will have an opportunity to listen to that message concerning the topic under consideration--economics and alienation and oppression, finances, and related issues.

Learning to search and to explore with expectance and hope is the type of learning intentionally fostered at the point of "interlude for scanning" in the creative educational sequence. It involves learning not to take for granted reality as it is--or what is presented as "reality"--but rather to question, criticize, and look for alternatives. This is particularly important in the face of the common tendency to arrive too soon at easy answers and to get emotionally involved in arguments about religious and financial-economic matters. Development of communication skills such as sensitive listening, both to external and internal messages, is also involved in this major learning task.

3. Intuition and Insight. Christian education is to facilitate creative discoveries in connection with the initial problems and quests of the people. Resolution often arrives rather suddenly, for example, in the fashion of clues for enhancing the sense of vocation, of witness, of stewardship, or the illuminating relevance of a given Biblical text or motif (e.g., contentment, compassion, or nonconformity). Insights often take the form of heightened awareness of hidden assumptions and contradictions as well as alternatives for transformation in terms of the concept and actual experience of Christian stewardship. Resolution usually involves not only an appropriate answer to the problem or conflict situation, but also a new way of looking at the problem, or a new set of questions. That is, the "raising of awareness"--in this special version of the

conscientization process-assumes a variety of meanings and directions.

Closely connected with learning to search and explore with expectance and hope previously mentioned, is learning to receive hospitably one's own insights. Christian education for liberation and creativity will intentionaly foster the inclination to attent to, value, and trust those intuitions as well as the disposition to actually learn from them and to share them in the context of the learning community of the church.

4. Release of Tension and Transformation of Energy. Insights experienced with intuitive and convincing force are usually associated with or followed by release and redirection of energy bound up with the original conflict. Tensions related to the problem situation tend to be dissolved, and there is a pleasant sense of freedom and transformation already occurring --for instance, in connection with the realization that it is indeed possible not to remain in the "rat race," or that fulfillment and wholeness are consistent with a life of service even within a materialistic and alienating socio-cultural milieu.

The spontaneous celebration of learning that is taking place is to be affirmed and refocused further as learning to celebrate. In light of the overall context of our study, this is particularly fitting due to the clear association that exists between liberation and celebration. In a profound sense, this also enlightens the political meaning of worship as response to God's recreating and liberating grace. Political, because of the very nature of the lordship of Christ and the rule of God that is confessed,[50] as indicated in the previous chapter.

5. Interpretation and Verification. This is the final movement in the transformational sequence of creativity. Interpretation is required in order to understand the connection between insights and conflicts, and also to test their correspondence with the public context of the conflicts. The method and process of conscientizaiton has illumined the fact that reflection and action are to be considered together in terms of praxis learning and transformation. This is the phase in the sequence when critical reflection concerning past, present and future becomes especially necessary, together with concrete responses ("action") in light of the Kingdom Gospel. In the case of our

example, the learners develop for instance a more clear appraisal of their economic situation--together with new visible expressions of fidelity voluntarily chosen (e. g., sharing resources, changes in budgeting and buying practices, working for economic justice). Again, the mutually informing relationship between reflection and action has to be underscored.[51]

The learning task of interpretation and responsible action is to be encouraged, not only for the benefit of the Christian learners but also because they are to be prepared "to account for the hope" that is in them, both in word (sound doctrine or "theory") and in deed (relevant "practice"). We are referring to an ongoing process. New questions and problems will elicit further engagement in the transformational movement that aims at the appropriation of the Gospel of the Kingdom of God.

c. Further Notes on Content

In previous sections we have already made reference to content in Christian education and to some principles as such. More will be said in this regard when we consider the category of timing. At this point we can indicate a few, more specifically content-focused implications for the discussion of content in connection with this study.

It can be said that the subject-matter of Christian education involves the whole field of relationships--including, of course, history and nature--in light of the Kingdom Gospel. In this sense, we can also indicate that Freire's contribution provides clues and concrete suggestions for a careful analysis of human relationships and for the choice of more "humanizing" alternatives to the situation in which people find themselves. However, there is something unique and special about the content of Christian education that is determined precisely by the very Gospel of the Kingdom and personal responses to the Gospel in faith and love. A sharper question is, then, how can the Christian faith be further nurtured or enhanced? The following comments are proposed in the face of that question.

In light of our study, one of the tasks of Christian education in terms of the content question is the "purification" of faith, that is to free the Christian faith from ideological trappings within a particular socio-cultural historical situation. Diverse kinds of

influences integrated in thought patterns, tend to
correlate with certain religious and theological men-
talities. Hence, quite often the "gospel" becomes a
palid and distorted version of the Christian faith.
Analysis, critique and reformulation are thus to be
encouraged.[52] Also by means of the dialogical approach
and the development of critical reflection, theological.
symbols, liturgical expression and sacraments can be
"decodified." That is, their transcendent meaning and
potential may be recaptured anew in terms of the actual
historical context of the faith community.

These formulations obviously negate the model of
faith as a finished product, or as a "deposit" of static,
sacred beliefs and propositions to be carefully transmitted as a parcel of truth. Religious language is
always subject to change, to reformulations and improvements. In other words, the renunciation of the opportunity and the invitation to re-create the very language
of faith is to be avoided. We are thus underscoring a
special dimension of "authorship" so intentionally
fostered in Freire's conscientization method and process
--and dramatically demonstrated in the literacy paradigm.
A new Christian language can always be developed in an
atmosphere of freedom. People can appropriate and
communicate the Gospel of the Kingdom in their own
terms and in their own words, with a langue that is
praxis-oriented--i.e., which expresses commitment to
God and to the neighbor--and efficacious for the interpretation and transformation of reality. Christian
education can facilitate the discovery and sharing of
new ways of expressing the faith in a learning process
in which method and dynamics intentionally become part
of the content and the very message.

5. Timing

This category refers to the question of when
education takes places and it involves several related
dimensions. It is obvious that learning as such occurs
continually, in different areas and diverse registers
of behavior, although it is particularly observable when
it is deliberately or intentionally fostered in specific
instances agreed upon by the persons involved. Further,
a learning sequence such as that including the movements of conscientization as creative process, can take
place in many different time frames as indicated in our
discussion above.

All of the church's life and mission involve varied forms of learning. A basic challenge is, then, to make accessible educational processes and experiences on the basis of the learning that occurs continually.

The matter of timing in Christian education has several interrelated aspects. In the face of our considerations, the discussion of this question provides the occasion to elaborate further on the four areas of biblico-theological reflection on the Kingdom. And this, in turn, reflects back to the categories and principles already dealt with, and especially the question of content in Christian education.

a. The timing question is to be seen in terms of the experience of the church, its past (history and the interpretation and announcement of "salvation history" especially, and its own tradition), and its future orientation (hope, the anticipation of the will of God, and the utopia of the Kingdom). This is to be realized in connection with the discernment of time in the social and cultural life, and God's time, in order to facilitate or point out the direction of appropriate--i.e., "timely," relevant and faithful--responses to the Kingdom Gospel.

b. Another dimension of the when educational question pertains to what we have called the "secular agenda." Discernment and appraisal of emergent events and trends in the social and cultural milieu are an indispensable component of the educational program of the church. This includes attending also to the positive--i.e., life-promoting, humanization enhancing --dimensions of reality, and discerning the work of God's Spirit outside the church. By "testing the spirits" of the age, the sense of timing and the historical consciousness can be augmented. Also, further motivation for learning as well as necessary subject-matter can be provided.

c. There must also be a reference to God's time. By this we mean responsiveness of the educational program and process to the activity of God in the midst of history. The challenge here is the development of sensitivity to the free movements of the creative and liberating will of God, in consistency with the eschatological perspective of the Gospel of the Kingdom. Hope and expectance in the face of mystery are thus to be affirmed.

139

d. Finally, together with the previous considerations, in mind, we need to focus on the learners' timing
(their readiness, and the schedule that is determined
by their motivations and plans) in terms of what we
have called the agenda of personal self and development.
Christian education is to be very sensitive to the
actual situation of the persons involved and to existential conflicts particularly. Personal timing, therefore, determines considerably the content of subject-
matter, to the extent that the stages of life and social
relationships are taken into account. In most situations the time dimension appears rather explicitly in
subjective terms--e.g., longings and plans, haunting
memories, the paralizing persistence of certain oppressive limitations, a sense of challenge and opportunity,
and so on. A corollary principle in this regard is that
Christian educators are to be especially careful when
engaging in the assessment of the needs of people.[53]

As emphasized before, these four "agendas" need to
be considered in close relation with one another. In
actual practice, personal developmental opportunities
and problems are to be dealt with in light of the
challenges of the times together with the historical
perspective of the church, and the search for the
revelation of God's timing. And the whole educational
process is to be "timed" in such a way that the persons
involved in learning together within the Christian
context may actually appropriate the Gospel of the Kingdom of God (content and purpose). The synthesis and
articulation of those fundamental principles in terms
of a curriculum theory, is the work of an organizing
principle.[54]

Our work with adolescents has been particularly
rewarding as far as the implications of Freire's approach
for Christian education is concerned. Their special
sense of timing within a usually demanding developmental
agenda, accounts for the inclusion of the following
brief references in this section.

Christian education of adolescents provides a
unique challenge for the provision of a context of trust,
freedom and mutual respect--i.e., a truly dialogical
setting and approach--given the common difficulties that
many adults have in relating to them. Adults (parents,
teacher, ministers) should realize that their own
personal situation needs to be seen in dynamic interaction with the adolescents'. Defensively enough, we
often try to just "teach" and "guide" teenagers from a

140

stance of assumed superiority and stability, conceived of in more or less authoritarian or maternalistic fashion, for instance.

Christian educators must elicit, welcome, and register carefully the "vocabular universe" of adolescents, with particular attention to words and themes with special existential meaning. Personal frustrations, desires, and needs are thus revealed, together with social and cultural references and implications. In Freire's terms, that is linguistic material with potential for conscientization. In our experience, the often mentioned identity struggle of the adolescent usually points to four interrelated dimensions of his/her situation: family relationships (discipline, emotional-economic dependence, separation from parents); sexuality and social relationships (sexual identity, special concerns with sex problems, love, friendship, recreation); vocation (interests, abilities, study and work, finances, service); philosophy of life (values, faith). The educator's own identity and existential struggles can always be related to those of the adolescents. In fact, it should be clear that our own attitudes, conceptions, beliefs, are especially subject to challenge and become the focus of conscientization when teaching and learning with adolescents.

Our "inventory" is thus gathered from the adolescents' experience, and it always includes a variety of "generative themes" and "limit-situations"--e.g., the question of authority--that can be subdivided in a number of actual conflicts or problem issues--e.g., specific situations involving discipline and freedom--that need to be confronted individually and also as a group. Adolescents themselves can help in the identification and selection of "themes" that will then become the focus for further sharing, discussion, critical reflection and action.

By means of "codifications" we attempt to move from the original perception and consciousness in regard to those issues, to the "maximum possible awareness" or critical and committed consciousness. The methods utilized in order to "codify" the themes, such as sketches, debates, role playing, assigned reading, and so on, should assume the form of problem situations to be engaged and solved together. In this connection it is always possible and necessary to let the Scripture illumine the discussion and generate what Groome calls "dialectical hermeneutic" between the adolescents'

141

experiences and dreams and the Christian message ("Story" and "Vision"). Regardless of specific issues being dealt with, adolescents' capacity for engaging in critical reflection and for suggesting utopian alternatives (Freire's "untested feasibilities") usually allows for consideration of several levels within a given conflict situation--e.g., from personal concerns with erotism and sexuality, to socio-cultural double standards and the place of sexual manipulation in commercial publicity.

Finally, actual faith responses in terms of commitment to action and further reflection are facilitated by the adolescents' idealism, sensitivity and passion. The responses may involve changes in attitudes, relationships, or different sorts of social involvement. Adolescent developmental traits are quite often reinforced through this very educational process, which is informed by the paradigm of conscientization as fostered creativity. Hence, the learning sequence and learning tasks previously discussed, should also have a special place within a Christian education program for youth.[55]

D. Other Suggested Implications

In this section we will briefly indicate some possibilities for further utilizing the contributions stemming from the work and thought of Paulo Freire in light of our study. The areas alluded to below have been selected on the basis of our own experience in professional practice in the fields of education and counseling, seminary teaching, and involvement in pastoral and educational work in the church.

1. Practical Engagements in Christian Education

This study may be taken into account in connection with the teaching of foundations and principles of Christian education and the church's educational ministry. Our discussion suggests some pointers for the integration of Christian education theory and practice. It also encourages the functional interrelation of diverse disciplines and learning experiences in the curriculum of theological education. Specifically, Freire's approach provides an outstanding example of how an educator goes about his task--including his contribution to philosophy of education--and provocative foundation material for Christian education.

Another area of application is curriculum planning and design on the basis of a Christian education theory that incorporates Freire's contribution. In this light, the "schooling-instructional paradigm" would be radically altered, including the expansion of the educational context far beyond the Sunday school set-ting and structures. Further, that curriculum -- systematic plan by which the church seeks to fulfill its teachIng ministry--would have, among others, the following characteristics: (1) It would call for a praxis, action oriented approach, i.e., more consistent with the biblical view of knowledge; (2) it would foster a dialogical and dialectical--rather than "didactic"--educational stance; (3) it would associate more closely the questions of "how" and "what" in our educational programs, with focus on interpretation (hermeneutics) and critical reflection and awareness; (4) it would have an "utopian," prophetic orientation-- "denouncing and announcing" in Freire's terms--openly directed towards the transformation of socialization patterns (i.e., the practice of "non-conformity"). This is another possible ramification of our study insofar as it provides general orientation for involve-ment in curriculum work, including actual writing and preparation of resource materials, and teachers' training.

2. Other Possible Ramifications

Together with Christian education in the narrow sense of the concept, other areas in the church and pastoral ministry could benefit from Friere's contribu-tion as reformulated in this study. For example, the "conscientization" dimensions of worship, pastoral care, and preaching, may be enlightened and underscored from that perspective. Further, there is a clear necessity for consistency among different aspects of the life and mission of the church in the face of the gift, the promise, and the responsibilities of the Kingdom. Our guiding principle can illumine ways whereby the gap, say, betweenthe so-called "pastoral" and "prophetic" ministries may be bridged,and personal and interpersonal dimensions of service may be perceived and enhanced in the framework of institutions and socio-political and cultural structures.56

3. Church-Sponsored Schools

This is an area that, in general terms, has not received adequate attention on the part of Christian education theorists, and one which very often is not properly dealt with in the seminary curriculum. However, private schools sponsored by Catholic and Protestant churches have been playing an important role in many communities for several centuries, and they have influenced and have been influenced by the public school system.

Parochial schools often include attempts to provide alternative educational contexts and curricula in terms of both a general approach and denominational perspective. When that is indeed the case, these institutions are conceived of as a special expression of the mission and the educational ministry of the church. Their explicit aim is to implement an educational plan that is consistent with the teachings of the church. The actual nature and profile of these schools depend on a variety of factors, such as religious denomination and the socio-cultural and economic situation. The purposes of these private, church-sponsored schools, are often stated in terms of providingand educational institution and program for children whose parents identify themselves with a given religious tradition, and serving the comunity through the school activities.

In our view, there are two major considerations to be further developed concerning Christian education in parochial and chruch-related schools in light of this study: the general question of philosophy of education, and the specific question of Christian education within the curriculum. In the first case, there are a number of important issues to be addressed in connection with the--implicit or explicit-- "Christian" (and, therefore, creative and liberating) inspiration of the educational plan. For example: How can the prevailing instructional model be corrected and improved while complying with the curriculum requirements established by the state? How is the distinctive educational philosophy articulated and communicated to parents, educators and learners? Is it consistently upheld with integrity in the educational context of the school and in the diverse teaching-learning processes and program?

144

In the case of Christian education as a special "subject"--that quite often functions only as an appendix which does not appeal to the students--there is first of all the question of its place within the educational plan and its connection with other areas of the curriculum: How do "Bible," "Religion," or "Christian Education" (both as courses and other specific activities) help to illumine the educational philosophy and to set a contextual tone that is conducive to the educational goals? Secondly, what is the theory under-girding that systematic teaching? In this light, it would seem that our discussion of Christian education principles concerning personnel in context, goal, process and scope, and timing is also applicable in the setting of parochial and other church--related schools.

CONCLUSION

In the introduction to this book, after discussing the challenge that motivated our study, its purpose was indicated as consisting primarily of the re-statement and integration of Freire's approach in order to accomplish the following objectives: (1) to make the integrity of his work and thought more comprehensive; (2) to spell out further the character and dimensions of creativity; (3) to make a contribution to Christian education theory. The content of our findings has been indicated in the constructive reformulations and in the stated implications of our study. In this final section, we will summarize how our discussion in fact illumines each one of these three areas of special concern and consideration.

On Freire's Contribution

In light of creativity, the integrity of Freire's thought and work has become more comprehensive. We have underscored the developmental structure of his educational method and made explicit its latent epistemology of the creative process. It is our claim that this re-statement of Freire's epistemological foundation adequately accounts for the dynamics and effectiveness of the conscientization process. We argue that our reformulation is also necessary in order for the Freire method to maintain its integrity and its thrust of "cultural action for freedom" and "education for liberation." We have thus expanded considerably Freire's own intuition and understanding concerning the association between his educational method on the linguistic-symbolic dimension, and the conscientization process on the level of self and social interaction.

Conscientization has a structure which is parallel to the phases of the creative process, and the method makes it possible to experience actual liberation. An arrested state of personal growth is thereby overcome, and new alternatives and power do become available for individuals and groups engaged in the educational program.

The possibility of relating more closely the epistemological foundation--and the conscientization method as such--to the religious inspiration and the theological concerns that are manifest in Freire's thought, is another outcome of our study. That is, our approach illumines that relationship by establishing a comprehensive frame of reference for Freire's

contribution. Our re-statement of the theological
foundation underscores Freire's Christian prophetic and
utopian perspective within a systematic presentation on
the centrality of the Gospel of the Kingdom of God.
The liberation thrust is reappraised together with an
emphasis on the resurrection motif. The potential of
the Freire method to facilitate greater freedom and
wholeness thus becomes clearer in light of the affirmation of the creative and liberating character of the
Christian Story and Vision. In this sense, conscientization may indeed become one specific way of actuali-
zing the God-given capacity to participate in the
struggle for liberation from oppression and alienation,
and to creatively shape human life and destiny.

On Creativity

This study of the conscientization method and
process has taken into account and relied on the contributions of creativity theorists, notably James E. Loder.
Our discussion of Freire's work and thought in turn
sheds some light on the nature and facets of creativity
itself.

Conscientization may be perceived as a variation on
the creativity model. The coordinators of the culture
circles aim at facilitating the occurrence of the very
creative process in the participants, including themselves. A special developmental sequence is raised to
the level of critical awareness, and a latent or
arrested state of development is called forth or
reconstructed in that educational setting. This is,
then, a clear instance in which the process is expected
to unfold both coopeartively as well as individually,
within the context of a creative group. Thus, different
dimensions (linguistic-symbolic, self) and levels (ego,
group process, sociocultural structure) may become
simultaneously engaged in conscientization as creative
process.

The social expressions of creativity can then be
appreciated from the perspective of "education for
liberation" and "cultural action for freedom."   The
conscientization method may exemplify the character of
a creativogenic social milieu, both because of the
process fostered in the culture circle as well as the
content--i.e., the efficacious vision of a revitalized
society and a reconstructed culture. Closely related
to that realization is the fact that the very scope of

a creativity may be intentionally expanded by means of an educational approach and program inspired in the conscientization model.

On Christian Education

Our study of Paulo Freire provides a base for enhancing Christian education theory. It assists us in pursuing the following tasks and directions, which must be perceived not only in a sequence but also realted to one another.

First, there is the need to analyze and critique any historico-cultural situation in terms of the nature and mission of the church and the place and role of Christian education particularly. Freire's insights on such areas as the dynamics of indoctrination and domestication, current instructional patterns, and alternatives in the nature and mission of the church and its educatioanl program, enlighten our understanding in this regard. The church reflects indeed the historico-cultural situation in which it exists, but it also confronts society and culture. It attempts to present more creative and liberating options than those of the prevailing values and practices. In this context, Christian education is affirmed as a useful means for discernment, criticism and reconstruction of culture.

In second place, Freire's contribution is helpful for the discussion of theory building. This is the case especially in light of the emphasis on the inter-relationship between practice and theory, and the action-reflection (praxis) model that Freire espouses. Further, as far as content is concerned, the focus on epistemological and theological foundations also provides important clues for theory building due to the fact that we are after a Christian education theory that is both educationally sound and theologically valid. We can thus engage cooperatively in a "methodological cycle" beginning with the church and its educational ministry in the midst of the historical situation. In view of special needs and possibilities that can be stated as identifiable foci of concern, we may utilize Freire's contribution in the articulation of both a basic theory of Christian education as well as the formulation of operative principles in practical areas such as method, curriculum and administration.

Third, our study leads to the statement of
Christian education principles--i.e., the content of
theory. Four main theoretical categories have emerged
in that light as essential questions to be addressed:
personnel in context, Christian education purpose,
process and content, and timing. On that basis, we are
able to develop a set of dependable guides to educational practice which stem from our foundations and reformulations. They are actually specific ramifications
of the guiding principle focused on the Gospel of the
Kingdom.

The unifying factor and ultimate inspiration of the
whole endeavor is provided by that guiding principle
which can also help us to gain a clear and adequate
understanding of both theory and practice. In our case,
the guiding principle ultimately serves as a reminder
of the church's call to be that revolutionary community
of Jesus Christ meant to be the promise and foretaste
of the new society and new humanity. The educational
ministry is supposed to communicate and sustain that
vision, and to foster its comprehension and fulfillment.

NOTES

INTRODUCTION

1. The original portuguese term, conscientizaçao, literally means "making conscious" (Spanish, conscientización--with or without "s" as in the English adaptation; German, Bewusstmachung. These are considered equivalent). According to Freire the term was popularized and given currency by another outstanding Brazilian Christian, D. Hélder Cámara, Archbishop of Recife. Paolo Freire, "Conscientisation," Cross Currents, 24:1 (Spring 1974), 23.

2. Conscientization, as Freire understands it, is a complex concept and for the purposes of this introduction we must point out the following:
First of all, it refers to a process (and not merely some methods and techniques) whose methodological implications will be referred to later on.
Secondly, the concept of conscientization is founded upon a dialectical and phenomenological approach to consciousness and the world: it involves intentionality, the affirmation of the subjective-objective dialectic, consciousness and the world dialectically constituting each other. (More about this will be said in Chapters 1 and 2).
Thirdly, conscientization is the critical development of the prise de conscience (become aware, the first level of apprehension of reality). Says Freire: "Conscientisation is a prise de conscience that goes deeper...implies going beyond the spontaneous phase of apprehension of reality to a critical phase, where reality becomes a knowable object, where man takes an epistemological stand and tries to know. Thus conscientisation is a probing of the ambience of reality. The more a person conscientises himself, the more he unveils reality and gets at the phenomenic essense of the object he stands in front of, to analyze it" (Ibid., pp. 24, 25).

3. Freire actually points out two kinds of-- "naive" or "shrewd"--misuses of his pedagogy of the oppressed: methodizing and mythologizing conscientization. See for instance, "Education, Liberation and the Church," Study Encounter ix: 1(1973): 1-16. In the first case Freire's approach is reduced to the level of small-group technique, that is without a deliberate concern for change in the social structure and therefore

without involving risk. By mythologizing conscientization Freire means idealization of praxis so that conscientization becomes a subjective idealism. He stresses the interdependence of action and reflection: consciousness transformation, a significant change of mind, necessitates some ongoing action aimed at changing the social reality of a given community. Conversely, decisive structural change cannot take place while the old mentality persists on the part of the persons involved. Freire relies on Marx (and particularly a Marxist cultural and class analysis) in order to prevent conscientization from becoming mythologized or methodized.

4. In our Bibliography, the works by Bugbee, Dewitt, Goldman, Harmon, Kane, McFadden, and Smith, are in this category.

5. This is the case of the doctoral studies of Bailey, Craig, Crawford, Harter, Parker, C. Pereira, Sherwin, Steckel and Thompson included in the Bibliography.

6. The works of C.E. Collins, Dawson, Elias, Fisher, and Streck, are comparative studies between Freire and Brameld, Jung, Illich, Oakershott, and Dewey, respectively.

FIRST PART -- THE EPISTEMOLOGICAL FOUNDATION:

EDUCATION AS KNOWING

1. Paulo Freire, Extension or Communication," Education for Critical Consciousness (New York: Seabury Press, 1973), p. 149.

2. This is so for several reasons. In the first place, epistemology is the study of how human beings take hold of their cosmos. Second, it is not only a necessary check on the credibility of knowledge, but a body of fundamental theory underlying the nature of the mind and how it functions. Thirdly, the relevance of epistemology can be seen in that theories of knowledge are, in a sense, direct pointers to theories of learning, and learning theory is central in any educational enterprise. See Van Cleve Morris and Young Pai,

Philosophy and the American School, An Introduction to the Philosophy of Education (Boston: Houghton Mifflin Co., 1976), pp. 169-170.

CHAPTER I

CONSCIENTIZATION AND HUMAN DEVELOPMENT

1. For references to the historico-cultural setting of Freire's early work, see Emmanuel De Kadt's Catholic Radicals in Brazil (London: Oxford University Press, 1970).

2. Paulo Freire, La Educación como Práctica de la Libertad (Montevideo: Tierra Nueva, 1972), p. 123.

3. Paulo Freire, Pedagogy of the Oppressed (New York: Seabury Press, 1970), pp. 92-93.

4. Ibid., p. 91.

5. Ibid., p. 93.

6. Ibid., p. 92.

7. Ibid., p. 107

8. Ibid., p. 116.

9. A very high phonemic-orthographic correspondence is characteristic of Spanish and Portuguese.

10. Freire, Education for Critical Consciousness, p. 51.

11. The phenomenological base of Freire's thought is very apparent, since the necessity for reflecting upon one's consciousness is an essential feature in his approach and methodology. Freire adopts Husserl's principles that the exploration of consciousness is a prerequisite to knowledge of reality, and that consciousness is able to reflect upon itself so as to unveil its own structure, consciousness of self. The phenomenological investigation of reality and consciousness itself is utilized in order to discover the modes of human knowing. From phenomenology Freire borrows

specially the notion of intentionality, which is for him the process through which consciousness and the world are dialectically constituting each other.

In this sense, conscientization implies first of all the affirmation of the subjective-objective dialectic. This conception has practical implications, such as the realization that there is a close relationship between the mythologizing an oppresive reality (concealing reality behind myths--e.g., the myth of the generosity of the elites) and mythologizing consciousness, which is precisely the negation of critical awareness. In this light we can perceive conscientization as the process whereby the critical attitude necessary to unmask the myths is awakened and developed, and the fear of freedom is thus removed. This is an example of how, by probing human consciousness and appearances, Freire aims at discovering the social conditioning of consciousness and the power of reflecting subjects to act creatively on their own behalf.

12. Paulo Freire, Cultural Action for Freedom (Cambridge: Harvard Educational Review, 1970), p. 32.

13. Ibid., p. 36.

14. Ibid., p. 40.

15. Ibid., p. 46.

16. William A. Smith developed an operational measure of the theoretical "conscientizaçao" concept, consisting of an instrument that elicits a sample of verbal responses and a system for classfying these statements as evidence of magical, naive, and critical consciousness. This coding system includes a division of three aspects (naming, reflecting, acting) for each level ("magical," "naive," and "critical"). "Conscientizacao: An Operational Definition" (Ed. D. dissertation, University of Massachusetts, 1975). On the basis of this study, a Critical Consciousness Inventory was constructed (C. C. I., Smith-Alschuler, 1976) as an operational description of the stages of consciousness as described by Freire. It consists of giving four Thematic Aperception Test-type pictures in order to elicit the subjects' responses to problematic situations. Those responses are then classified and coded according to the level of consciousness that they represent. This instrument has been tested in other

studies related to the conscientization method and process and suggested applications, by researchers from the University of Massachusetts.

17. Piaget is the major representative of structuralism in human development. In light of his structural-developmental approach, he demonstrates that the cognitive structures applicable to all realms of knowledge, develop through descernible stages from birth to adolescence. In Piaget's theory of cognitive development, the final stage is the stage of formal operations, which is characterized by the use of propositional and combinatorial operations. Particularly important for our topic is the new facilitated reversal of the direction of though between reality and possibility. This is indeed a turning point in the development of the structure of intelligence, which can express itself in terms of a more complex and mature equilibrium that is both stable and flexible.

Barbel Inhelder and Jean Piaget put it this way: "The most distinctive property of formal thought is this reversal of direction between reality and possibility; instead of deriving a rudimentary type of theory from the empirical data as in done in concrete operations, formal thought begins with a theoretical synthesis implying that certain relations are necessary and thus proceeds in the opposite direction . . . This type of thinking proceeds from what is possible to what is empirically real." The Growth of Logical Thinking from Childhood to Adolescence (New York: Basic Books, 1958), p. 251. Formal-operational intelligence corresponds to the peak of intellectual maturity in the structural sense, the optimal structure of the human mind for Piaget.

18. "Initiative adds to autonomy the quality of undertaking, planning and 'attacking' a task for the sake of being active and on the move . . . The danger of this stage is a sense of guilt over the goals contemplated and the acts initiated in one's exuberant enjoyment of new locomotor and mental power: acts of aggressive manipulation and coercion which soon go far beyond the executive capacity of the organism and mind and therefore call for an energetic halt in one's contemplated initiative . . . the child is at no time more ready to learn quickly and avidly, to become bigger in the sense of sharing obligation and performance than during this period of his development. He is eager and able to make things cooperatively, to combine with other

children for the purpose of constructing and planning, and he is willing to profit from teachers and to emulate ideal prototypes." Childhood and Society, 2nd ed. (New York: Norton, 1963), pp. 255-258.

See also Erikson's discussion of initiative in "Growth and Crises of the Healthy Personality" in Identity and the Life Cycle, (New York: Norton, 1980), pp. 78-87. Psychoanalytic ego psychology as represented by Erikson has made a special contribution to our understanding of cognitive and self dynamics. Another suggestive example we find in the just mentioned book is the reference to identity and ideology in the study of ego identity in the adolescent age. It also applies to our subjetct and may be related directly to the previous discussion. Erikson concludes: "Thus, identity and ideology are two aspects of the same process. Both provide the next higher form of identification, namely, the solidarity linking common identities" (p. 168).

19. Paulo Freire, Risk, 11:1 (1975), p. 15. This movement has been clearly registered in an IDAC (Institute of Cultural Action) document as follows: "During the Brazilian experience, Freire's pedagogy proposed that people should learn democracy by practicing it. Ten years later, his thought is much more radical without having lost its dialectical movement. Now he says that pedagogy will be revolutionary when it has as its goal the conscious, creative action and reflection of the oppressed masses on their liberation." Rosiska Darcy de Oliveira and Pierre Dominice, "Freire-Illich: The Pedagogy of the Oppressed--The Oppression of Pedagogy," IDAC, Doc. No. 8, p. 24.

20. Jerome S. Bruner also puts it clearly: ". . . a pedagogical theory is perforce quite different from and hardly as neutral as the usual type of scientific theory. . . A theory of instruction is a political theory in the proper sense that it derives from consensus concerning the distribution of power within society--who shall be educated and to fulfill what roles? . . . The psychologist or educator who formulates pedagogical theory without regard to the political, economic, and social setting of the educational process courts triviality and merits being ignored in the community and in the classroom . . . Pedagogical theory, then, is not only technical but cultural, ideological and political. If it is to have its impact, it must be self-consciously all of these." The Relevance of Education (New York: Norton, 1973), pp. 100, 106.

21. "Desmitificación de la Concientización, "Mensajero (Quito, enero 1973), pp. 34-40.

22. The clue of the relationship between Hegelian thought and Freire's educational approach can be found in Hegel's Phenomenology of Mind (New York: Harper & Row, 1967): ". . . just when the master has effectively achieved lordship, he really finds that something has come about quite different from an independent consciousness. It is not an independent, but rather a dependent consciousness that he has achieved . . . The truth of the independent consciousness is accordingly the consciousness of the bondsman. This doubtless appears in the first instance outside itself, and not as the truth of self-consciousness. But just as lordship showed its essential nature to be the reverse of what it wants to be, so, too, bondage will, when completed pass into the opposite of what it immediately is: being a consciousness repressed within itself, it will enter into itself and change round into real and true independence" (pp. 236, 237).
The core definition in Pedagogy of the Oppressed refers to an educational approach which searches for the restoration of intersubjectivity and is animated by an authentic humanist (not humanitarian) generosity. This "pedagogy of the oppressed" actually presents itself as a pedagogy of the human being (p. 39). Why can this be the only pedagogy able to reach that objective? To this question, Freire replies that the great humanistic and historical task of the oppressed is to liberate themselves and their oppressors as well. And he adds that considering that the oppressed are subordinated to the consciousness of the "master" (as Hegel affirms) true solidarity with them means fighting at their side to transform the objective reality which has made them beings for another (Ibid. pp. 28, 34).
Freire refers to two distinct stages in the pedagogy of the oppressed. In the first, the oppressed unmask the world of oppression and, through praxis, commit themselves to its transformation. In the second stage, when the reality of oppression has already been transformed, that pedagogy is no longer a "pedagogy of the oppressed" but a pedagogy of all human beings in the process of permanent liberation. In both stages, it is always through action in depth--"cultural revolution" --that the culture of domination is culturally confronted. (Ibid. p. 40).
From a Hegelian perspective this would imply the movement from abstract reason (as oppressed consciousness) to liberating praxis (as negation of the oppressed

consciousness) and the "synthesis," the (complex) new reason as consciousness in the search for liberation in a project of social change. The differences between Hegel and Freire with regard to historico-political context should not be underestimated: Hegel deals with Europe's imperial consciousness and his philosophy involves an affirmation of the German nation-state from the "center" so to say. Freire, on the contrary, from the "periphery" attempts to facilitate the liberation of oppressed people, by means of enhancing popular consciousness (whereas Hegel aims at consciousness' growth towards--Europe's--Absolute Knowledge).

23. Karl Mannheim, Ideology and Utopia (New York: Harcourt, Brace & World, 1936), part II.

24. Cf. the presentation of the Spanish sociologist Ruiz Olabuénaga, in Paulo Freire, Concientización y Andragogia (Buenos Aires: Paidós, 1975).

25. Freire's educational philosophy does not lend itself to simple analysis and to identification with any specific "school." His thought flows first of all from his personal and professional experiences, and it is eclectic. Freire presents a synthesis of several philosophical strains which are blended with his basic humanistic--classic and otherwise--stance. We agree with Denis E. Collins that there are five major sources to be singled out with regard to Freire's philosophical foundation: personalism, existentialism, phenomenology, Marxism, and Christianity. See Collins' introduction to Freire: Paulo Freire: His Life, Works and Thought (New York: Paulist Press, 1977). Apart from several notes on foundation materials that appear in this chapter, we include a reference to Freire's intellectual background in Chapter 3 ("Freire and Liberation Theology").
Considering the fact that philosophy of education as a discipline has traditionally broken itself down into opposing schools, Freire's synthesis of those various strains of thought into his own approach to education for liberation can be regarded as a valuable contribution to that discipline. On another level of discussion, Freire's ability to utilize diverse foundation materials may account for the attraction that his ideas and writings arouse among people with very different backgrounds and viewpoints.

26. Both approaches are change- and social-change centered, but progressivism focussess more on the present and on cultural transition, and tends to fit in the

category of political liberalism. Reconstructionism is more future-oriented, aimed at cultural rebuilding, and politically "radical." The very concepts of "progress" and "reconstruction" seem to point to important and diverse philosophical connotations and educational implications.

27. The presence of existential thought is pervasive throughout Freire's work. Human beings are beings-in-the-world, beings in the process of constructing themselves. They can encounter themselves by turning from their actualities to their potentialities, and these potentialities are discovered in relationships with others. Man's ontological vocation is to be a subject for transformation of self and world. The human experience of being-in-the-world runs the risk of estrangement, alienation in a world which fosters massification. Only through the experience as existence is communication of intersubjectivities possible, through dialogue (an existential necessity) that takes place in terms of commitment to the challenges of the world, that is commitment with fidelity and hope.
Freire underscores the fact that human beings are beings of relationships and, as such, they "ad-mire" and transform that world, nature, their own person, and history. Man's real self is a pure possibility unless and until it realizes and establishes itself in the midst of existential decisions. True humanity is a process of becoming more and more responsive and responsible. "Humanization" is for Freire a process of dialectical and intersubjective interrelation in which (intersubjective) mediation may be altered by means of "prescription": one consciousness prescribes the human contours of the other. A kind of robbery thus takes place, whenever persons are forbidden to be, to pronounce their word. Project to be realized and developed, word to be owned and pronounced, are central concepts in Freire's reflection on the human experience. An authentic existence involves, then, a painful tension between the struggle for personalization and the risk of alienation. Freire announces freedom and the hope in the new human being, the "critical" person, while denouncing the robbery of humanity by those who oppress.

28. Freire, Pedagogy of the Oppressed, chapter 3.

29. In his comparative study of Paulo Freire and Theodore Brameld, Denis Collins found out that their educational philosophies do not differ greatly, although Brameld's reconstructionist thought is understood as a

radical refinement of progressivism. Collins concludes:
"Divergencies seemed to stem more from choice of terminology employed by each man to explicate his thought as
well as from the different cultural origins of Freire
and Brameld , rather than from any major philosophical
disagreement. They both wish to reconstruct society and
their educational theories share that commong aim . . .
Both are radical utopian thinkers . . . Both underscore
a need to unite anthropology with philosophy to assit
men to discover educational remedies for human culture
which is not yet sufficiently developed to provide participation in political life for the majority of mankind.
Both esteem the social nature of knowing; both prize dialogue and intersubjectivity as value-means for modern
education. No substantial difference was found between
Freire's desire for education through investigation,
thematization, and problematization leading to authentic
praxis and Brameld's proposed education through practice
in consensual validation leading to social-self-realiza-
tion. Comparison and contrast of the educational philosophies of Freire and Brameld also suggested that they
address themselves to different phases of the task of
reconstructing society. "Two Utopians: A Comparison
and Contrast of the Educational Philosophies of Paulo
Freire and Theodore Brameld," (Ed. D. dissertation, University of Southern California, Berkeley, 1973), pp.
196, 200.

    30. Danilo R. Streck, "John Dewey's and Paulo
Freire's Views on the Political Function of Education,
with Special Emphasis on the Problem of Method" (E.D.
dissertation, Rutgers University, 1977).

    31. George Novack presents a thorough Marxian
critique of pragmatism in terms of questions of scientific method, logic, the nature of experience, the criteria of truth, and the anatomy of society. A typical
summary statement of the contrast between the two positions follows. It is representative of a reconstructionist approach as opposed to a progressive-instrumentalist
one, and representative also of the stated opposition
between a "revolutionary-prophetic" stance versus a
"modernist-reformist" one, in Freire's terminology. Says
Novack: "The record of their mutual relations, the testimony of their principal representatives, the difference in their class connections, the conflicts in their
methods and leading principles as applied to specific
cases, all serve to demonstrate the fundamental opposition between Pragmatism and Marxism. Whatever points
they have in common are subsidiary to their major

disagreements. The two are not harmonious and reconci-
liable but basically incompatible worldviews and methods of thought. They express the outlooks of two different social forces with opposing interest and aspira-
tions. Marxism is the militant ideology of the revolutionary working class on its way to power and of the
most advanced sections of humanity on the way to emancipation from capitalism and all forms of class domination. Pragmatism is the conciliatory philosophical instrument of the middle class on the downgrade, trying to
clutch at any means for salvation." George Novack,
Pragmatism versus Marxism, An Appraisal of John Dewey's
Philosophy (New York: Pathfinders Press, 1975), p. 278.

32. Berger is concerned with radical intellectuals'
uncritical identification with and commitment to mytho-
logical (and, therefore, "non-scientific") statements
about reality. He develops a methodological critique
against "consciousness raisers" who assume that they
know better how to describe the "way things are" for
other people (particularly the poor and under-educated)
than do those who participate in their own situations.
A definition of the world is thus imposed upon the oppressed. Rather than "consciousness raising" we have
here--Berger argues--a case of "conversion" from one
world view to another. The real question, then, is who
decides what the situation is? The attitude of "cognitive respect"--based on the postulate of the equality
of the worlds of consciousness--is thus underscored.
It means that one takes with utmost seriousness the way
in which others define reality and it is closely related
to the theoretical attitude and category of "value-
freeness" in science. This is carefully distinguished
from the social scientist's necessity to make clear moral
choices about the implications of certain cultural norms
and from "cognitive participation" as a political category. Peter Berger, "The False Consciousness of Consciousness Raising," Worldview, 18:1 (January 1975), pp.
33-38. Now, Berger himself, as a social scientist and
social critic, has been engaged in a "consciousness
raising" mission of his own, as in the study of the
"precarious vision" or the "seeing through" and "looking
behing" functions of sociological imagination. Furthermore, it is fair to point out that Freire is alert to
the danger of substituting his own consciousness for
that of the people and that he insists that anyone in a
position of educator, expert or leader must first acquire the "ontological humility" required to see the
distortions inherent in that role image. And this is
achieved by becoming vulnerable to the people themselves,

listening to their verbal, imaginative and aspirational language, dialoguing with them in a mode of respectful reciprocity so as to become a co-transformer along with them of the given oppressive social reality.

33.   There is an additional problem with regard to Freire's anthropology and "humanization" in particular. He seems to suggest that human beings have, essentially, an unchanging nature whose basic features are freedom, consciousness, transcendence, temporality, and intentionality.   It has been pointed out that there is a contradiction between this kind of "natual law" view of man (espoused by essentialists and perennialists) and the dialectical or Hegelian-Marxian view, such as Freire expresses in his approach to culture and history.   Cf. John J. Dewitt, "An Exposition and Analysis of Paulo Freire's Radical Psycho-Social Andragogy of Development" (Ed. D. dissertation, Boston University, 1971) pp. 183ff.

34.   The anxieties, desires and longings of the people are taken into account in terms of the lacks and problems as felt by them.   However, what really counts in Freire's "problem posing" method is facilitation of awareness as both "critical transitivity" and consciousness.   Manifestations such as affect and fantasy, for instance, do not share the privileged status of reasoning processes in the crucial concept of "praxis."   The strength of the epistemological approach may thus become a weakness.

35.   There are elements of Marxist thought which are absent, or at least not explicit in Freire, such as those pertaining to specific political formulations (dictatorship of proletariat, concrete programs of revolutionary action, etc.).   Marxism provides mainly epistemological (and ideological) support in terms of Freire's understanding of dialectics.   From Marxian dialectics, he assimilates such concepts as the necessity of class struggle, the unity of action and reflextion, human work as praxis, and the function of ideology.   The Marxian foundation often appears mediated by a variety of sources and authorities such as Althusser, Fromm, Mao, Marcuse, Kulakowski.   This poses a consistency problem given the opposing interpretations involved at crucial points (for instance regarding the continuity of Marx's thought from the Manuscripts to das Kapital).   In Chapter 3 this discussion and critique of the Marxian foundation is expanded, in the context of theological considerations. At this point, we need to elaborate on Marx's concept of alienation which is also important in Freire's thought.

Marx understands alienation in light of Hegel's phenomenology: alienation is part of a process of development of consciousness and being. He attempted to restate scientifically what--in his view--Hegel had said in a confused philosophical way: "The outstanding achievement of Hegel's Phenomenology--the dialectic of negativity--is, first, that Hegel grasped the self-creation of man as a process, objectivation as loss of object, as alienation and transcendence of this alienation, and that he, therefore, grasps the nature of labor and conceives objective man (true, because real man) as the result of his own labor." Karl Marx, Early Writings, transl. and ed. by T. B. Bottomore (New York: McGraw-Hill, 1964), p. 202.

Marx's "materialist" conception replaces the Hegelian idea of a process that takes place in the mind and terminates in "Absolute Knowledge" with that of the acquisitive movement as a practical appropriation of the world in the drive toward material enrichment. Furthermore, there is a major change in terms of moral perspective. That which in Hegel is the overcoming of alienation (i.e., freedom via the cognitive appropriation of the world) in Marx becomes greater alienation and bondage (i.e., acquisition, the self-aggrandizement movement of capital is dehumanizing). And yet, paradoxically enough, capital's destructiveness eventually facilitates its own destruction. Humanization is finally achieved not just in spite of but by means of a dehumanizing process.

The "negation of the negation" in this context means the self-abolition of the proletarian as such, the overcoming of alienation, that which communism is supposed and expected to achieve. Finally, the Hegelian vision of the goal of history is reproduced in terms of radical self-transformation and a special knowing relationship of self and the world.

In "mature" Marx, self-alienation is seen as a social conflict and struggle between "labor" and "capital." Robert Tucker puts it thus: The capitalist . . . is the personification of the life-urge to self-aggrandizement in terms of wealth . . . The worker on the other hand is the embodiment of living labor power, creative capacity in human form, personified labor time. Neither is man, although the essential human attribute--creativity--remains with the worker. Accordingly, Marx considers the worker to be the incarnation of the real self." Philosophy and Myth in Karl Marx, 2nd ed. (Cambridge: University Press, 1972), p. 217. It is Tucker's thesis that Marx actually projected self-alienation--essentially inner reality, as an impersonal social

process: alienated man became bifurcated. Hegel had
represented the universe as a subjective process and
Marx ended up by representing a subjective process as
the universe, the social cosmos. The background of
German philosophy and, perhaps, Marx's own personal conflictive experience, might account for that (mythic)
portrait of capitalist society.

36. Freire, Pedagogy of the Oppressed, pp. 22, 23.

37. Cf. Tucker, Philosophy and Myth in Karl Marx,
chapter XV: "The Myth and the Problem of Conduct" in
reference to Marx's mythical thinking.

38. See William S. Griffth's essay: "Paulo Freire:
Utopian Perspective on Literacy Education for Revolu-
tion," Paulo Friere: A Revolutionary Dilemma for the
Adult Educator, Stanley M. Grabowski, ed. (Syracuse:
Syracuse University, 1972), pp. 67-82.

39. Freire, Pedagogy of the Oppressed, p. 23.

CHAPTER 2: CONSCIENTIZATION AS CREATIVITY

1. Paulo Freire, Educación y Cambio (Buenos Aires:
Ediciones Búsqueda, 1976), pp. 27, 74.

2. See Stephen Crites, "The Narrative Quality of
Experience," Journal of the American Academy of Religion,
39 (September, 1971), pp. 291-311.

3. Several sources have been taken into consideration, and more directly the work of Arieti, Barron,
Klinger, Koestler, May, Rugg, and--mainly--Loder.

4. Freire, "El Compromiso del Profesional con la
Sociedad," in Educación y Cambio, pp. 7-20.

5. When discussing Max Weber on this matter, Peter
Berger writes: "The intrinsic relations among theory,
policy, and morality may be further clarified by a consideration of the concept of 'value-freeness' . . . The
ideal of 'value-freeness' is that the scientific observer
of human affairs should subdue his own values for the
sake of understanding. It is virtually identical with
the notion that science should be objective . . . 'Value-
freeness' is an ideal for theoretical understanding . . .

means that one tries to understand, even if that understanding is contrary to one's wishes . . . In all this,
'value-freeness' pertains to the theoretical attitude;
it cannot pertain to action. One may aspire to value-
free science; value-free policy is an absurdity . . .
It is a moral, not a methodological principle that a
social scientist is responsible for the political uses
to which his findings are put. If, in a given situation,
one says that social scientists should support the revolution rather than support those trying to suppress it,
one is making a moral judgment rather than taking a
philosophical position on the possibilities of scientific
understanding." Pyramids of Sacrifice (Garden City,
N.Y.: Doubleday, 1976), pp. 134-136.

    6. Systems of knowledge could be seen as one of
those realities which in the New Testament are called
the "powers" (exousiae). Sometimes those "powers" can
be the network of persons and agencies which make decisions and exert pressure. These "powers" can also be
ways in which the world and people, culture and history
are understood. "Powers" are thus patterned ways of
perceiving and understanding reality. The confession of
the lordship of Christ over the "powers" in this context
means that the Christian scholar is called to faithfulness in the use of concepts and theories, and in participating in scholarly groups or professional endeavors.
As in the case of other kinds of "powers" a two-sided
tendency can be discerned: they are used to give order
to life (ultimately by the Spirit of Christ the Lord)
and they also become more or less autonomous and alienating or oppressive. /Cf., Hendrik Berkhof, Christ and
the Powers (Scottdale, Pa.: Herald Press, 1977) /. The
Christian scholar belongs to the community of faith
which claims prior loyalty. Where the loyalties are in
tension, where they conflict or where they complement
each other, these are questions that need to be approached within that hermeneutic community, including
the participation of those who do not enjoy scholarly
or professional status. The reaffirmation of the lay-
people in this kind of discerning process is precisely
one of Freire's consistent emphases.

    7. Ethics in a Christian Context (New York:
Harper & Row, 1963), p. 101. A summary statement of
Lehmann's approach follows: "When we say, then, that
God is a 'politician,' it is the Aristotelian definition
and the biblical description of what is going on that
we have in mind. According to the definition, we may
say that politics is activity, and reflection on activity,

which aims at and analyzes what it takes to make and to keep human life human in the world. According to the description, what it takes to make and to keep human life human in the world is 'the unsearchable riches of Christ . . . the plan of the mystery hidden for ages in God who created all things; that through the church the manifold wisdom of God might now be made known to the principalities and powers in the heavenly places . . . until we all attain . . . mature manhood, to the measure of the stature of the fullness of Christ.'" (p. 85)

". . . by the operative (real) presence and power of the Messiah-Redeemer in the midst of his people, and through them of all people, the will to power is broken and displaced by the power to will what God wills. The power to will what God wills is the power to be what man has been created and purposed to be. It is the power to be and to stay human, that is, to attain wholeness or maturity. For maturity is the full development in a human being of the power to be truly and fully himself in being related to others who also have the power to be truly and fully themselves. The Christian koinonia is the foretaste and the sign in the world that God has always been and is contemporaneously doing what it takes to make and to keep human life human. This is the will of God . . ." (p. 101).

8. The creative sequence may actually have an apparent starting point in other phases or movements with which it is usually characterized (e.g., insights--step 3--and/or interpretations--step 5--often move us back to assessing original conflicts). However, the completion of the process--including of course the subjective experience of successful resolution--necessitates the recognition of an original problem situation or baffled struggle.

9. James E. Loder, The Transforming Moment (San Francisco: Harper & Row, 1981), p. 32.

10. Harold Rugg, Imagination (New York: Harper & Row, 1963), p. 309.

11. Arthur Koestler, The Act of Creation (New York: Macmillan, 1964), p. 658. See also Rollo May, Freedom and Destiny (New York: Norton, 1980), pp. 170-173, for a discussion on pause, freedom and creativity.

12. J. Randall Nichols discusses the communication process in terms of creative imagination in his study

"Conflict and Creativity: The Dynamics of the Communication Process in Theological Perspective" (Th.D. dissertation, Princeton Theological Seminary, 1971). "The
importance of such an approach to communication can be
seen most clearly and most strategically when the creative imagination point of view is contrasted with a
transmission of information outlook. The thrust of such
a creative approach runs counter to the naive assumption
that in communication 'meaning is transferred' or 'information is transmitted' in some quantum-like fashion.
The creative model thus provides a more systematic statement of the ideational dynamic whereby an isomorphism of
intention between receiver and sender is reached, but
through what could be called a transgeneration rather
than a trans-mission of any conceptual arrangement . . ."
    "Communication processes modeled around the crea-
tive act thus prove to be essentially assymmetrical:
the receiver's behavior is not a mirror image of a
sender's, in the typical source-encoder model fashion.
What communication 'does' is to structure a situation of
optimal incompletion and uncertainty in order to evoke
in a receiver imaginal responses which complete the ill-
formed pattern. It is as though communication depended
upon messages' creating a problematic situation in which
a receiver 'discovers' the inner structure of the problem
presented, fashions a creative solution, and interprets
the resulting imaginal offerings of his preconscious as
knowledge in terms of the structural properties of the
problem to which it is addressed" (pp. 254, 255). Cf.
Paulo Freire, "Extension or Communication" in Education
for Critical Consciousness (New York: Seabury Press,
1973), pp. 91-164.

    13. Koestler, The Act of Creation, pp. 35, 36, 45.

    14. James E. Loder, Religious Pathology and
Christian Faith (Philadelphia: Westminster Press, 1966),
p. 193.

    15. Koestler, The Act of Creation, p. 659.

    16. Eric Klinger, Structure and Functions of Fan-
tasy (New York: Wiley-Inter-science, 1971), pp. 218-219.

    17. Freire, "Education as the Practice of Freedom"
(Education for Critical Consciousness), p. 47.

    18. Freire, La Educación como Práctica de la Li-
bertad, p. 144.

19. Loder, The Transforming Moment, p. 34.

20. Loder, Religious Pathology and Christian Faith, p. 195.

21. This topic is systematically discussed in Julio Barreiro, Educación Popular y Proceso de Concientización (Buenos Aires: Siglo XXI, 1974).

22. Loder, The Transforming Moment pp. 129-133. See also Loder's "Creativity in and Beyond Human Development." In Aesthetic Dimensions of Religious Education. Edited by Gloria Durka and Joanmarie Smith (New York: Paulist Press, 1979), pp. 222 ff.

23. Rollo May, The Courage to Create (New York: Norton, 1975), p. 93.

24. The term structuralism as used here has a broad, comprehensive meaning. Structuralism states that there are innate formal capacities or properties ("structures") in the human mind which determine the limits within which psychic, social, cultural types of behavior occur. Those structures are deep, latent capacities which emerge to shape surface or manifest behavior as a result of the interaction between the person and the environment.
The structuralists further believe that the structure underlying all human behavior and mental functioning, can be discovered through proper analysis, that it has meaning and cohesiveness and generality. Howard Gardner summarizes this well: "Two assumptions mark the structuralist enterprise overall. One is the belief that through careful examination of groups which, like children or primitives, differ from the contemporary Western adult, new light can be cast on the whole human experience; the second is the faith that what is distinctive about human beliefs, development, and institutions is a reflection of the fundamental nature of human thought, and hence the biological structure of the 'human mind.'" The Quest for Mind, Piaget, Lévi-Strauss and the Structuralist Movement (New York: Random House, 1972), pp. 13.

25. See Lévi-Strauss' classical paper "The Structural Study of Myth," in Structural Anthropology (New York: Basic Books, 1963), pp. 206-231. It is a paradigmatic deep structural analysis in which he presents a formula that corresponds, in his view, to every myth:

$$F\ (a) : F_y\ (b) :: F_x\ (b) : F_{a-1}\ (y)$$

The formula is designed to account for the relationship
between a whole series of variants of a myth and the
socio-historical context from which it springs. It
reflects a teleological view in light of which the deep
structure of a myth appears as the resolution of contradictions involving diverse orders, such as the cognitive,
the sociological, and the cosmological.

Notice that the formula includes a mediator (b)
which has a dual function: F_y is positive or constructive, and F_x is negative or destructive. In this structure there is a built-in double negation that is a key
factor: $F_x(b)$ negates or cancels an original negative
situation, $F_x(a)$. Now, the F_x of (b) must have the
same or sufficient "power" as the F_x of (a) if the
double negation or cancellation is to be effective in
freeing the liberated state (a-1) to live in and become
a function of the positive function of the "mediation,"
$(F_{a-1}\ (y))$. Hence, double negation by the "mediator"
is the condition or pre-requisite for establishing not
just a liberation of the original arrested situation
but a gain over it.

26. A collection of people's stories, discussions
and reflections, can be read in Spanish, in Se Vive como
se Puede (Buenos Aires: Shapire/Tierra Nueva, 1974).

27. In the face of our analysis, it would seem
possible to read this crucial aspect of conscientization
in terms of the Lévy-Strauss formula. That reading
would synthesize the sequence and pattern of literacy/
conscientization in the following fashion:

A situation of
lack and the
setting of the
conflict

$F_x(a)$: the "necrophilic" (x) function (F)--
i.e. dehumanizing--of the oppressive
structures (a) (resulting in privation
and alienation...)

is to

$F_y(b)$: the "biophilic" (y) function (F)--
i.e. life enhancing, humanizing--of
the liberating agent (b) (a hermeneutic community which facilitates the
overcoming of alienation and oppression through solidarity, dialogue,

mediation ⟨   critical reflection and action),

as

double
negation

$F_x^{\sim}(b)$ :: the destructive or negative (x) function (F) of the liberating agent (b)
--i.e. annihilating of internal and
external oppressive structures (the
corrective, confrontational dimension
of conscientization, or "denouncing")

is to

outcome: lack
liquidated, task
accomplished
(and beyond...)

$F_{a-1}(y)$: the radical concellation of oppressive
conditions and privations (a-1) function(F) of
the liberating-creative process--life
enhancing, community building--(y) of
the learning community.

We start with the initial situation of privation
and oppression that calls for a liberating process to
take place. The outcome is much more than the return
to an initial situation of relative equilibrium--"lack
of lack"--or simply the point of departure. A helicoi-
dal step happens involving the cancellation of the initial situation plus the enablement (power) obtained
through the negation of the negative, that is the correction of alienating and oppressive conditions. Thus,
the effects of the inversion of the initial state via
the mediating and liberating process continue to be perceived and felt beyond the immediate resolution--i.e.
the achievement of literacy skills, realization of potentialities on the levels of self and community.

28. Freire's approach and reflections include
material for an analysis of the suggested complementarity

between Hegel's "teleology of consciousness" and Freud's
"archeology of the unconscious." Paul Ricoeur --Freud
and Philosophy (New Heaven: Yale University Press,1970)
points out that Freud's problematic is already in Hegel,
whose teleology of the achievement of consciousness
arises on the basis of life and desire. There is a
striking parallel in what can be called the dialectical
world view of both Hegel and Freud. For Hegel, bifurca-
tion or discord is the source of the need for philosophy;
Freud refers to ambivalence as the birthplace of psychology. Their visions of the world, man and history
emphasize development through conflict, the motivating
power of human passions producing unintended results,
the irony of sudden reversals, and so on. The Freudian
contribution in this context facilities the understanding
of Hegelian thought, particularly in that the psychological dimension and structure of that thought and system
is illuminated. For example, it is possible to visualize
better what Hegel means when he refers to the desire and
impulse to abolish the independence of the object,which
is to be "consumed" (literally, of course, in the case
of actual hunger). Consumption, literally or otherwise,
is aimed at self-affirmation, which allows us to establish a connection with Freud's "omnipotence of desire,"
ego's "narcisism" and "voracity."

The complementarity between Hegelian and Freudian
thought is also very suggestive on the level of socio-
anthropological and political analysis that Freire takes
into account in his own dialectical approach, Cf. the
studies of the colonizer-colonized dialectic, in Albert
Memmi, Portrait of the Colonizer and the Colonized (New
York: Orion Press, 1965); Franz Fanon, The Wretched of
the Earth (New York: Grove Press, 1968).

29. Freire, Cultural Action for Freedom, p. 22.

30. In Ruth Nanda Anshen, ed., Language: An Enquiry into its Meaning and Function (New York: Harper,
1957), pp. 155-173.

31. Ibid., p. 158.

32. We referred above to the clue of the relationship between Hegelian thought and Freire's educational
approach in terms of the classical master-slave paradigm,
that is, with particular emphasis on the content of such
a proposition. Closely connected with that, there is
another important reference to underscore now, and it
has to do more specifically with the process of self-
consciousness development.

The psychology of Hegelian spirit has an important congnitive dimension insofar as Hegel associates knowing with self-discovery. Psychologically speaking, then, an intimate connection is established between self- and cognitive-dynamics, particularly in terms of the dialectic of negativity: knowing involves self-expansion through "aggression" against the object; spirit's self-realization occurs within a process of successive transcending of limits, self-aggrandizement (to be seen in Hegel's system, of course, in the larger context of his theory of history as the self-realization of "God"). If this is actually the case--and much more could be said regarding Hegel's dialectic (i.e., the pattern of development through inner conflict) or "psychodynamics of the spirit"--one important implication follows in light of our present concerns: Marx probably misread Hegel by selectively emphasizing (and projecting?) a supposedly esoteric economics, while underestimating the heavily psychological and "intellectualizing" character of Hegel's thought.

Freire is actually proposing a context and a (dialectical) process whereby negation of negation is to take place thus facilitating affirmation. Literacy/concientization involve the progressive overcoming of cognitive lacks, and self-enhancement. Concientization (which includes expansion of self and consciousness) is supposed to be a continuing, never ending conquering and mastering process, analogous to Hegel's self-infinitizing process.

33.   "The conformist has been forced into denying the self, not as the result of existential or valid social limits, but rather as a result of the frequent experiences of being confined, restricted and limited. A distinction must be made here between natural limits and imposed limitations. Limits provide the structure through which individual identity emerges and grows. They enable the organism to use its capacities within its own defined structure and are meaningful as the inherent requirements of a situation. Limitations are induced and imposed from without and are external and extraneous. They are blocks and deterrents to growth and hinder creative emergence." Clark Moustakas, Creativity and Conformity (New York: Van Nostrand, 1967), pp. 36, 37. Although missing this useful distinction between limits and limitations, Rollo May describes well the limits of creativity, particularly in the discussion of the dialectics of imagination and form (The Courage to Create, Chapter 6).

34. The two characteristics of creative groups underscored by Paul Matussek are fitting in regard to the personal and social context of the Freire method. Members of a creative group identify themselves very strongly with the common objective; and the great interest in achieving the group objective is conducive to better learning. These are groups with a great deal of solidarity, coopearation and openness, that highly motivate indivudal members to realize their best potentialities. La creatividad desde una perspectiva psicodinámica (Barcelona: Ed. Herder, 1977), pp. 227-233. The character of a creativogenic social milieu is spelled out by Silvano Arieti in Creativity - the Magic Synthesis (New York: Basic Books, 1976), especially chapters 13 and 14.

35. Rollo May discusses "creative courage" as "the discovery of new forms, new symbols, new patterns in which a new society can be built . . . This is why authentic creativity takes so much courage: an active battle with the gods is occurring . . . the actual (as contrasted to the ideal) gods of our society--the gods of conformism as well as the gods of apathy, material success, and exploitative power . . . The rage is against injustice . . . ultimately it is rage against the prototype of all injustice--death. /The possibility of revelation / the politically rigid cannot stand . . . creative persons of all sorts are the potential destroyers of our nicely ordered systems." (The Courage to Create, pp. 21, 27, 30, 32, 76.)

36. William A. Lessa and Evon Z. Vogt, Reader in Comparative Religion, An Anthropological Approach, 3rd edition (New York: Harper & Row, 1972), pp. 503-512.

37. Ibid., p. 505.

38. Ibid., p. 511.

39. Loder, personal communication and unpublished paper "Creativity in and Beyond Human Development."

40. Loder's discussion is brought to focus on Luther and the German reformation but with a major reformulation in order to preserve the integrity of the human spirit and the self-understanding of the prophet. He observes that the normative frame of reference derived from sociological functionalism and psychoanalytic thought obscures the genius of the corporate human spirit as it works through and individual for the

reorganization of an entire social milieu. He argues in favor of the human spirit--instead of tension-management and pattern maintenance--as the fundamental reality against which all revitalization movements are to be measured. The alternative understanding--assuming the validity of Wallace's patterning of revitalization-- reads as follows: "Transformation is the product of the mediational work of the divine presence . . . and needs to be seen as the movement of God's Spirit renewing and restoring his people through an intrinsically creative process that has an integrity of its own . . . whenever socialization patterns work to suppress, divide or diffuse the life of the human spirit will erupt with dramatic force to redress the balance of forces for the health of the social organism. If that redressing of balance is mediated by Christ, as it was in Luther's case, it is impossible not to see the interconnection between Luther's personal transformation and the transformation of his society as the work of the Holy Spirit." (Paper, pp. 32, 33).

41. In a group in which conscientization is being experienced successfully, people may enter a kind of euphoric state, characterized by a sense of quasi-omnipotence derived from the social situation (circles of culture) which fosters self-affirmation and solidarity. This would amount to the subjective manifestation of "self-aggrandizement." In light of the creativity paradigm, this phenomenon, if persistent, can be seen as an expanded phase of discharge and transformation of energy, without adequate interpretation and action.

42. All proximate healing, saving figures expand the human spirit and tend to hypostatize their liberating function. This natural tendency of the human spirit represents a longing not just for the saving figures but for that which they do, their liberating and creative action in itself has a substance which is transferrable. With every new exertion of that action there is an incremental magnification of both the significance of the mediators and of this creative power.

43. The following example is illustrative of the attempt to correlate Freire and theology. In her book Human Liberation in a feminist Perspective, A Theology (Philadelphia: Westminster Press, 1974), Letty Russell states that conscientization is parallel to the Christian experience of conversion: "There is no doubt that a formal analogy exists between conversion and conscientization in the way they happen in human experience.

The difference is one of emphasis. In conversion, stress
is placed on God's action while in conscientization
stress is placed on human initiative . . . the process
is similar and the Holy Spirit can and does work through
both . . . In classical reformation theology faith was
spelled out under three interrelated rubrics . . .
These same elements are clear in Freire's typology of
the process of conscientization: logos, or critical
awareness, corresponds to notitia; praxis, or commitment
to action-reflection, is similar to assensus; and utopia,
or vision of trust which makes possible a transformed
self and world, corresponds to fiducia. Together they
make up the same important whole in the process of new
life" (pp. 122-125). The formal analogy that Russell
describes is assumed to include also content or substance; the power or energy for transformation is supposed to be essentially the same, the Holy Spirit being
somehow engaged in the two processes (conscientization
and conversion). They are practically identified since
the difference is claimed to be merely a matter of "emphasis" and perspective.

SECOND PART -- THE THEOLOGICAL FOUNDATION:
EDUCATION AND THE KINGDOM

CHAPTER 3: FREIRE AND LIBERATION THEOLOGY

1. El Mensaje de Paulo Freire (Madrid: Marsiega,
1976), p. 20.

2. Paulo Freire, "Conscientizar para Liberar"
Contacto 8:1 (1971): 43-51.

3. This is the topic of one of the special doctoral studies on Freire, Michael P. Kane, "An Interpretation of Humanism in the Thought of Paulo Freire" (Ed.
D. dissertation, George Peabody College for Teachers,
Vanderbilt University, 1980).

4. cf. Pierre Teilhard de Chardin, The Phenomenon
of Man (New York: Harper & Bros., 1959).

5. See John L. Elias, Conscientization and Deschooling - Freire's and Illich's Proposals for Reshaping
Society, Philadelphia: Westmister, 1976.

6. By Anabaptism we refer to the Christian movement which started in the sixteenth century as part of the Radical Reformation and which was characterized--in the perspective of present-day heirs of this movement-- by a peculiar "vision," thus referred to by Harold S. Bender: The Anabaptist vision included three major points of emphasis: first, a new conception of the essence of Christianity as discipleship; second, a new conception of the church as a brotherhood; and third, a new ethic of love and non-resistance. "The Anabaptist Vision," in Guy F. Hershberger, ed., The Recovery of the Anabaptist Vision (Scottdale, pa.: Herold Press, 1957), p. 42. For detailed expositions of Anabaptist approaches to the church, biblical interpretation, social ethics, missions and theology, see the books by Bender, Burkholder-Redekop, Durnbaugh, Friedman, Klaaseen, Kraus, Ramseyer and Yoder, cited in the bibliography. Our own understanding will become more apparent in the following sections in this chapter and the next, as we develop our theological reflections in critical and constructive fashion.

7. Paulo Freire, Las iglesias, la educación y el proceso de liberación humana en la historia (Buenos Aires: La Aurora, 1974), pp. 5, 8.

8. Ibid., p. 21.

9. Ibid., pp. 17, 18.

10. Many authors have referred to the religious structure of Marx's thought and/or to the implicit "theology" in it (incidentally, the distinction and relationship between the "religious" and the "theological" is not always established). Several issues are indeed apparent from this perspective, such as: the holistic structure of Marxism, attempting to provide an all-inclusive Weltanschauung; its concern with history and the story of innocence-fall-redemption and the return to paradise; the promise of home for the new humanity; the basically moralizing motif of "praxis" and so on. In his "The Theological Structure of Marxist Atheism," Gaston Fessard wisely underscores three points: the unity of Man-Nature as parallel to the Man-God in the incarnate Word; private property and original sin; the proletariat and redemption. Concilium Vol. 16 (New York: Paulist Press, 1966), pp. 7-24.

11. Freire, Las iglesias, pp. 28, 29.

12.   Ibid., p. 30.

13.   Ibid., p. 38.

14.   Paulo Freire, "Carta a un Joven Teólogo," Fichas Latinoamericanas 1 (Diciembre, 1974), pp. 51-53.

15.   Freire's conception at this point is similar to Freud's, for whom the aim of psychoanalysis is the expansion of awareness. Put in terms of the structure of the psyche, the Ego is to grow and become more and more powerful to the detriment of the impulsive Id and the repressive Super-Ego. The expected result is indi- viduals better equipped to cope with internal and ex- ternal reality, and to become masters of their own destiny.

16.   Both "targets" were attacked on the basis of Marx's radical and passionate humanism and his early conviction that philosophy is not meant to merely in- terpret the world but to transform it (Thesis on Feuer- bach).

17.   In our view, Kierkegaard's attack on the Christendom establishment is, in a sense, a counterpart of Marx's critique, but in the name of Christianity. That seems to be basically consistent with our own Ana- baptist perspective at this point. Cf., Vernard Eller's Kierkegaard and Radical Discipleship (Princeton: Uni- versity Press, 1968).

18.   In the light of the influence of enlightenment humanism in Marx's rejection of all religion as an in- version of the criticism of reality, it could still be argued that atheism is an integral aspect of Marxian materialism. The view that religion originated as an idealistic justification for economic manipulation of one group by another, the subsequent belief that the radical alteration of economic relations would eventually determine the disappearance of religion, and the impli- cations of those two ideas, are expressions of an atheistic worldview.

19.   The reiterated use of theological language on the part of Marx, both "young" and "old," is noteworthy: In the case of the "young" Marx, his religious-moralistic orientation and the corresponding theological structure are manifest within a philosophico-anthropological frame- work with strong existentialist and humanistic flavor (the human struggle is set almost in terms of the

individual against society). In the "old" Marx, they appear within a socio-politico-economic analysis, in terms of the class struggle within capitalist society. Here, an objective, "scientific" contribution is attempted.

20. Freire, "Carta a un Joven Teólogo." p. 53.

21. Ibid.

22. Ibid.

23. Freire, "Tercer Mundo y Teología," Fichas Latinoamericanas 1, p. 54.

24. Paulo Freire, La educación como práctica de la libertad, pp. 38, 39.

25. Freire, Pedagogy of the Oppressed, p. 48.

26. "Christology" here is not used in the sense traditionally understood (the part of dogmatic theology that studies the Person and attributes of Christ, and in particular the union in Him of divine and human natures; or the part of Christian doctrine concerned with the revelation of God in Christ, in terms of Incarnation). Rather than a dogmatic-normative approach ("how must Jesus Christ be understood"?) We are dealing with a descriptive and analytic one ("how is Jesus Christ perceived and described?" "how can we comprehend and interpret that image?").

The question about "who is Jesus Christ today" has been considered very seriously in Latin American theological circles. Catholics and Protestants have produced several papers around that very question. They show a remarkable commonality in pointing to the prevailing images and symbols. The typology confirms first of all and predominantly the suffering, defeated, passive Christ as described by John A. Mackay half a century ago /The Other Spanish Christ, A Study in the Spiritual History of Spain and Suth America (New York: Macmillan, 1932). / There is also Christ as a "frozen" heavenly king, idealized and "glorified" and presented in imperial garments (i.e., assimilated to the colonizers' king). The sweeping radical conclusion of the authors who share the position of liberation theology is as follows:

Both images, the "defeated" Christ and the "heavenly monarch," are the two faces of Christology of oppression. The Christ of "constituted impotence," of resignation, and who refuses to struggle because he is alienated, defeated. The Christ of "constituted power" of submission, who does not struggle because he is dominated. Saúl Trinidad, "Cristología, Conquista-Colonización," Cristianismo y Sociedad, XIII: 43-44 (1975), pp. 23, 24. This political interpretation indicates that the production and popularization of such representations of Christ clearly favors the interests of those in power. What Mackay had already perceived and clearly stated in the context of his own approach, our Latin American authors refer to again by adding a different perspective via a Marxist analysis. A liberating and revolutionary Christ is then presented and opposed to the "Christology of oppression." On the basis of sociology of knowledge, a reference is made to contrasting global perceptions of reality originated, in turn, in diverse social praxis and definite ideological options. Therefore, as Hugo Assmann puts it: "the conflict of christologies cannot be analyzed nor solved outside the dialectic of socio-political conflicts, which has always been its real historical conditioning factor.. Any other way of approaching the problem is bound to be saturated with idealism. . . the conflict of christologies is not about to be solved because there is no immediate perspective of solution for the serious social contradictions in our 'Christian' America." (Ibid., pp. 44,45).

The conclusion is, then, that we shall keep having reactionary and revolutionary Christs for a while, and that the former will still be presented as the only authorized version, sanctifying and cementing the existing social order. In this view, faith in a liberating Christ is associated with a partisan option in favor of the oppressed classes, and his liberating power is to be found in the midst of the class struggle. Christ's power is not to be understood as substantive or non-power (something to have or to get) but as verb-power (the praxis or power). The corollary of this discussion is predictable: it is in the struggle in favor of the poor and exploited where Christianity is found free of bourgeoisie's ideology and false consciousness; only there can we find the true face of Christ and the liberating power of the Gospel of the Kingdom of God. Systematic presentations of Latin American Christological discussions are found in the following works, to be considered extensively in the next chapter: Leonardo Boff, Jesus Christ Liberator, A Critical Christology for Our Time (Maryknoll, N.Y.: Orbis Books, 1978); Jon

Sobrino, <u>Christology at the Crossroads</u>, A Latin American
<u>Appraisal</u> (Maryknoll, N.Y.: Orbis Books, 1978).

27. This concept is well illustrated in the case
of Freire's more recent educational endeavors in Africa.
<u>Pedagogy in Process, The Letters to Guinea-Bissau</u> (New
York: Seabury Press, 1978).

28. Freire, <u>Las iglesias</u>, p. 20.

29. Ibid., p. 43 ff.

30. Freire, "Tercer Mundo y Teología," p. 55.

31. Freire, <u>Pedagogy of the Oppressed</u>, p. 77.

32. Gustavo Gutiérrez, leading Catholic theologian
of liberation, put it this way: "What ultimately brings
Christians to participate in liberating oppressed
peoples is the conviction that the gospel message is
radically incompatible with an unjust society. They see
clearly that they cannot be authentic Christians unless
they act . . . In Latin America, the church must realize that it exists in a continent undergoing revolution,
where violence is present in different ways . . . its
missions must be achieved keeping that into account.
The church has no alternative. Only a total break with
the unjust order to which it is bound in a thousand
conscious or unconscious ways, and a forthright commitment to a new society, will make men in Latin America
believe the message of love it bears." "A Latin American Perception of a Theology of Revolution," in L.
Colonnese, ed., <u>Conscientization for Liberation</u> (Washington, D.C.: United States Catholic Conference, 1971),
pp. 72, 76-77.

33. See note number 37 below.

34. Malcolm Warford, "Between the Plumbing and
the Saving: Educatin, Theology, and Liberation,"
<u>Living Light</u> II:1 (Spring 1974), pp. 60-77.

35. For instance, Gustavo Gutiérrez takes Freire
into account in his discussion of the liberation process in Latin America, eschatology and politics, and
utopia and political action, in his well known <u>A Theology</u>
<u>of Liberation</u> (Maryknoll, N.Y.: Orbis Books, 1973).

36. Criticism of liberation theology relevant to
our study has been formulated from different perspectives

such as the following: Jurgen Moltmann's "Open Letter
to José Míguez Bonino" (Christianity and Crisis, 29
March 1976, 57-63) summarizes and European political
theology position; an appraisal by North American evangelicals is found in Evangelicals and Liberation, edited
by Carl E. Armerding (Nutley, N.J.:   Presbyterian and
Reformed Publishing Co., 1977); a Latin American Evangelicals' critique is systematically presented in J.
Andrew Kirk, Liberation Theology - An Evangelical View
from the Third World (Atlanta: John Knox Press, 1979).
See also Richard Shaull's "The Liberation of Theology,"
in Gustavo Gutiérrez and Richard Shaull, Liberation and
Change (Atlanta: John Knox Press, 1977), and Brian
Mahan and Dale L. Richesin, eds. The Challenge of Lib-
eration Theology - A First World Response (Maryknoll,
N.Y.:   Orbis Books, 1981).

37. For example, when Gustavo Gutiérrez discusses
Jesus and the political world, at the center of his
treatment of eschatology and politics in A Theology of
Liberation, he concentrates on three major critical
issues: the relationship with the zealots, Jesus'
attitude towards the leaders of the Jewish people, and
his death at the hands of the political authorities.
Gutiérrez focuses only on the prophetic confrontation
without referring to the constructive alternative of
the proclaimed and coming Kingdom. Hence, the "positive"
dimension of the political relevance of Jesus is not
properly taken into account.
It is important to notice that many Latin American
Roman Catholics are reacting against a predominantly
"priestly" theological conception on the part of their
tradition (which tended to canonize the status quo) by
adopting a strong "prophetic" stance. The problem,
though, is that their prophetic hermeneutical criteria
often betray a natural theology via Teilhard the
Chardin -type of evolutionistic conception, or a populist
or Marxist ideology relatively autonomous as criteria
of interpretation. A Catholic hermeneutic principle,
rooted in the concept of natural law and the evolutionary character of revelation in the tradition of the
church can bestow upon certain human discoveries (in
science, philosophy, for instance) a position of almost
equality with that of the biblical text. Thus, many
liberation theologians have recourse to the re-reading
of a given text in the light of the Marxist analysis.
Consequently, quite often theology and philosophy of
history tend to be derived more from Marxist and other
sources than from biblical eschatology. In our own
perspective, Scripture is given a greater value in

comparison to other elements of the theological reflection process such as ecclesiastical tradition and socio-political analysis of the historical situation.

38. John H. Yoder, The Politics of Jesus (Grand Rapids, Mich: Eerdmans, 1972), p. 100.

39. Alternative interpretations of Exodus are found in J. Marvin Breneman, ed., Liberación, Exodo y Biblia (Miami: Caribe, 1975) and John H. Yoder "Exodus and Exile: The Two Faces of Liberation" Cross Currents (Fall 1973) 297-309. See also Severino Croatto, Exodus: A Hermeneutics of Freedom (Maryknoll, N.Y.: Orbis Books, 1981).

40. Yoder, The Politics of Jesus, pp. 223 ff.

41. We would make a difference between a Christian eschatology and a Marxist teleology. Both concepts refer to the end of history, but mere teleology in this context presuposes that history has meaning in and of itself, whereas eschatology asserts that history acquires its meaning from the outside. For a "teleological" interpretation of the meaning of history, this meaning is to be found in the future, in the temporal culmination of history: history approaches the divine, so to speak. According to the "eschatological" (and apocalyptic) intepretation, meaning is not something that history has but that it receives: the divine breaks into history.

42. In that light it is possible to understand why Freire falls into some major contradictions, for instance, when he justifies the curtailment of freedom for the sake of advancing the revolutionary cause, and not trusting the oppressed before liberation, with whom dialogue is not always possible (Pedagogy of the Oppressed, pp. 134, 169, 170-171).

43. Freire's anthropology combines elements of scholastic philosophy and contemporary existentialism. It does not take consistently into account the diverse sources of limitations to human freedom. Consequently, it tends to present a too simplistic and optimistic view of the actual possibilities of socio-political trans-formation. Further, this radical change is referred to often as if it were merely a matter of perceiving its necessity and then willing its occurrence. The Marxist influence certainly does not help to correct these appreciations, which fail to take into account the

complexity of the problem of the human predicament and the pervasive presence of radical evil in particular.

44. The view of man which emerges in the discussion of class--namely, man as worker--is also fundamental for a biblical anthropology. J. Míguez Bonino suggests among other things, that there is a striking similarity between the understanding of alienated character of work and the Pauline refection of the "works of the law" in which man's actions are also objectified as something valuable in themeselves, apart from the doer and the neighbor, as a "work" which can be merchandised in order to buy "justification." Doing Theology in a Revolutionary Situation (Philadelphia: Fortress Press, 1975), p. 108 ff.

45. José Míguez Bonino, Christians and Marxists (Grand Rapids, Mich.: Eerdmans, 1976), p. 97 ff.

46. Ibid., p. 29 ff.

47. Liberation theologians stress that orthopraxis, rather than orthodoxy, becomes the criterion for theology: obeying the Gosper rather than defining, prescribing or defendind it. Interestingly enough, this reference to the theological task and mission resembles a sixteenth Century Radical Reformation emphasis on the matter, except for the exclusive normativeness of the biblical documents in the case of the Anabaptists. The "epistemology of obedience" is summarized in the well-known statement of Hans Denck: "No man may truly know Christ, except he follow him in life" (mit dem Leben), Schriften, 2 Teil. Walter Fellmann, ed. (Gutersloh, 1956), p. 45.

48. Proletarians are often idealized as bearers of revelation and of the new order. The assumption here is that the oppressed, once liberated, will somehow be different persons, able and willing to use their freedom wisely and to avoid futher exploitation. It is believed, à la Fromm, that the "necrophilic" tendencies will be essentially eliminated in the context of a humanistic socialism. There appears to be a flagrant contradiction between an inherently good human nature, idealistically assumed, and the reality of a wicked social structure. Furthermore, the social analysis in tersms of oppressed and oppressors is also a very simplistic one. The very concept of oppression is often dealt with in rather vague abstract terms (e.g., Pedagogy of the Oppressed, pp. 40-45). For a discussion of

pervasive oversimplification in Marxian sociological analysis, see Talcott Parsons, Sociological Theory and Modern Society (New York: Free Press, 1967), chapter 3.

49. The important point here is not so much whether we should be more or less optimistic, but rather what the source of our optimism will be. We would affirm, optimistically enough, human potential for creativity on the basis of the power of the resurrected Christ. This proposition is elaborated in the next chapter.

50. John H. Yoder, The Original Revolution (Scottdale, Pa.: Herald Press, 1971).

51. Yoder thus underscores some features of this new society: a voluntary association through repentance and commitment; mixed regarding its composition (races, sexes, cultures, religious backgrounds, social classes); formed by members with a new life style: redemptive response of forgiveness for the offenders, suffering in the face of violence, sharing of material possessions, shared leadership and personal gifts. It is commissioned to confront injustice and corruption through the building up of a new order without the violent destruction of the old one; with a different model for interpersonal relations (between the sexes, in the family, business, politics, recreation) in terms of a special vision of the meaning and value of the human being; with a different attitude toward the state and the enemies, etc..

CHAPTER 4: KINGDOM GOSPEL AND CREATIVITY

1. For a useful discussion of "Anabaptist" and "Evangelical" theological and ecclesiological stances, see Norman Kraus, ed., Evangelicalism and Anabaptist (Scottdale, Pa.: Herald Press, 1979), especially Chapter 9. We are actually alluding to an Evangelical movement characterized by a strong concern for social action for justice, peace and reconciliation, such as advanced in Sojourners magazine for example.

2. "A Preliminary Dialogue with Gutiérrez's A Theology of Liberation," in Carl E. Armendig, ed., Evangelicals and Liberation, pp. 10-42.

3. Ibid., p. 20.

4. An interesting discussion of this very theme is found in two works by Paul Verghese, from the perspective of the Christian Orthodox tradition: The Joy of Freedom (Richmond: John Knox Press, 1967) and The Freedom of Man An Inquiry into Some Roots of Tension Between Freedom and Authority in Our Society (Philadelphia: Westminster, 1972). According to Verghese, difficulties with our understanding of freedom stem in part from an excessive reliance upon St. Augustine's thought. Augustine discussed freedom to choose between good and evil (libertas major) and freedom from sin (libertas minor) in the bossom of God. "He chose the latter and abhorred the former . . . The first one had got him into trouble to start with." (Joy of Freedom, p. 79.) Verghese affirms that the essence of freedom is neither freedom to choose nor emancipation from constraint but rather creativity: "The essence of freedom lies in spiritual creativity, in being the originator of the causal chain . . ." (p. 79).

In order to obtain what he perceives as a more balanced appreciation of freedom, Verghese has recourse to the thought of Gregory of Nyssa. In Freedom of Man he amplifies his critique of those theologians who solely propose the human need to be emancipated from internal or external oppression and to attain power to choose. Freedom from bondage is a necessary (negative) phase of freedom, but only the prelude to the discovery of a more positive and creative freedom based upon the worship of God for whom freedom is essential. Man shares in God's image and nature and human freedom includes such elements as spontaneity and boldness.

5. This point is discussed by Orlando Costas in The Church and Its Mission: A Shattering Critique from the Third World (Wheaton, Ill.: Tyndale House Publishers, 1974). Costas argues that in the theology of liberation, "hope is not grounded also on a God who is ahead, coming to us, and pulling us toward him, but on a God who has come along with us and is leading us to the future which is in the making . . . Both the prophetic and the apocalyptic vision seem to be supported in the New Testament . . . These two eschatological visions are integrated in the ministry of the Spirit. On the one hand, he is the continuation of the incarnation, the one who makes Christ present in the historical situations of life. On the other, he is the Spirit of promise." (p. 261.).

6. Boff, Jesus Christ Liberator, Chapter 7.

7. Ibid., p. 135.

8. Ibid., pp. 290, 291.

9. Ibid.

10. Sobrino, Christology at the Crossroads, p. 377.

11. Ibid., p. 380.

12. Ibid., p. 381.

13. Philippians, 3:10.

14. James E. Loder refers to resurrection in terms of transformational negation (i.e., the negation of the negation such that a new integration emerges, establishing a gain over the original negated state or condition). Christ crucified and resurrected in taken as a paradigm of the mediator of transformation at the level of existential negation: ". . . Christ becomes the adequate 'grammar' for existential transformation because in his crucifixion he takes ultimate annihilation into himself and in his resurrection existential negation is negated. The Christ event thus creates an ontological gain for those whose existential nature is defined by his nature." /"Negation and Transformation: A Study in Theology and Human Development," in Towards Moral and Religious Maturity, The First International Conference on Moral and Religious Development (Morristown, N.J.: Silver Burdett Co., 1980), p. 169./ See also Loder's The Transforming Moment, sixth chapter, "From Negation to Love."

15. Useful discussions of the Kingdom of God can be found in the works of the following authors included in the bibliography: Gray, Harkness, Hiers, Ladd, Lundstrom, Padilla, Pannenberg, Perrin, Rottenber, Schnackenburg, Scott, and Weiss.

16. The arrangement of these sections follows closely that of John H. Yoder's paper "La Expectativa Mesiánica del Reino y su Carácter Central para una Adecuada Hermenéutica Contemporánea," in C. René Padilla, ed. El Reino de Dios y América Latina (El Paso: Casa Bautista de Publicaciones, 1975), pp. 103-120. Our own theological thought, whic h has been influenced by Yoder's discussion, will be blended with those christological considerations by liberation theologians which are consistent with Freire's contribution and with our biblico-

theological perspective. We will not dwell on critique
at this point, since in the previous chapter we exposed
those areas in liberation theology which need to be corrected and the direction that such a correction should
take.

17. Boff, Jesus Christ Liberator, pp. 53, 55.

18. Sobrino, Christology at the Crossroads, pp.
61 ff, 354 ff.

19. Boff, Jesus Christ Liberator, p. 64.

20. Sobrino, Christology at the Crossroads, pp.
68 ff.

21. Boff, Jesus Christ Liberator, pp. 90, 91, 95.

22. Ibid., p. 281.

23. Gustavo Gutiérrez stresses the importance of
the rediscovery of the eschatological dimension in
theology which has led to consider the central role of
historical praxis: "The Bible presents eschatology as
the driving force of salvific history radically oriented
toward the future. Eschatology is thus not just one
more element of Christianity, but the very key to understanding the Christian faith." (A Theology of Liberation,
p. 162.)

24. Sobrino, Christology at the Crossroads, pp.
119, 120.

25. See the section "Another Look at the Prophetic
Church," p. 78.

26. Sobrino, Christology at the Crossroads, p.
xiii.

27. Ibid., p. 50.

28. Boff, Jesus Christ Liberator, p. 69.

29. Sobrino, Christology at the Crossroads, p. 56.

30. This is considered in detail in Yoder's
Politics of Jesus. The difference with regards to most
liberation theologians on this point is the empahsis
on the creative alternatives represented by Jesus

besides and beyond the confrontation of oppressive power structures.

31. In Norman Perrin's terms, the symbol "was effective precisely because it evoked the myth by means of which they had come to understand themselves as the people of God, the beneficiaries of his kingly activity in the world. The symbol is dependent upon the myth, and it is effective because of its power to evoke the myth. The myth in turn derives its power from its ability to make sense of the life of the Jewish people in the world." Jesus and the Language of the Kingdom: Symbol and Metaphor in New Testament Interpretation (Philadelphia: Fortress Press, 1976) p. 23. See also Bernard B. Scott, Jesus, Symbol-Maker for the Kingdom (Philadelphia: Fortress Press, 1981).

32. Boff, Jesus Christ Liberator, p. 60.

33. A good summary of the meaning of shalom appears in John Driver's Community and Commitment (Scottdale, Pa.: Herald Press, 1976), p. 71: Shalom is a broad concept, essential to the Hebrew understanding of relationship between people and God. It covers human welfare, health, and wellbeing in both spiritual and material aspects. It describes a condition of wellbeing resulting from sound relationships among people and between people and God. According to the prophets, true peace reigned in Israel when justice (or righteousness) prevailed, when the common welfare was assured, when people were treated with equality and respect, when salvation flourished according to the social order determined by God in the convenant which He had established with His people. In fact, the prophet understood that God's covenant with Israel was a "covenant of life and peace" (Malachi 2:5). On the other hand, when there was greed for unjust gain, when judges could be bought for a price, when there was not equal opportunity for all, when suffering was caused by social and economic oppression, then there was no peace, even though false prophets insisted on the contrary (Jeremiah 6:13-14). For the Hebrews, peace was not merely the absence of armed conflict. Rather shalom was assured by the prevalence of conditions which contribute to human wellbeing in all its dimensions. Not merely tranquility of spirit or serenity of mind, peace had to do with harmonious relationships between God and His people. It had to do with social relationships characterized by justice. Peace resulted when people lived together according to God's intention. Peace, justice, and salvation are

synonymous terms for general wellbeing created by right
social relationships.
   See also Walter Brueggeman, Living Toward A Vision:
Biblical Reflections on Shalom (Philadelphia: United
Church Press, 1982); Edward Powers, Signs of Shalom
(Philadelphia: United Church Press, 1973). For a dis-
cussion of the Gospel as the Gospel of Peace, see
Marlin E. Miller, "The Gospel of Peace," in Robert L.
Ramseyer, ed., Mission and the Peace Witness (Scottdale,
Pa.: Herald Press, 1979), pp. 9-23.

   34. paul's use of the Kingdom motif is rather
limited and it includes an apparent distinction between
Christ's Kingdom and God's Kingdom (e.g., I Corinthians
15:24). However, in terms of our present discussion,
we can affirm that "lordship" is essentially another
symbol for the same confession.

   35. Boff, Jesus Christ Liberator, p. 79.

   36. Ibid., p. 281.

   37. Sobrino, Christology at the Crossroads, p.
127.

   38. The expression "upside-down Kindom" is developed at length in the book by Donald B. Kraybill,
The Upside-Down Kingdom (Scottdale, Pa.: Herald Press,
1978). It is a challenging study of the KIngdom of God
in the Synoptic Gospels.

   39. Boff, Jesus Christ Liberator, p. 64.

   40. Yoder, "La Expectativa Mesiánica del Reino,"
p. 110.

   41. Sobrino, Christology at the Crossroads, pp.
51, 55.

   42. See our critical note on this regard: Chapter 3, pp. 75-77.

   43. Ruben Alves, A Theology of Human Hope (Washington, D.C.: Corpus Books, 1969), p. 142.

   44. Ibid., p. 136.

   45. Yoder, "La Expectativa Mesiánica del Reino,"
pp. 114, 115.

46. There is an interesting coincidence at this point with Thomas H. Groome's reflections on the subject: Christian Religious Education - Sharing our Story and Vision (New York: Harper & Row, 1980), pp. 35-55.

47. Yoder, "La Expectativa Mesiánica del Reino," p. 115.

48. Boff, Jesus Christ Liberator, p. 97.

49. Gutiérrez, A Theology of Liberation, p. 261.

50. By guiding principle we understand the nucleus or heart of the matter to be communicated to those who participate in the diverse dimensions of Christian education: an essential principle for the interpretation of objectives, method, curriculum and administration guidelines. We are taking into consideration D. Campbell Wyckoff's theoretical approach /see his The Gospel and Christian Education, A Theory of Christian Education for Our Times (Philadelphia: Westminster, 1959) /. Five features are particularly noteworthy in Wyckoff's contribution: It suggests a comprehensive pattern for theory building; it calls for serious consideration of the social cultural milieu; it emphasizes consistently educational and theological integrity and soundness; it does not impose a restrictive biblico-theological perspective; it stresses and represents the interrelation and interdependence of practice and theory.

51. Wyckoff, The Gospel and Christian Education, p. 87 ff.

52. In her essay "Theology and Religious Education," Marvin Taylor, ed., Foundations for Christian Education in an Era of Change (Nashville: Abingdom, 1976), pp. 30-40, Sara Little presents five alternatives concerning the relation between theology and education. Those alternatives are: theology as content to be taught, theolgoy as norm, theology as irrelevant, "doing" theolgoy as educating, and education in dialogue with theology. She suggests that none of those is "the" way to relate education and theology and that today, the relationship between theology and education is somewhat more mystifying to representatives of both fields than it used to be a few decades ago. We find Little's guidelines for the educator in knowing how to deal with theology today useful in terms of our own study. In light of Freire's theological foundations, we can

briefly illustrate the four ways in which theological
insights can relate to the educational process and
program:
    a. There is a message of the Gospel of the Kingdom
to be discovered and shared. The story of God's love
and liberating-re-creating deeds is to be appropriated,
"learned" in actual praxis, together with the vision of
God's coming Kingdom.
    b. That message, as content, helps shape the pro-
cess by which it is communicated. It serves as norm
for selection, interpretation and evaluation of educational practices and programs (e.g., indoctrination is
to be avoided, dialogue fostered).
    c. These theological foundations involve a dynamic
conception of "ortho-praxis." Theologizing and the process of education become intimately related. Both
should take place in the context of "hermeneutic learning communities."
    d. Finally, the "dialogue" between theology and
education is very apparent in Freire's own work and
reflections. The two disciplines and endeavors benefit
mutually from such an interface.

THIRD PART -- RAMIFICATIONS FOR THEORY AND PRACTICE

CHAPTER 5: IMPLICATIONS FOR CHRISTIAN EDUCATION

    1. A theory of the cultural process, the church
and education, is precisely articulated by D. Campbell
Wyckoff in chapters 1, 2, and 3 of The Gospel and
Christian Education.

    2. Ibid., pp. 13, 47-48.

    3. The purpose of Mackay's research and writing
was to contribute a pioneer's comprehensive picture of
the religious situation in Latin America on the basis
of the problem posed by the apparent contradiction
between the presence of (nominal) Christianity and the
need for radical "evangelization" and Christian nurture.
The major hypothesis with which the study was undertaken
is that "A true appreciation of this continent's spiritual pilgrimage depends on a knowledge of the psychic
forces emanating from Spain and Portugal, which have
moulded all life and history of the countries which
compose it, from the time of the Conquest until now."
(The Other Spanish Christ, p. ix.) Mackay reveals a

vast acquaintance with a number of sources, particularly
historical, philosophico-theological and literary studies.
   It is not possible to classify Mackay's approach
narrowly, but at several points it comes close to a
kind of "psycho-historical" perspective, in Erikson's
terms /see, for instance, "On the Nature of Psycho-
Historical Evidence: In Search for Gandhi," B. Mazlich,
ed., Psychoanalysis and History (New York: Universal
Library, 1971) /. What is lacking in Mackay's contribution is an assessment of the Protestant missionary
movement in terms of its correlation with the neo-
colonialist expansion of Britain and the United States
/see J. Míguez Bonino, "The Recent Crisis in Missions,"
G. H. Anderson and T. F. Stransky, eds., Mission Trends,
1 (New York: Paulist Press, 1974), pp. 37-48 /. The
serious question there is that--in attenuated form, to
be sure--many Protestant agencies and programs repeated
the colonizers' pattern, from a "Christ-of-culture" in
the metropolis, to a "Christ-transformer-of culture" in
the so-called mission field /adapting freely H.R. Niebuhr's typology in Christ and Culture (New York:
Harper & Row, 1951), chapters 3 and 6 /.

   4. Mackay, The Other Spanish Christ, p. 124.

   5. Ibid., pp. 102, 63.

   6. Journal of American Folklore, 71 (1958) 34-39.
Wolf concludes that indeed there is a symbolic identi-
fication of the Virgin with life, hope and health, and
Christ with defeat, despair and death. Wolf also points
to the fact that in Hispanic artistic tradition in gen-
eral, Christ is never depicted as an adult man, but
either as a helpless child, or-- more often--as a figure
that is beaten, tortured, defeated and killed. Victor
Turner refers to the Virgin of Guadalupe in "Hidalgo:
History as Social Drama." Dramas, Fields and Metaphors,
Symbolic Action in Human Society (IThaca: Cornell
University Press, 1974).

   7. Mackay, The Other Spanish Christ, p. 98.

   8. Ibid., pp. 101-102.

   9. Ibid., p. 111.

   10. Curiously enough, Fromm-one of Freire's mentors
--reports that he adopted the use of this term (which

also appears in Freire's writings) from Miguel de Una-
muno who inspired Mackay. Erich Fromm, Anatomy of Human
Destructiveness (Greenwich, Conn.: Fawcett, 1973), p.
368.

11. Mackay, The Other Spanish Christ, chapter
VIII.

12. Wyckoff, The Gospel and Christian Education,
pp. 13-14.

13. Mackay, The Other Spanish Christ, p. 105.

14. Freire, "Cultural Freedom in Latin America,"
in Louis M. Colonesse, ed., Human Rights and the Liberation of Man in the Americas (Notre Dame: University
of Notre Dame Press, 1970), p. 169.

15. Memmi, The Colonizer and the Colonized. Cf.
Franz Fanon, The Wretched of the Earth.

16. For an excellent study of the history of the
church in Latin America, see Enrique Dussel, A History
of the church in Latin America: Colonialism and Liberation (1492-1979) (Grand Rapids: Eerdmans, 1981). A
team of historians, sociologists and theologians is
engaged currently in a thorough investigation of the
history of the church in different regions and countries,
under the auspices of CEHILA (Organization for the
Study of the History of the Church in Latin America),
which is ecumenical in nature.

17. Hubertus Halbfas, Theory of Catechetics (New
York: Herder and Herder, 1971).

18. Cecilio de Lora, "A Fuller Account of Catechetics in Latin America since Medellín (1968-1975),"
Lumen Vitae 30: 3-4 (1975) 357-374. After Vatican II
and the Medellín CELAM Conference, Roman Catholics have
been active in studying and implementing substantial
modifications in their approach to practical theology,
and education particularly.

19. See Alvaro Barreiro, Basic Ecclesial Communities: The Evangelization of the Poor (Maryknoll, N.Y.:
Orbis Books, 1982) and John Eagleson and Sergio Torres,
eds., The Challenge of Basic Christian Communities
(Maryknoll, N.Y.: Orbis Books, 1981).

20. Orlando Costas, "La Realidad de la Iglesia Latinoamericana," in C. René Padilla,ed., Fe Cristiana y
Latinoamérica Hoy (Buenos Aires: Certeza, 1974), pp.
65-66.

21. Gerson A. Meyer, "Patterns of Church Education
in the Third World," in Marvin J. Taylor, ed., Foundations for Christian Education in an Era of Change, pp.
231-233.
We could provide numerous specific examples of the
kind of problems identified by Meyer and others in general terms. Several students at the Seminario Evangélico de Puerto Rico, representing various denominations,
have recently analyzed diverse areas that present concrete challenges in this regard: goals and objectives,
programs and materials, methods and administration.
Their study was done in the context of a seminar on conscientization and a course in foundations and principles
of Christian education. It is interesting to notice the
similarity of this critique of Christian education in the
United States, as stated by John H. Westerhoff, for instance, in Will Our Children Have Faith? (New York:
Seabury Press, 1976), especially chapter 1. This similarity is to be accounted for in terms of the two following factors: the transplanting to Latin America and
subsequent reinforcement of the schooling-instructional
paradigm (Westerhoff's term), and the considerable commonality of foundation material between Westerhoff's
approach and our own.

22. Ibid., p. 235.

23. See Luis F. Reinoso, "Veinte años de CELADEC:
Un intento de fidelidad al Espíritu." Educación 8 (Julio
1982) 4-11, and CELADEC books included in our Bibliography.

24. Daniel S. Schipani, El Reino de Dios y el Mi-
ministerio Educativo de la Iglesia (Miami: Caribe,
1983).

25. It is not hereby suggested, however, that these
kinds of resources should be employed exclusively, not
even in Latin America. It is evident that our own approach is very much indebted to other sources, notably
the thought of James Loder (creativity and interdisciplinary studies), John H. Yoder (Anabaptist theology), and D. Campbell Wyckoff (Christian education
theory and practice). The following clarification is in
order.

Even if we recognize the need for Latin Americans to take some distance regarding North American and European influence in Practico-theological enterprises and training, we must also affirm the possibility of meaningful interaction and cooperation. Christian education is a special case in this regard. And this is so, first of all, because of the fact that any given culture can serve--and there is none that cannot serve--as an expression of God's Kingdom Gospel. On the other hand, all cultural contexts are subject to correction and improvement precisely in light of that Gospel. Therefore, a corollary of this is that we can benefit a great deal from mutual exposure in the context of a common understanding of the church as a worldwide fellowship. Elementary as this observation seems to be, it is also fundamental for any serious consideration of possibilities of partnership work with an ecumenical spirit. In fact one of the earliest ecumenical movements and actual cooperative endeavors has been associated with Christian education. In spite of different agendas and priorities, it is clear that the task of Christian education also presents basic common and similar challenges in terms of the educational needs and ministry of the church as such, on different levels and dimensions.

26. Wyckoff , The Gospel and Christian Education, pp. 75-76, 173.

27. Since we are adopting Wyckoff's general framework for understanding Christian education theory (see note number 50, Chapter 4), it is helpful to summarize the definitions and interconnections of key concepts that we have been utilizing: Theory is to serve as a body of principles acting as the connecting link between the foundation disciplines (theology, the church's life and work, philosophy and philosophy of education in particular, history and history of education, psychology and other behavioral sciences and their focus on the educational process, etc.) and the operational aspects of Christian education. In other words, a self-consciously constructed theory makes the bridge between foundational disciplines and the major educational questions.

The foundation disciplines are to inform the principles of Christian education, and those principles link together the two major concerns of Christian education theory: theology and the science of education. The foundation disciplines are the resources which provide clues and answers (as well as new questions) to the educational problems and questions that the theorist

propounds to them in the light of the categories which
directly refer to the focus of concern. The posing of
the questions in terms of theoretical categories (e.g.
objectives, process) is an essential procedure in the
building of Christian education theory because, from
them, dependable operating principles can be derived.
The principles (dependable guides to practice) constitute
the content of theory, to be drived from and appraised
in terms of the resources (information, experience,
ideas) stemming from the foundation disciplines. The
interrelation and interdependence of theory and practice
is thus consistently underscored. In our particular
case, that is on the basis of Freire's contribution,
this interdependence is to be perceived and realized as
a specific instance (i.e. methodologically speaking) of
the action-reflection dynamics and dialectics.

28. "What's New' Is the Wrong Question," unpublished
paper, Princeton Theological Seminary (Spring 1976), p.
10.

29. Margaret Webster, "Imperative for Religious
Education: The Integration of Theory and Practice."
Religious Education 77:2 (March-April 1982) pp. 126-128.

30. For alternative ways of discussing Christian
education theory, see Charles F. Melchert, "Theory in
Religous Education," in Marvin J. Taylor, ed., Foundations of Christian Education in an Era of Change, pages
20-29; compare with H. Edward Everding, "A Hermeneutical
Approach to Education Theory," Ibid., 41-53. In his
book An Invitation to Religious Education (Mishawaka,
Ind.: Religious Education Press, 1975), Harold W.
Burgess examines in detail four distinct approaches:
traditional theological, contemporary theological, socio-
cultural and social-science. The analysis of content of
alternative theories is presented in terms of a set of
six investigative categories (aim, content, teacher,
student, environment and evaluation).

31. The guiding principle fulfills a crucial per-
ception-facilitating and focusing function. As Loder
puts it: "The guiding priciple articulates, in a way
that is both theologically and behaviorally sound, the
nature of the essential reality with respect to which
all the various subdivisions and aspects of Christian
education are to be defined, directed and evaluated. As
we know, what questions one can ask and what actions one
can take depends greatly on how and what one can perceive. The guiding principle tells one in the field how

to perceive him/herself in relation to the fundamental
reality that is at stake." "Transformation in Christian
Education," Religious Education 76:2 (March-April 1981)
p. 216.

32. Our guiding principle emerged from the critical
and constructive theological reflections, and its biblico-
theological basis has been clearly established. In the
face of the previous discussion as well as the formulations leading to the principle of the Kingdom Gospel,
it could be said that our perspective leans in the direction of a "contemporary theological" approach, in
Burgess' typology (An Invitation to Religious Education,
chapter IV).

33. Among other things, this is particularly problematic in light of Jesus' reference to the children and
the Kingdom. For example, Mt. 18: 1-5 points to some
interesting "Kingdom principles":
    a. (the child as a metaphor for the disciple and a
vehicle of revelation) "unless you change and become like
children. . ." Could it be that conscientization has
something to do with the exposing and critique of our
own illusions of self-righteousness, sufficiency and
greatness? In this connection, Hans-Ruedi Weber rightly
states: ". . . a reversal in the teaching/learning
situation occurs, which indicates at the same time a
reversal of being: the first must be last; the least
one is great, the person who humbles him or herself like
a child is the greatest in the Kingdom of Heaven."
/Jesus and the Children, Biblical Resources for Study
and Preaching (Atlanta: John Knox Press, 1979), p. 43.7
This seems to point to one of the manifold surprises of
the "upside-down Kingdom."
    b. (the child as a special object of hospitable
acceptance, respect and loving care) "whoever receives
(or, welcomes) one such child in my name receives me."
This second principle may be related also to our concerns
in that it includes providing an adequate Christian education environment. By "adequate" here we mean one that
takes into account the child's total person and his/her
developmental agenda, in the context of family and society.
    The question for us at this point is how can the
Kingdom-focused Christian education--and especially
conscientization as creativity--relate to "pre-formal"
children (i.e. before the development of formal operational thinking, necessary for conscientization)? A
somewhat similar question has been addressed by C. Daniel
Batson in his essay "Creativity and Religious

Development: Toward a Structural-Functional Psychology of Religion." (Th.D. dissertation, Princeton Theological Seminary, 1971), pp. 305-316. Batson proposed a process-oriented education for creative Christian growth through imaginal thought. Religious education for pre-formal children is conceived of basically as preparation for eventual constructive handling of existential religious conflicts. The following emphases are suggested by Batson for such an education:

a. The child should be given experience in the supportive context of the church as an accepted, loved participant.

b. The child should have an opportunity to develop his abilities to interpret significant experiences in his life through imaginal thought and symbolization of these thoughts (e.g. by playing, and "make believe" play particularly).

c. "Along with the development of symbolic facility, the child should be allowed to deal with the conflictual material which comes out of his interactions with his family, peers, teachers, etc., and encouraged to express his interpretation of these events symbolically . . . the concern is to help the child develop pro-social means of expressing his reactions to and interpretations of significant encounters in his life" (p. 312).

d. The content of the educational process comes mainly from the learner, not the teacher. It is the children themselves who provide the subject matter, and pre-formal Christian education should be set in the context of a "responsive environment," where the child is able to receive feedback on whether his symbolizations communicate and what sort of response his behavior generates. See also Batson's article "Creative Religious Growth and Pre-Formal Religious Education," Religious Education 69:3 (May-June 1974): 302-315.

Thomas H. Groome, whose work has several points in common with our own, also argues convincingly that children are ready for his "shared praxis approach" from the age of seven or eight onward (i.e. the beginning of concrete operational thinking in Piaget's theory). In fact he contends that to begin at this "pre-formal" stage is necessary for children to be more likely to come at a later age to a personal, creative and mature Christian faith. Groome shows that children can engage in "critical reflection" for instance by attempting to comprehend the reasons and consequences of present action. Also, the "action" dimension of the educational process can be realized with specific concrete experiences that children have in close relationship with reflection, in a setting where effective collaboration and incipient dialogue are encouraged. Finally, the Christian Story and its Vision (the Kingdom of God) can be made present also to children within their lived experience, as a concrete encounter for them. See: <u>Christian Religious Education</u>, pp. 250 ff.

It is clear that the implementation of those principles necessitates skillful and committed educators whithin a Christian community which provides the required context for learning.

34. Westerhoff proposed a "community of faith-enculturation" pradigm in which the total life of a faith community becomes the natural context of education, and intentional religious socialization and means: "We need to stop thinking of 'school' or 'instruction' and center our educational concern on the church's rites and rituals, the formal and informal experiences persons have in community, the interactions between the generations, the church's environment, structure, organization and budget, the role models presented, the status assigned particular persons, and the actions witnessed and encouraged in a host of often unconscious ways . . . While this paradigm maintains a necessary particularity for education--deliberate, systematic and sustained efforts--and a place for schooling and instruction, it broadens church education to include, consciously and intentionally, as the primary context and means of education, every aspect of our individual and corporate lives within an intentional, convenanting, tradition-bearing faith community. Only as we rethink the radical nature of Christian community and reform our institutions so that they might faithfully strive to transmit their cumulative tradition through ritual and life, to nurture adn convert persons to Christian faith through commong experience and interaction, and to prepare and motivate persons for individual and corporate action in society can true Christian education emerge . . . To accomplish this end, we need to ask what it means to be Christian together and how it is that persons develop mature faith." /"Church Education for Tomorrow," <u>The Christian Century</u> (December 31, 1975), p. 1202.7

35. Our purpose in the following discussion is to refer, from a practical educational perspective, to the church's call to be a vanguard of God's Kingdom. However, we do not assume that actual churches can easily meet all of these criteria. Rather, here as well as in the next sections, we aim at providing a framework for the evaluation and enhancement of the educational

potential of the church in the face of that call and that vision. The challenge, then is to move further in that direction.

36. Romans 12:5, N.E.B.

37. I Corinthians 12:26.

38. Most of the criteria and principles discussed in this section 2 are recognized in different ways by creativity theorists in terms of conditions which foster the creative process. In our particular case, they are presented in the light of the foundations spelled out in the previous chapters.

39. Loder, "Negation and Transformation," p. 191.

40. Ibid., p. 190.

41. Romans 12:3 ff.; I Corinthians 12:14 ff.

42. C. Daniel Batson puts it well in terms of his focus on education for creative Christian growth: "Interaction with a broad social environment and the needs of that environment, is necessary 1) as a catalyst for the creative growth process, 2) as context for the natural expression for renewed involvement in one's expanding world, the result of a positive restructuring of perceptual-conceptual conflict, and 3) to provide feedback on the functional validity of one's new perception-conceptions. As one's conceptual structure in the religious domain increases in complexity, he is able to process more information in a more sensitive manner, and, if this growth is to be in the direction of increased ability to see and minister to the needs of those in one's world (as the Christian language system would seem to require), the Church should not only allow for but encourage this movement into the world." ("Creativity and Religious Development: Toward a Structural-Functional Psychology of Religion," pp. 302-303.)

43. "The notion of a smooth learning sequence, or growth without conflict is extremely dubious from the standpoint of any effort to induce and strengthen the creative process. Moreover, the teacher does not learn as he teaches if he will not engage the conflictual struggles which involve students; students will not learn if they refuse to accept their responsibility to teach each other and the teacher." /Loder, "The Medium

for the Message," in Colloquy of Christian Education, edited by John H. Westerhoff (Philadelphia: United Church Press, 1972), p. 77 7

44. Westerhoff, Will Our Children Have Faith?, pp. 41, 76.

45. James R. Schaefer, Program Planning for Adult Christian Education (New York: Newman, 1972) p. 83.

46. Cf. Thomas H. Groome, Christian Religious Education, pp. 57 ff.

47. Freire, Pedagogy of the Oppressed, pp. 77-81.

48. In order to avoid repetition in the description of the sequence, the reader is invited to review the discussion of conscientization as fostered creativity, in Chapter 2.

49. "The ultimate and decisive conflict is not 'my suffering," 'their suffering' or 'our suffering.' Rather, what is God doing in this world . . . to create a people who are truly human according to the humanity of Christ? That is the conflict to face and embrace with perseverance because in its many particular forms which always engage human suffering, that is the conflict that initiates transformation as Christ's living answer." Loder, "Transformation in Christian Education," p. 218.

50. See Millard C. Lind, Biblical Foundation for Christian Worship (Scottdale, Pa.: Herald Press, 1973).

51. In Groome's "shared praxis" approach, these dynamics are seen in terms of present dialectical hermeneutics, specifically as the fourth and fifth movements of the educational sequence: dialectical hermeneutic between the Christian Story and participants' stories, and dialectical hermeneutic between the Christian Vision and participants' visions. This last movement includes an opportunity for decision-making and choosing a faith response, in Groome's paradigm.
At this point we should indicate that, in spite of the considerable commonality of concerns, foundation material, and constructive propositions between Groome's work and our own, some differences also have to be pointed out. For one thing, Groome's treatment of Paulo Freire--to whom he is partially indebted--is one-sided in that he does not take into accout fundamental

contradictions on both epistemological and theological grounds. Secondly, our conception of the nature and mission of the church could be seen from a Catholic perspective such as Groome's as essentially "sectarian." One of our main concerns in this sense is that the church is to maintain its freedom and integrity and avoid becoming part of the power structure of society. In light of historical and theological perspectives concerning the place and the role of the church in Latin America--from the colonization period to Christian-sponsored revolutionary movements and liberation theology--this seems to be, indeed, a valid concern. Now, Groome does realize this kind of problem and in fact he condemns "the marriage of throne and altar" and related perversities of the church's nature and mission. However, he does not articulate his critique theologically, neither does he formulate an alternative theology of the church vis à vis the traditional Catholic doctrine on the matter.

52. As Bruce O. Boston put it: ". . . to take the reflexive aspects of liberation education seriously is to reflect upon, criticize, redirect, and transform the appearances of Christian faith until its rationale begins to appear. Each doctrine, each ethical precept, each teaching of Christ and/or the church, each bit of the tradition will be perceived differently . . . They will become problems to be solved rather than data to be banked. Once the rationale begins to appear, we will begin to pronounce ourselves in our own world and not simply echo the utterances of others . . . a reflective style in Christian education will mean the self-conscious recognition that our current educational practice is already a method of politicizing, socializing, and culture-building. Equipped with the tools of conscientization we can uncover our real concerns, whether or not they are being met, or whether what we do in Christian education is a way of side-stepping those concerns in the name of the gospel." "Conscientization and Christian Education," Learning for Living, 13:3 (January 1974): 100-105.

53. In his article "Paulo Freire and Other Unheard Voices," Religious Education 74:2 (September-October 1979): 543-554, Maurice L. Monette discusses the political and ethical assumptions of the need-assessment approach to program planning in adult education. On the basis of Freire's perspective, Monette argues convincingly against different ways of unilaterally prescribing the "needs" of others, and of merely catering to their wants or felt needs, thereby promoting an individualistic

ethic which fails to foster social awareness and responsibility. He concludes that an "education designed to
promote justice would administratively and programatically
be based on a listening process which would encourage a
critical analysis of needs both as perceived by the
educator and by the educatees. This process involves
discerning the educators' own assumptions and--in light
of such critical reflection--the construction of educational policy, not on the basis of prescriptive needs or
marketing demands, but on the basis of an informed analy-
is of (1) political and cultural forces to be fostered;
(2) assumptions concerning the type of persons to be
nurtured; (3) and assumptions concerning the desired
shape of the educational relationship." (p. 554).

54. Says Wyckoff : "When we seek an organizing
principle, we are seeking an answer to the question,
'What is the soundest possible basis upon which the
educational plan of the church may be put together?'"
("Understanding Your Church Curriculum," Princeton
Seminary Bulletin 63:1 (1970) p. 78. In the face of our
strongly church-focused biblico-theological foundations,
the very life and work on the community of believers
becomes the organizing principle. At the same time, we
can underscore an important relationship and a certain
tension between, on the one hand, the reality and utopian
eschatological vision of the Kingdom of God (and the
educational guiding principle inspired by the Kingdom
Gospel) and, on the other hand, the historical experience
of the church (and the curricular organizing principle
defined in terms of that actual experience). "If, then,
the organizing principle of the curriculum is the church's
experience, the heart of the matter is involvement, with
all our varied need and developing experience, in the
life and work of the worshipping and witnessing community in a cycle of orientation, action, and reflection."
(Ibid., p. 83.)

55. For further reading in connection with this
topic see: A. Roger Gobbel, "Christian Education with
Adolescents: An Invitation to Thinking." The Living
Light, 17:2 (1980) 134-143; Kieran Scott, "Youth Educa-
tion as Problematizing Political Forms." Religious
Education, 77:2 (March-April 1982) 197-210; Michael
Warren, "Youth Politicization: A Proposal for Education
Within Ministry." Religious Education, 77:2 (March-
April 1982) 179-196.

56. For example, Rubem Alves proposed that pastoral care must be politically understood, in his article "Personal Wholeness and Political Creativity: The Theology of Liberation and Pastoral Care." He underscores the determining influence of the actual institutional setting and the social function of pastoral care. Alves is very critical of every form of pastoral assistance--especially "consolation"--that fails to recognize the socio-political roots of human misery and oppression /Pastoral Psychology 26 (Winter 1977): 124-236/. It seems that those considerations could be further amplified--including suggested corrections in terms of conscientization--on the basis of Freire's approach. An attempt in this general direction is made by Charlotte Holt Clinebell in Counseling for Liberation (Philadelphia: Fortress Press, 1976) concerning consciousness raising and changing attitudes and roles related to sex. A specific study of Freire's relevance in this regard is Janet Perry Bailey's "Consciousness Raising Groups for Women: Implications of Paulo Freire's Theory of Critical Consciousness for Psychology and Education (Ed. D. dissertation, University of Massachusetts, 1977).

BIBLIOGRAPHY

Alas, Higinio, y Cabrera, Sergio. Auto-educación Comu-
nitaria de Adultos. Proceso de Conscientización y
Alfabetización. Buenos Aires: Búsqueda, 1976.

Alonso, Antonio. Iglesia y Praxis de Liberación. Salamanca: Sígueme, 1974.

Althusser, Louis. For Marx. New York: Random House,
1969.

Alves, Rubem A. A Theology of Human Hope. St. Meinard,
Ind.: Abbey Press, 1969.

_____. Tomorrow's Child. New York: Harper & Row,
1972.

_____ y otros. De la Iglesia y la Sociedad. Montevideo: Tierra Nueva, 1971.

Anderson, Gerald H., and Stransky, Thomas F., eds. Mission Trends No. 3--Third World Theologies. New
York: Paulist Press/Grand Rapids: Eerdmans, 1976.

_____. Mission Trends No. 4--Liberation Theologies.
New York: Paulist Press/Grand Rapids: Eerdmans,
1979.

Anshen, Ruth N., ed. Language: An Enquiry into its
Meaning and Function. New York: Harper, 1967.

Arias, Esther and Mortimer. The Cry of My People. Out
of Captivity in Latin America. New York: Friendship Press, 1980.

Arieti, Silvano. Creativity: The Magic Synthesis. New
York: Basic Books, 1976.

Armerding, Carl E., ed. Evangelicals and Liberation.
Nutley, N.J.: Presbyterian and Reformed Publishing
co., 1977.

Assmann, Hugo. Teología desde la Praxis de la Liberación. Salamanca: Sígueme, 1973.

205

Bailey, Janet Perry. "Consciousness Raising Groups for Women: Implications of Paulo Freire's Theory of Critical consciousness for Psychology and Education." Ed.D. dissertation, University of Massachusetts, 1977.

Barker, Kenneth. Religious Education, Catechesis and Freedom. Birmingham: Religious Education Press, 1981.

Barndt, Deborah J. "People Connecting with Structures: A Photographic and Contextual Exploration of the Conscientization Process in a Peruvian Literacy Program." Ph.D. dissertation, Michigan State University, 1978.

Barreiro, Alvaro. Basic Ecclesial Communities - The Evangelization of the Poor. Maryknoll, N.Y.: Orbis, 1982.

Barreiro, Julio. Educación Popular y Proceso de Concientización. Buenos Aires: Siglo Veintinuo, 1974.

Barron, Frank. Creative Person and Creative Process. New York: Holt, Reinhart and Winston, 1969.

_____. Creativity and Personal Freedom. Princeton: Van Nostrand, 1968.

Barros, Raimundo C. La Educación ¿Utilitaria o Liberadora? Madrid: Editorial Marsiega, 1974.

Batson, C. Daniel. "Creative Religious Growth and Pre-Formal Religious Education." Religious Education 69:3 (May-June 1974): 302-315.

_____. "Creativity and Religious Development. Toward a Structural Functional Psychology of Religion." Th.D. dissertation, Princeton Theological Seminary, 1971.

_____. "How far does one Teach the Truth which Admits of Being Learned? Toward a Model of Education for Creative Growth." Religious Education 66:3 (May-June 1971): 180-191.

_____, Beker, J. Christiaan, and Clark, W. Malcolm. Commitment Without Ideology. Philadelphia: United Church Press, 1973.

Baum, Gregory. Religion and Alienation. New York: Paulist Press, 1975.

Bender, Harold S. These Are My People, Scottdale, Pa.: Herald Press, 1962.

Bender, Ross T. The People of God. Scottdale, Pa.: Herad Press, 1971.

Berger, Peter L. Pyramids of Sacrifice. Garden City, N.Y.: Doubleday, 1976.

_____. "The False Consciousness of Consciousness Raising." Worldview, January 1975, pp. 33-38.

_____ and Luckmann, Thomas. The Social Construction of Reality. Garden City, N.Y.: Doubleday, 1966.

Berkhof, Hendrik. Christ and The Powers. Scottdale, Pa.: Herald Press, 1977.

Bloch, Ernst. Man on His Own. New York: Herder and Herder, 1970.

Bochair, Ernestine B. "Toward a Theory of Adult Education: An Elaboration of Certain Concepts from the Works of Paulo Freire and Selected Adult Educators." Ed.D. dissertation, Florida State University, 1976.

Boff, Clodovis. Comunidades Eclesiales de Base y Prácticas de Liberación. Bogotá: Indo-American Press Service, 1981.

Boff, Leonardo. Jesus Christ Liberator. A Critical Christology for Our Time. Maryknoll, N.Y.: Orbis Books, 1978.

_____. Way of the Cross-way of Justice. Maryknoll, N.Y.: Orbis Books, 1978.

Boston, Bruce O. "Conscientization and Christian Education". Learning for Living 13:3 (January 1974):

_____. "Paulo Freire-Notes of a Loving Critic." In Paulo Freire: A Revolutionary Dilemma for the Adult Educator. Edited by Stanley Grabowski. Publications in Continuing Education and ERIC Clearinghouse on Adult Education. Syracuse University, 1972.

Bosco Pinto, Joao. Educación Liberadora. Dimensión Metodológica. Bogota: Asociación de Publicaciones Educativas, 1973.

Bottomore, T.B., ed. Karl Marx, Early Writings. New York: McGraw-Hill, 1964.

Breneman, J. Mervin, ed. Liberación, Exodo y Biblia. Miami: Caribe, 1975.

Bright, John. The Kingdom of God. Nashville: Abingdon Press, 1953.

Brown, Robert McAfee. Theology in a New Key. Philadelphia: Westminster, 1978.

Brueggeman, Walter. Living Toward a Vision: Biblical Reflections on Shalom. 2nd ed. Philadelphia: United Church Press, 1982.

Bruner, Jerome. On Knowing. New York: Atheneum, 1976.

_____. The Process of Education. Cambridge: Harvard University Press, 1960.

_____. The Relevance of Education. New York: Norton, 1973.

Brusselmans, Christiane, Convenor. Toward Moral and Religious Maturity: The First International Conference on Moral and Religious Development. Morristown: Silver Burdett, 1980.

Buber, Martin. Between Man and Man. New York: Macmillan, 1965.

_____. I and Thou. New York: Charles Scriber's Sons, 1970.

Bugbee, John A. "On the Quality of the Moral Partisanship of the Pedagogy of Paulo Freire." Ph.D. dissertation, Indiana University, 1973.

Burgess, Harold W. An Invitation to Religious Education. Mishawaka, Indiana:Religious Education Press, 1975.

Burkholder, John R., and Redekop, Calvin, eds. Kingdom, Cross and Community. Scottdale, Pa.: Herald Press, 1976.

Calderón Manrique, Jaime. La Teología de la Liberación y el Educador Cristiano. Bogotá: Indo-American Press Service, 1980.

Chomsky, Noam. Cartesian Linguistics. New York: Harper and Row, 1966.

CELADEC. Educación Cristiana - Educación Popular. Lima: CELADEC, 1982.

_____. Realidad Latinoamericana y Alternativa Pedagógica. Lima: CELADEC, 1981.

Clasby, Miriam. "Education as a Tool for Humanization and the Work of Paulo Freire." Living Light 8:1 (Spring 1971): 48-59.

Collins, Colin B. "The Ideas of Paulo Freire and an Analysis of Black Consciousness in South Africa." Ph.D. dissertation, University of Toronto, 1974.

Collins, Denis E. Paulo Freire: His Life, Works and Thought. New York: Paulist Press, 1977.

_____. "Two Utopians: A Comparison and Contrast of the Educational Philosophies of Paulo Freire and Theodore Brameld." Ed.D. dissertation, University of Southern California School of Education, 1973.

Colonnese, Louis M., ed. Conscientization for Liberation. Washington, D.C.: Division for Latin America, United States Catholic Conference, 1971.

_____, ed. Human Rights and the Liberation of Man in the Americas. Notre Dame: University of Notre Dame Press 1970.

Confederación Interamericana de Educación Católica. Metodología de una Educación en y para la Justicia. Bogotá: Indo-American Press Service, 1980.

Conteris, Hiber, y otros. Conciencia y Revolución. Montevideo: Tierra Nueva, 1970.

Costas, Orlando E. Christ Outside the Gate. Mission Beyond Christendom. Maryknoll, N.Y.: Orbis, 1982.

_____. The Church and Its Mission: A Shattering Critique from the Third World. Wheaton, Ill.: Tyndale, 1974.

Craig, Gillian M. "The Development of a Freire-Based Literacy/Conscientization Program for Low Literate Women in Prison." Ph.D. dissertation, Pennsylvania State University, 1981.

Crawford, Linda M. "Paulo Freire's Philosophy: Derivation of Curricular Principles and their Application to Second Language Curriculum Design." Ph.D. dissertation, University of Minnesota, 1978.

Crites, Stephen. "The Narrative Quality of Experience." Journal of the American Academy of Religion 39 (September 1971): 291-311.

Croatto, Severino. Exodus. A Hermeneutic of Freedom. Maryknoll: Orbis, 1981.

Dawson, Jay P. "The Intersection of Paulo Freire and C.G. Jung: A Paradigm for Education." Ed.D. dissertation, Columbia University Teachers College, 1979.

de Kadt, E. Catholic Radicals in Brazil. London: Oxford University Press, 1970.

de Lora, Cecilio. "A Fuller Account of Catechetics in Latin America since Medellín (1968-1975)." Lumen Vitae 30:3-4 (1975): 357-374.

Dewey, John. Democracy and Education. Compiled by Martin S. Dworkin. Classics in Education, No. 3. New York: Teachers College Press, 1971.

_____. Dewey on Education. Compiled by Martin S. Dworkin. Classics in Education, No. 3. New York: Teachers College Press, 1971.

_____. Experience and Education. New York: Collier Books, 1938.

De Witt, John J. "An Exposition and Analysis of Paulo Freire's Radical Psycho-Social Andragogy of Development." Ed.D. dissertation, Boston University School of Education, 1971.

Diálogo Paulo Freire-Iván Illich. Buenos Aires: Búsqueda, 1975.

Driver, John. Community and Commitment. Scottdale , Pa: Herald Press, 1976.

Driver, John. Kingdom Citizens. Scottdale, Pa.:
    Herald Press, 1980.

Durnbaugh, Donald F. The Believers' Church. New
    York: Macmillan, 1968.

Dussel, Enrique D. A History of the Church in Latin
    America: Colonialism and Liberation (1492-1979).
    Grand Rapids: Eerdmans, 1981.

_____. "Historical and Philosophical Presuppositions
    for Latin American Theology." In Frontiers of
    Theology in Latin America. Edited by Rosino Gi-
    bellini. Maryknoll, N.Y.: Orbis Books, 1979.

_____. History and the Theology of Liberation.
    Marynoll, N.Y.: Orbis Books, 1976.

_____. Método para una Filosofía de la Liberación.
    Salamanca: Sígueme, 1974.

_____. Teología de la Liberación y Etica. Buenos
    Aires: Latinoamérica Libros, 1974.

Elias, John L. Conscientization and Deschooling.
    Philadelphia: Westminster, 1976.

_____. "Paulo Freire: Religious Educator." Reli-
    gious Education 71:1 (January-February 1976):
    40-56.

Ellul, Jacques. Violence. Reflections from a Christian
    Perspective. New York: Seabury Press, 1969.

Erikson, Erik H. Chilhood and Society. New York:
    Norton, 1963.

_____. Identity and the Life Cycle. New York:
    Norton, 1980.

_____. The Life Cycle Completed. New York:
    Norton, 1982.

Escobar, Samuel. "El Reino de Dios, la Escatología y la
    Etica Social y Política en América Latina." In El
    Reino de Dios y América Latina. Edited by C. René
    Padilla. El Paso, Tex.: Casa Bautista de Publica-
    ciones, 1975.

_____ and Driver, John. Christian Mission and Social
    Justice. Scottdale, Pa.: Herald Press, 1978.

Everding, H. Edward, Jr. "A Hermeneutical Approach to Educational Theory." In Foundations for Christian Education in an Era of Change. Edited by Marvin J. Taylor. Nashville: Abingdon, 1976.

Ewert, David M. "Freire's Concept of Critical Consciousness and Social Structure in Rural Zaire." Ph.D. dissertation. University of Wisconsin, 1977.

Fanon, Franz, The Wretched of the Earth. New York: Grove Press, 1968.

Fenton, Thomas P., ed. Education for Justice. A Resource Manual. Maryknoll, N.Y.: Orbis, 1975.

Fessard, Gaston. "The Theological Structure of Marxist Atheism," In Concilium 16 (New York: Paulist Press, 1966).

Fisher, John S. "Political Education: The Views of Michael Oakershott and Paulo Freire." Ph.D. dissertation, Claremont Graduate School, 1980.

Fowler, James W. "Faith Development Theory and the Aims of Religious Socialization." In Emerging Issues in Religious Education. Edited by Gloria Durka and Joanmarie Smith. New York: Paulist Press, 1976.

_____. Stages of Faith: The Psychology of Human Development and the Quest for Meaning. San Francisco: Harper & Row, 1981.

_____. "Stage Six and the Kingdom of God." Religious Education, 75:3 (May-June 1980): 231-248.

Franco, Fausto. El Hombre: Construcción Progresiva. La Tarea Educativa de Paulo Freire. Madrid: Editorial Marsiega, 1973.

Freire, Paulo. "Carta a un Joven Teólogo." Fichas Latinoamericanas 1 (Diciembre 1974): 52, 53.

_____. "Conscientizar para Liberar." Contacto 8:1 (1971): 43-51.

_____. Conscientización. Buenos Aires: Búsqueda, 1974.

Freire, Paulo. "Conscientization." Cross Currents 24:1 (Spring 1974): 23-31.

_____. Cultural Action for Freedom. Cambridge, Mass.: Harvard Educational Review, 1970.

_____. "Cultural Freedom in Latin america." In Human Rights and the Liberation of Man in the Americas. Edited by Louis M. Colonnese. Notre Dame: University of Notre Dame Press, 1970.

_____. "Desmitificación de la Conscientización." Mensajero, Enero 1973, pp. 34-40.

_____. "Education as Cultural Action." In Conscientization for Liberation. Edited by Louis M. Colonnese. Washington, D.C.: Division for Latin America, United States Catholic Conference, 1971.

_____. "Education for Awareness: A Talk with Paulo Freire." Risk, 6:4 (1970): 7-19.

_____. Education for Critical Consciousness. New York: Seabury Press, 1973.

_____. "Education, Liberation, and the Church." Risk, 9:1 (1973): 34-38.

_____. Educación y Cambio. Buenos Aires: Búsqueda, 1976.

_____. El Mensaje de Paulo Freire. Teoría y Práctica de la Liberación. Madrid: Marsiega, 1976.

_____. La Educación como Práctica de la Libertad. Montevideo: Tierra Nueva, 1972.

_____. Las Iglesias, La Educación y El Proceso de Liberación Humana en la Historia. Buenos Aires: La Aurora, 1974.

_____. Pedagogy in Process. New York: Seabury Press, 1978.

_____. Pedagogy of the Oppressed. New York: Seabury Press, 1970.

_____. "Tercer Mundo y Teología." Fichas Latinoamericanas I (Diciembre 1974): 54, 55.

Freire, Paulo y otros. _Educación para el Cambio Social_. Buenos Aires: Tierra Nueva, 1974.

Freud, Sigmund. _Creativity and the Unconscious. Papers on the Psychology of Art, Literature, Love, Religion_. New York: Harper & Row, 1974.

Friedmann, Robert. _The Theology of Anabaptism_. Scottdale, Pa.: Herald Press, 1973.

Fromm, Erich. _Anatomy of Human Destructiveness_. Greenwich, Conn.: Fawcett, 1973.

_____. _Beyond the Chains of Illusion. My Encounter with Marx and Freud_. New York: Simon and Schuster, 1962.

_____. _Escape from Freedom_. New York: Holt, Rinehart & Winston, 1941.

_____. _Marx's Concept of Man_. New York: Frederick Ungar Publishing Co., 1966.

_____. _On Disobedience and Other Essays._ New York: Seabury, 1981.

_____. _The Heart of Man_. New York: Harper & Row, 1964.

_____. _The Sane Society_. New York: Holt, Rinehart & Winston, 1955.

Furter, Pierre. _Educación y Reflexión_. Buenos Aires: Shapire/Tierra Nueva, 1974.

_____ y Fiori, Ernani. _Educación Liberadora, Dimensión Política_. Bogotá: Asociación de Publicaciones Educativas, 1973.

Gardner, Howard. _The Quest for Mind-Piaget, Lévi-Strauss and the Structuralist Movement_. New York: Random House, 1972.

Garret, James L., ed. _The Concept of the Believers' Church_. Scottdale, Pa.: Herald Press, 1968.

Gibellini, Rosino. _Frontiers of Theology in Latin America_. Maryknoll, N.Y.: Orbis Books, 1979.

Gobbel, A. Roger. "Christian Education with Adolescents: An Invitation to Thinking." The Living Light 17:2 (1980): 134-143.

Goldman, Ronald S. "An Interpretation of Paulo Freire's Theory of Education." Ed.D. dissertation, University of Massachusetts, 1978.

Goldman, Lucien. The Human Science and Philosophy. London: Jonathan Cape, 1969.

González, Justo L. Revolución y Encarnación. Río Piedras, Puerto Rico: Librería La Reforma, 1967.

Gottwald, Norman K., ed. The Bible and Liberation. Political and Social Hermeneutics. Maryknoll, N.Y.: Orbis, 1983.

Goulet, Denis. A New Moral Order. Development Ethics and Liberation Theology. Maryknoll, N.Y.: Orbis Books, 1974.

Grabowski, Stanley M., ed. Paulo Freire: A Revolutionary Dilemma for the Adult Educator. Publications in Continuing Education and ERIC Clearinghouse on Adult Education. Syracuse University, 1972.

Gray, John. The Biblical Doctrine of the Reign of God. Edinburgh: T. & T. Clark, 1979.

Griffith, William S. "Paulo Freire. Utopian Perspectice on Literacy Education for Revolution." In Paulo Freire: A Revolutionary Dilemma for the Adult Educator. Edited by Stanley M. Grabowski. Syracuse: Syracuse Univesity, 1972.

Groome, Thomas H. Christian Religious Education. Sharing Our Story and Vision. New York: Harper & Row, 1980.

_____. ""Conversion, Nurture and Educators." Religious Education 76:5 (September-October, 1981): 482-496.

Guevara, Ernesto. Obra Revolucionaria. México: Ediciones ERA, 1967.

Gutiérrez, Gustavo. A Theology of Liberation. Maryknoll, N.Y.: Orbis Books, 1973.

Gutiérrez, Gustavo. "A Latin American Perception of a Theology of Revolution." In Conscientization for Liberation. Edited by Louis M. Colonnese. Washington, D.C.: United States Catholic Conference, 1971.

_____. "Liberation Praxis and Christian Faith." In Frontiers of Theology in Latin America. Edited by Rosino Gibellini. Maryknoll, N.Y.: Orbis Books, 1979.

_____. The Power of the Poor in History. Maryknoll, N.Y.: Orbis, 1983.

_____ and Shaull, Richard. Liberation and Change. Atlanta: John Knox Press, 1977.

Habermas, Jurgen. Knowledge and Human Interest. Boston: Beacon Press, 1973.

_____. Theory and Practice. Boston: Beacon Press, 1973.

Halbfas, Hubertus. Theory of Catechetics. New York: Herder and Herder, 1971.

Harkness, Georgia. Understanding the Kingdom of God. Nashville, Tenn.: Abingdon Press, 1974.

Harmon, Maryellen C. "Paulo Freire: Implications for a Theory of Pedagogy." Ed.D. dissertation, University of Massachusetts, 1975.

Harter, Terry. "A Critique of North-American Protestant Theological Education form the Perspective of Ivan Illich and Paulo Freire." Ph.D. dissertation. Boston University Graduate School, 1980.

Hegel, G.W.F. Phenomonology of Mind. New York: Harper & Row, 1967.

Heiss, Robert. Hegel, Kierkegaard, Marx. New York: Dell Publishing Co., 1975.

Hershberger, Guy F., ed. The Recovery of the Anabaptist Vision. Scottdale, Pa.: Herald Press, 1957.

Hiers, Richard M. The Kingdom of God in the Synoptic Tradition. Gainsville: University of Florida Press, 1970.

Horning, Warren G. "Paulo Freire's Contribution to the Theological Education of Protestant Laity in Chile." D. Min. dissertation, School of Theology at Claremont, 1974.

Hunter, Archibald M. Christ and the Kingdom. Edinburgh: Saint Andrew Press, 1980.

Husserl, Edmund. Ideas: General Introduction to Pure Phenomenology. New York: Macmillan, 1931.

_____. The Idea of Phenomenology. The Hague: M. Nijhoff, 1964.

Illich, Ivan. "Crítica a la Liturgía de la Enseñanza." En Paulo Freire y otros. Educación para el Cambio Social. Buenos Aires: Tierra Nueva, 1974.

_____. En América Latina ¿Para qué Sirve la Escuela? Buenos Aires; Búsqueda, 1974.

Inhelder, Barbel, and Piaget, Jean. The Growth of Logical Thinking from Childhood to Adolescence. New York: Basic Books, 1958.

Instituto Fe y Secularidad. Fe Cristiana y Cambio Social en América Latina. Salamanca: Sígueme, 1973.

Jakobson, Roman. "The Cardinal Dichotomy in Language." In Language: An Enquiry into its Meaning and Function. Edited by Ruth N. Anshen. New York: Harper, 1957.

Jorge, J. Simoes. A Ideología de Paulo Freire: Sao Paulo: Loyola, 1979.

_____. Sem Odio Nem Violencia. A Perspectiva da Libertaçao segundo Paulo Freire. Sao Paulo: Loyola, 1979.

Kagan, Jerome, ed. Creativity and Learning. Boston: Beacon Press, 1967.

Kane, Michael. "An Interpretation of Humanism in the Thought of Paulo Freire." Ed.D. dissertation, George Peabody College for Teachers, Vanderbilt University, 1980.

Kauffmann, Walter. Hegel: A Re-interpretation. Garden City. N.Y.: Doubleday & Co., 1965.

Kennedy, William B. "Education for Liberation and Community." Religious Education 70:1 (January-February, 1975): 5-44.

Kierkegaard, Soren. Attack Upon "Christendom" 1854-55. Princeton, N.J.: Princeton University Press, 1944.

_____. Philosophical Fragments, 2nd ed. Princeton, N.J.: Princeton University Press, 1962.

_____. Training in Christianity. Princeton, N.J.: Princeton University Press, 1941.

Kirk, Andrés. Jesucristo Revolucionario. Buenos Aires: La Aurora, 1974.

_____ y otros. Hombre Marxista y Hombre Cristiano. Barcelona: Ediciones Evangélicas Europeas, 1977.

Kirk, J. Andrew. Liberation Theology: An Evangelical View from the Third World. Richmond: John Knox, 1979.

_____. Theology Encounters Revolution. Downers Grove: Inter Varsity Press, 1980.

Klaassen, Walter, ed. Anabaptism in Outline. Selected Primary Sources. Scottdale, Pa.: Herald Press, 1981.

Klinger, Eric. Structure and Function of Fantasy. New York: Wily-Inter-Science, 1971.

Koestler, Arthur. The Act of Creation, A Study of the Conscious and Unconscious in Science and Art. New York: Macmillan, 1964.

Kolakowski, Leszek. Towards a Marxist Humanism. New York: Grove Press, 1968.

Kraus, C. Norman. The Authentic Witness. Grand Rapids, Mich.: Eerdmans, 1979.

_____. The Community of the Spirit. Grand Rapids, Mich.: Eerdmans, 1976.

_____, ed. Evangelicalism and Anabaptism. Scottdale, Pa.: Herald Press, 1979.

Kraybill, Donald B. The Upside-Down Kingdom. Scottdale, Pa.: Herald Press, 1978.

Kubie, Lawrence S. Neurotic Distorsion of the Creative
Process. New York: Ferrar, Staus & Giroux, 1961.

Ladd, George E. Jesus and the Kingdom. New York:
Harper & Row, 1964.

_____. The Gospel of the Kingdom. Grand Rapids,
Mich.: Eerdmans, 1959.

Leaver, V. Wayne. "Preparing a Local Church for Social
Action. An Adaptation of Paulo Freire." Ph.D.
dissertation, Wesley Theological Seminary, 1974.

Lederach, Paul M. Reshaping the Teaching Ministry.
Scottdale, Pa.: Herald Press, 1968.

_____. Teaching in the Congregation. Scottdale,Pa.:
Herald Press, 1979.

Lefebre, Henri. The Sociology of Marx. New York:
Random House, 1968.

Lévi-Strauss, Claude. Structural Anthropology. New
York: Basic Books, 1963.

Libanio, J.B. Formación de la Conciencia Crítica 2.
Aportes Socio-Analíticos. Bogota: CLAR, 1980.

_____y Monnerat Celes, L.A. Formación de la Concien-
cia Crítica 3. Aportes Psico-Pedagógicos. Bogota:
CLAR, 1980.

Lischer, Richard. Marx and Teilhard. Two Ways to the
Humanity. Maryknoll, N.Y.: Orbis, 1979.

Little, Sara. "Theology and Religious Education." In
Foundations for Christian Education in an Era of
Change. Edited by Marvin J. Taylor. Nashville:
Abingdon, 1976.

Loder, James E. "Creativity in and Beyond Human Development." In Aesthetic Dimensions of Religious Education. Edited by G. Durka and J. Smith. New York:
Paulist Press, 1979.

Loder, James E. "Developmental Foundations for Christian Education." In Foundations for Christian Education in an Era of Change. Edited by Marvin J. Taylor. Nashville: Abingdon, 1976.

_____. "Negation and Transformation. A Study in Theology and Human Development." In Towards Moral and Religious Maturity. The First International Conference on Moral and Religious Development. Morristown, N.J.: Silver Burdett Co., 1980.

_____. Religious Pathology and Christian Faith. Philadelphia: Westminster Press, 1966.

_____. "The Medium for the Message." In A Colloquy on Christian Education. Edited by John W. Westerhoff, III. Philadelphia: United Church Press, 1972.

_____. The Transforming Moment. New York: Harper & Row, 1981.

_____. "Transformation in Christian Education." Religious Education 76:2 (March-April 1981): 204-221.

Londoño, Alejandro. Colegios para el Cambio. Bogotá: Indo-American Press Service, 1977.

_____. Dinámica de la Concientización. Bogotá: Ediciones Paulinas, 1975.

Lonergan, Bernard J.F. Insight. A Study of Human Understanding. New York: Philosophical Library, 1970.

Lundstrom, Gosta. The Kingdom of God in the Preaching of Jesus. Richmond: John Knox, 1963.

McCann, Dennis P. Christian Realism and Liberation Theology. Practical Theologies in Creative Conflict. Maryknoll, N.Y.: Orbis, 1981.

McFadden, John P. "Consciousness and Social Change: The Pedagogy of Paulo Freire." Ph.D. dissertation, University of California at Santa Cruz, 1975.

McGovern, Arthur F. Marxism: An American Christian Perspective. Maryknoll, N.Y.: Orbis Books, 1980.

Mackay, John A. The Other Spanish Christ. A Study of the Spiritual History of Spain and South America. New York: Macmillan, 1932.

McNeil, Jesse J. "A Critical Analysis of Planning for Social Change: A Freirean Perspective Toward the Building of Planning Competence." Ed.D. dissertation, University of Massachusetts, 1975.

Mahan, Brian, and Richesin, L. dale, eds. The Challenge of Liberation Theology. A First World Response. Maryknoll, N.Y.: Orbis, 1981.

Mannheim, Karl. Idiology and Utopia. New York: Harcourt, Brace & World, 1936.

Maranda, Elli K. and Maranda, Pierre. Structural Models in Folklore and Transformational Essays. The Hague: Mouton, 1971.

Marcel, Gabriel. Man Against Mass Society. Chicago: Gateway, 1962.

Marcuse, Herbert. An Essay on Liberation. Boston: Beacon Press, 1969.

_____. One Dimensional Man. Boston: Beacon Press, 1964.

Marsh, William Harry. "An Evaluative Study of the Philosophical Justification of Paulo Freire's Dialogic Pedagogy and its Potential for Use in Formal Schooling ." Ed.D. dissertation, Memphis State University, 1978.

Marx, Karl. A Contribution to the Critique of Political Economy. Edited by M. Dobb. Translated by S.W. Ryazanskaya. New York: International Publishers, 1970.

_____. Capital. Edited by Frederich Engels. Translated by Samuel Moore and Edward Aveling. New York International Publishers, 1967.

_____. Economics and Philosophic Manuscripts of 1844. Translated by Martin Milligan. Moscow: Foreign Languages Publishing House, 1961.

_____. "Theses on Feuerbach." In The German Ideology. New York: International Publishers, 1947.

Marx, Karl and Engels, Friedrich. Marx and Engels on Religion. Introduction by Reinhold Niebuhr. New York: Schoken Books, 1964.

Matussek. Paul. La Creatividad, Desde una Perspectiva Psicodinámica. Barcelona: Herder, 1977.

May, Rollo. Freedom and Destiny. New York: Norton, 1980.

_____. Power and Innocence. A Search for the Sources of Violence. New York: Norton, 1972.

_____. The Courage to Create. New York: Norton, 1975.

Melchert, Charles F. "Theory in Religious Education." In Foundations for Christian Education in an Era of Change. Edited by Marvin J. Taylor. Nashville: Abingdon, 1976.

Memmi, Albert. Portrait of the Colonizar and the Colonized. New York: Orion Press, 1965.

Metz, René y Schlick, Jean, eds. Ideologías de Liberación y Mensaje de Salvación. Salamanca: Sígueme, 1975.

Metzler, James A. "Shalom Is the Mission." In Mission and the Peace Witness. Edited by Robert L. Ramseyer. Scottdale, Pa.: Herald Press, 1979.

Meyer, Alfred G. Marxism. The Unity of Theory and Practice. Ann Arbor, Mich.: The University of Michigan Press, 1963.

Meyer, Gérson A. "Patterns of Church Education in the Third World." In Foundations for Christian Education in an Era of Change. Edited by Marvin J. Taylor. Nashville: Abingdon, 1976.

Migliore, Daniel L. Called to Freedom. Liberation Theology and the Future of Christian Doctrine. Philadelphia: Westminster, 1980.

Míguez Bonino, José. Christians and Marxists. Grand Rapids, Mich.: Eerdmans, 1976.

_____. Doing Theology in a Revolutionary Situation. Philadelphia: Fortress Press, 1975.

Míguez Bonino, José. "El Reino de Dios y la Historia."
In El Reino de Dios y América Latina. Edited by
C. René Padilla. El Paso, Tex.: Casa Bautista de
Publicaciones, 1975.

_____y otros. Jesús: Ni Vencido ni Monarca Celestial.
Buenos Aires: Tierra Nueva, 1977.

Miller, Marlin E. "The Gospel of Peace." In Mission
and the Peace Witness. Edited by Robert L. Ramseyer. Scottdale, Pa.: Herald Press, 1979.

Miller, Randolph C. The Theory of Christian Education
Practice. Birmingham: Religious Education Press,
1981.

Miranda, José P. Marx Against The Marxists. Maryknoll,
N.Y.: Orbis Books, 1980.

_____. Marx and the Bible. Maryknoll, N.Y.: Orbis
Books, 1974.

Moltmann, Jurgen. "Open Letter to José Míguez Bonino."
Christianity and Crisis, 29 March 1976, pp. 57-63.

_____. The Crucified God. New York: Paulist Press,
1977.

Monette, Maurice. "Paulo Freire and Other Unheard
Voices." Religious Education 74:5 (September-
October 1979): 543-554.

Moore, Barry D. "Two Approaches to Educational Planning:
Freire and Worth." Ph.D. dissertation, University
of Alberta, 1973.

Morris, Van Cleve and Pai, Young. Philosophy and the
American School. An Introduction to the Philosophy
of Education. Boston: Houghton Mifflin Co., 1976.

Mounier, Emmanuel. Manifiesto al Servicio del Personalismo. Personalismo y Cristianismo. Madrid: Taurus, 1972.

Moustakas, Clark. Creativity and Conformity. New York:
Van Nostrand, 1967.

_____. Creative Life. New York: Van Nostrand, 1977.

Nevin, Hugh G., Jr. "Values Clarification: Perspectives in John Dewey and Paulo Freire." Ed.D. dissertation, Columbia University Teachers College, 1977.

Nichols, J. Randall. "Conflict and Creativity: The Dynamics of the Communication Process in Theological Perspective." Th.D. dissertation, Princeton Theological Seminarym 1970.

Niebuhr, H. Richard. Christ and Culture. New York: Harper and Brothers, 1951.

Niebuhr, Reinhold. Moral Man and Inmoral society. New York: Scribners, 1932.

Novack, George. Pragmatism versus Marxism. An Appraisal of John Dewey's Philosophy. New York: Pathfinders Press, 1975.

Novaes, María H. Psicología de la Aptitud Creadora. Buenos Aires: Kapelusz, 1973.

O'Donnell, James G. "Education as Awakening." Religious Education 76:5 (September-October 1981): 517-524.

Oglesby, Carl and Shaull, Richard. Containment and Change. New York: Macmillan, 1967.

Ollman, Bertell, Alienation. Marx's Concept of Man in Capitalist Society. Cambridge, Mass.: University Press, 1975.

Padilla, C. René. "El Reino de Dios y la Iglesia." In El reino de Dios y América Latina. Edited by C. René Padilla. El Paso, Tex.: Casa Bautista de Publicaciones, 1975.

_____. "The Kingdom of God and the Church." Theological Franternity Bulletin, 1:2 (1976): 1-24.

_____, ed. El Reino de Dios y América Latina. El Paso, Tex.: Casa Bautista de Publicaciones, 1975.

_____, ed. Fe Cristiana y Latinoamérica Hoy. Buenos Aires: Certega, 1974.

Pannenberg, Wolfhart. Theology and the Kingdom of God. Philadelphia: Westminster Press, 1969.

Parker, Harriet L. "A Freirian Model: In-Service Teacher Education." Ed.D. dissertation, University of Massachusetts, 1979.

Parsons,Talcott. Sociological Theory and Modern Society. New York: Free Press, 1967.

Pereira, Carlos A. "The Implementation of Paulo Freire's Educational Philosophy in an American Setting." Ed.D. dissertation, Boston University School of Education, 1977.

Pereira Paiva, Vanilda. Paulo Freire E O Nacionalismo-Desenvolvimentista. Río de Janeiro: Civilizacao Brasileira, 1980.

Perrin, Norman. Jesus and the Language of the Kingdom. Philadelphia: Fortress Press, 1976.

Piaget, Jean. Genetic Epistemology. Translated by Eleanor Duckworth. New York: Norton, 1970.

_____. Six Psychological Studies. Translated by David Elkind. New York: Random House, Vintage Books, 1967.

_____. To Understand is to Invent: The Future of Education. New York: Penguin Books, 1973.

_____ and Inhelder, Barbel. The Psychology of the Child. New York: Basic Books, 1969.

Pixley, George V. God's Kingdom. A Guide for Biblical Study. Maryknoll, N.Y.: Orbis Books, 1981.

_____ and Bastian, Jean-Pierre. Praxis Cristiana y Producción Teológica. Salamanca: Sígueme, 1979.

Polanyi, Michael. Personal Knowledge-Towards a Post-Critical Philosophy. Chicago: University of Chicago Press, 1958.

Powers, Edward. Signs of Shalom. Philadelphia: United Church Press, 1973.

Pueblo Oprimido, Señor de la Historia. Montevideo: Tierra Nueva, 1972.

Raines, John C. and Dean, Thomas, eds. Marxism and Radical Religion. Essays Towards a Revolutionary Humanism. Philadelphia: Temple University Press, 1970.

Ramseyer, Robert L., ed. Mission and the Peace Witness. Scottdale, Pa.: Herald Press, 1979.

Redekop, Calvin. The Free Church and Seductive Culture. Scottdale, Pa.: Herald Press, 1979.

Resnik, Rosa P. "Indigenization of Social Work: Conscientization and Social Work in Chile." DSW dissertation, Yeshiva University, 1976.

Ricoeur, Paul. Freud and Philosophy. New Heaven, Conn.: Yale University Press, 1970.

_____. Interpretation Theory. Fort Worth, Tex.: The Texas Christian University Press, 1976.

Rottenberg, Isaac C. The Promise and the Presence - Toward a Theology of the Kingdom of God. Grand Rapids, Mich.: Eerdmans, 1980.

Rugg, Harold. Imagination: An Inquiry Into the Sources and Conditions that Stimulate Creativity. New York: Harper & Row, 1963.

Ruiz Olabuénaga, José I. y otros. Paulo Freire, Concientización y Andragogía. Buenos Aires: Paidós, 1975.

Russell, Letty M. Human Liberation in a Feminist Perspective: A Theology. Philadelphia: Westminster Press, 1974.

Sanz Adrados, Juan José. Educación y Liberación en América Latina. Bogotá: Universidad Santo Tomás, 1979.

Sartre, Jean Paul. El Hombre y las Cosas. Buenos Aires: Losada, 1965.

_____. Search for a Method. New York: Vintage Books, 1968.

Savage, Peter. "The Church as the Community of the Kingdom." Theological Fraternity Bulletin, 3-4 (1979): 1-24.

Scannone, Juan Carlos. Teología de la Liberación y
    Praxis Popular. Salamanca: Sígueme, 1976.

_____. "Theology, Popular Culture, and Discernment."
    In Frontier of Theology in Latin America. Edited
    by Rosino Gibellini. Maryknoll, N.Y.: Orbis
    Books, 1979.

_____y otros. Cultura Popular y Filosofía de la Li-
    beración. Buenos Aires: Fernando García Cambeiro,
    1975.

Schacht, Richard. Alienation. Garden City, N.Y.:
    Doubleday & Co., 1971.

Schipani, Daniel S. "Conscientization and Creativity:
    A Reinterpretation of Paulo Freire Focused on his
    Epistemological and Theological Foundations, with
    Implications for Christian Education Theory."
    Ph.D. dissertation, Princeton Theological Seminary,
    1981.

_____. El Reino de Dios y el Ministerio Educativo de
    la Iglesia. Miami: Caribe, 1983.

_____. "Paulo Freire: Education, Liberation and the
    Church." International Reformed Bulletin 62-63
    (1975): 17-24.

Schnackenburg, Rudolf. God's Rule and Kingdom. New
    York: Herder and Herder, 1963.

Scott, Bernard B. Jesus, Symbol-Maker for the Kingdom.
    Philadelphia: Fortress, 1981.

Segundo, Juan Luis. Masas y Minorías en la Dialéctica
    Divina de la Liberación. Buenos Aires: La Aurora,
    1973.

_____. The Liberation of Theology. Maryknoll, N.Y.:
    Orbis Books, 1976.

Se Vive Como se Puede. 4a. edición. Buenos Aires:
    Shapire/Tierra Nueva, 1976.

Seymour, Jack L. and Miller, Donald E., eds. Contempo-
    rary Approaches to Christian Education. Nashville:
    Abingdon, 1982.

Shaeffer, James R. Program Planning for Adult Christian Education. New York: Newman, 1972.

Sharif, Salim Akhtar. "The Problem of Poverty in Rural India: A Proposed Model in the Community Development Program of India, Using the Pedagogy of the Consciousness Raising (Paulo Freire's and Ivan Illich's Educational Methods) and Growth Group Models." D.Min. dissertation, School of Theology at Claremont, 1976.

Shaull, M. Richard. "Iglesia y Teología en la Vorágine de la Revolución." in De La Iglesia y la Sociedad. Montevideo: Tierra Nueva, 1971.

Sherwin, Harriet B. "Paulo Freire: His Philosophy and Pedagogy and Its Implications for American Education." Ph.D. dissertation, University of California at Berkley, 1973.

Shockley, Grant S. "Liberation Theology, Black Theology, and Religious Education." In Foundations for Christian Education in an era of Change. Edited by Marvin J. Taylor. Nashville: Abingdon, 1976.

Sider, Donald J. "An Evangelical Theology of Liberation." In Perspectives in Evangelical Theology. Edited by Kenneth S. Kantzer and Stanley N. Gundry. Grand Rapids, Mich.: Baker House, 1979.

_____. Christ and Violence. Scottdale, Pa.: Herald Press, 1979.

Silva Gotay, Samuel. El Pensamiento Cristiano Revolucionario en América Latina y el Caribe. Salamanca: Sígueme, 1981.

Smith, William A. "Conscientizacao': An Operational Definition." Ed.D. dissertation, University of Massachusetts, 1975.

Sobrino, Jon. Christology at the Crossroads. Translated by John Drury. Maryknoll, N.Y.: Orbis Books, 1978.

Solle, Dorothee. Political Theology. Philadelphia: Fortress Press, 1974.

Stace, W.T. The Philosophy of Hegel. New York: Dover Publications, 1955.

Steckel, Richard A. "The Transferability of Paulo Freire's Educational Ideals to American Society." Ed.D. dissertation, Boston University, 1975.

Streck, Danilo R. "John Dewey's and Paulo Freire's Views on the Political Function of Education, with Special Emphasis on the Problem of Method. Ed.D. dissertation, Rutgers University, 1977.

Taylor, Marvin J., ed. Foundations for Christian Education in an Era of Change. Nashville: Abingdon, 1976.

Teilhard de Chardin, Pierre. The Phenomenon of Man. New York: Harper & Bros., 1959.

Temas de Educación y Política. Lima: Centro de Publicaciones Educativas-Tarea, 1976.

Thompson, Donald C. "The Application of Paulo Freire's Approach to United States Adult Education." Ed.D. dissertation. University of California at Los Angeles, 1976.

Torres Novoa, Carlos Alberto. La Praxis Educativa de Paulo Freire. México: Gernika, 1978.

_____, comp. Entrevistas con Paulo Freire. México: Gernika, 1978.

Trocmé, André. Jesus and the Nonviolent Revolution. Scottdale, Pa.: Herald Press, 1973.

Tucker, Robert. Philosophy and Myth in Karl Marx, 2nd ed. Cambridge, Mass.: University Press, 1972/

Verghese, Paul. The Freedom of Man. An Inquiry into Some Roots of the Tension Between Freedom and Authority in Our Society. Philadelphia: Westminster, 1972.

_____. The Joy of Freedom. Richmond, Va.: John Knox Press, 1967.

Vernon, P.E., ed. Creativity. Baltimore: Penguin Books, 1970.

Vidales, Raúl. "Methodological Issues in Liberation Theology." In Frontiers of Theology in Latin

America. Edited by Rosino Gibellini. Maryknoll, N.Y.: Orbis Books, 1979.

Wallace, Anthony F.C. "Revitalization Movements." In Reader in Comparative Religion, An Anthropological Approach, pp. 503-512. Edited by William A. Lessa and Evon Z. Vogt. New York: Harper & Row, 1972.

Warford, Malcolm L. "Between the Plumbing and the Saving--Education, Theology and Liberation." Living Light, 11:1 (Spring 1974): 60-77.

_____. The Necessary Illusion-Church,Culture and Educational Change. Philadelphia: Pilgrim Press, 1976.

Weber, Max. Economy and Society. An Outline of Interpretive Sociology. Edited by Guenther Roth and Claus Wittich. New York: Bedminster Press, 1968.

Weiss, Johaness. Jesus' Proclamation of the Kingdom of God. Philadelphia: Fortress Press, 1971.

Westerhoff, John H. "Church Education for Tomorrow. The Christian Century, December 31, 1975. pp. 1201-1204.

_____. Will Our Children Have Faith? New York: Seabury Press, 1976.

_____. ed. A Colloquy on Christian Education. Philadelphia: United Church Press, 1972.

_____, ed. Who are We. The Quest for a Religious Education. Birmingham, Ala.: Religious Education Press, 1978.

Whitehead, Alfred North. The Aims of Education and Other Essays. New York: The Press, 1929.

World Council of Churches. Educación para la Liberación y la Comunidad. Buenos Aires: La Aurora, 1975.

Wren, Brian. Education for Justice. Maryknoll, N.Y.: Orbis, 1977.

Wyckoff, D. Campbell. The Gospel and Christian Education. A Theory of Christian Education for Our Times. Philadelphia: Westminster Press, 1959.

Wyckoff, D. Campbell. Theory and Design of Christian Education Curriculum. Philadelphia: Westminster Press, 1961.

_____. "Understanding Your Church Curriculum." The Princeton Seminary Bulletin. 63:1 (1970) 77-84.

_____. "'What's New' Is the Wrong Question." A Paper presented at the Christian Education Theory Seminar, Princeton Theological Seminary, Spring 1976.

Wynn, John Charles. Christian Education for Liberation. Nashville: Abingdon, 1977.

Yoder, John H. "Exodus and Exile The Two Faces of Liberation." Cross Currents (Fall 1973): 297-309.

_____. "La Expectativa Mesiánica del Reino y su Carácter Central para una Adecuada Hermenéutica Contemporánea." In El Reino de Dios y América Latina. Edited by C. René Padilla. El Paso, Tex.: Casa Bautista de Publicaciones, 1975.

_____. The Original Revolution. Scottdale, Pa.: Herald Press, 1971.

_____. The Politics of Jesus. Grand Rapids, Mich.: Eerdmans, 1972.